KED D

EXPERIENCING AMERICA'S PAST
A Travel Guide to Museum Villages

EXPERIENCING AMERICA'S PAST

A Travel Guide to Museum Villages

Second Edition

Gerald and Patricia Gutek

University of South Carolina Press

Copyright © 1994 University of South Carolina

*Published in Columbia, South Carolina, by the
University of South Carolina Press*

Manufactured in the United States of America

Library of Congress Cataloging-in-Publication Data

Gutek, Gerald Lee.
    Experiencing America's past : a travel guide to museum villages /
Gerald and Patricia Gutek. — 2nd ed.
        p.   cm.
    Includes bibliographical references and index.
    ISBN 0-87249-667-8 (pbk. : acid-free)
    1. Historic sites—United States—Guidebooks.   2. Historical
museums—United States—Guidebooks.   3. Villages—United States—
Guidebooks.   4. United States—History, Local.   5. Historic
buildings—United States—Guidebooks.   I. Gutek, Patricia, 1941–
. II. Title.
E159.G87   1994
917.304′929—dc20   94-11291

CONTENTS

Introduction

Revising *Experiencing America's Past* has been a labor of love. Preparing the second edition of *America's Past* gave us a good excuse to revisit our favorite museum villages. We found that we were just as excited and enthusiastic about them the second time as we were when they were new discoveries. Our first visit to a museum village was to New Harmony, Indiana, more than twenty-five years ago, and we still find these historic sites our favorite travel destinations.

In this second edition of *Experiencing America's Past*, as in the first edition, are forty-three museums. However, we have added some excellent museum villages that we hadn't visited prior to the publication of the first edition. Thirty-two of the sites found in the first edition also appear in the second edition, along with eleven sites not previously included.

Because there are hundreds of American museum villages, the selection process is always difficult but eventually the best museums emerge. Since this is a national rather than a regional guidebook, only what we considered to be the finest, most interesting, and unique representatives of the museum village genre have been included.

To obtain up-to-date information about the forty-three sites, the directors of the museums were contacted. We invited them to review our copy and suggest changes. Every director or another member of the museum's staff responded to our queries, and we appreciate the time they took from their busy schedules to help us with our project.

VISITING A MUSEUM VILLAGE

Visiting a museum village is a way of rediscovering our roots as Americans. Trips to these restored cross sections of American life can satisfy many purposes, ranging from pure recreation to escape to education. Unlike a visit to a typical museum, where the exhibits are protected in glass cases, the exploration of a historic village enables you to be a time-traveler, nearly an active participant in the past. It offers the opportunity to step out of the hurried pace of modern life and to recapture life in an earlier time. It can be a totally enriching experience.

This introduction provides a general perspective or orientation to make your exploration of America's past a heightened and enriching experience. To begin, let's identify the various types of museum villages that you will discover in your travels.

Types of Museum Villages

Museum villages are generally carefully selected and arranged collections of original buildings grouped to illustrate the way of life—architecture, economics, industry, furniture, society, and culture—of a community representative of a particular period. Among the various types of museum villages are the *restored* village, once an actual community, with original buildings on their original sites; the *recreated* village, composed of either original buildings or well-researched, newly constructed facsimiles brought together on an arbitrary site; and the *reconstructed* village, rebuilt on its original site but consisting primarily of new structures.

The Restored Village

In most instances, the buildings in a restored village were actually lived in by the community members. The buildings, furnishings, and environment are restored to a particular period. Examples of restored villages are Colonial Williamsburg in Virginia; Historic Deerfield in Massachusetts; Historic New Harmony in Indiana; Old Salem in Winston-Salem, North Carolina; and the various Shaker communities.

Many restored villages were once the locations of religious communal societies such as the Shakers, the Rappites at Old Economy Village in Pennsylvania, the Separatists at Zoar in Ohio, and the Inspirationists at Amana in Iowa. These groups sought to create perfect communities, often in isolated regions, where they could practice their religion without interference. The communities of religious societies such as the Shakers and Rappites endured for a much longer time than those of secular groups such as the Owenites at New Harmony. A shared set of beliefs generally sustained the religious communitarians, but the nonreligious groups often disintegrated because of internal conflicts.

At times, extensive rebuilding has been done in restored villages. The plan is generally to restore the buildings to their original sites as they were at a particular time in history. These restorations follow the architectural design and style of the original buildings. Furniture and other artifacts usually date from the period portrayed in the village but are not necessarily original to that site.

The Recreated Village

In a recreated community, historic buildings such as homes, shops, stores, and offices are transported to a particular location, usually from the nearby vicinity. These buildings are then restored to the period that the village is meant to portray, and authentic artifacts are assembled for display. Examples of recreated villages are Old World Wisconsin; Greenfield Village, Michigan; and Old Sturbridge Village, Massachusetts. Some of these villages were developed because antique collectors' collections outgrew their space. In studying historic preservation, we often see this pattern: one or two people with a passion for collecting and the means and good taste with which to do it, leaving a valuable legacy for society. The Wells brothers at Old Sturbridge Village, the Rockefellers at Colonial Williamsburg, Henry Ford at Greenfield Village, and Electra Havemeyer Webb at Shelburne Museum all carried out massive tasks of restoration and preservation that are to America's benefit.

The Reconstructed Village

In some instances, where an actual village has been completely destroyed, total reconstruction has been done. Using archaeological research, the foundations of the original buildings are located. Based upon historical documents such as drawings, blueprints, or diaries, facsimile structures are built. This has often been done in the case of forts and military installations. An example is New Salem in Illinois, where Abraham Lincoln once lived.

A Total Environment

Regardless of its type, the museum village has the advantage of depicting a complete historical environment in relationship to its natural setting. It portrays religious, cultural, social, and economic life by showing us where people prayed, worked, and lived. Entering their homes, their shops, and their churches transports us not only to another time but also tells us who we are and who we might become.

A Visitor's Overview of the Historic Village

To appreciate a historic village, you should be a traveler in space and time rather than a harried tourist. Allow yourself to become a part of the museum village experience by taking the time to place it in context.

Many museum villages have visitors' centers that provide brochures, maps, and guides. Some time spent at the visitors' center before you begin your journey through the village streets and shops will give you an overall perspective. Rather than seeing isolated buildings, you can gain a total mental landscape. If the visitors' center has a film or slide presentation, take the time to view it. Many of the larger historic villages have such visual presentations. Smaller villages that operate with limited staffs and budgets may be unable to provide a visitors' orientation, but they should not be overlooked; they still have much to offer. In these instances, travelers should do their own preliminary orientation. In either case, the descriptions in this book provide background information for your journey into the American heritage.

In addition to the orientation at the visitors' center, some museum villages provide guided tours, on which a trained guide will narrate the history, tell you about the people, and describe the art and artifacts of the community. If such a tour is available, it will further enhance your visit.

After getting a perspective of the museum village, begin your personal exploration. See the village in terms of the functions that its buildings performed in the total life of the people who lived there.

Each traveler has his or her own interests, and a historic village can satisfy all of them. Some people may be interested in the style of architecture, which may range from colonial to Federal to crude log cabin or to sophisticated plantation manor. Others may be interested in the decorative arts and artifacts—the utensils, wall hangings, chinaware, quilts, and furniture. Still others may want to concentrate on the gardens. It is possible to see how families lived by studying the design of their homes, or to see how they shopped by visiting their stores, or to see how they were educated by visiting the town school.

USING THE BOOK

The museum villages described in this book are organized into the following geographic regions: New England, the Middle Atlantic, the South and Southeast, the Midwest, and the Southwest and West. The regional arrangement facilitates planning trips to a number of villages located in the same geographic area. Within a region, the museum villages are then grouped by state.

Each entry for a museum village begins with a listing of facts, identifying and categorizing the village, giving its location, address, phone number, operating months and times, and pointing out restaurants, shops, facilities, and special features. We have indicated admission fees, but it should be noted that these are subject to change. In our descriptions, we have used the following abbreviations: NR, which signifies that the site is included in the National Register of Historic Places; NHL, which identifies the site or structure as a National Historic Landmark; and HABS, which identifies the structure as being included in the Historic American Building Survey.

To facilitate your travel planning, we have included a "Where to Stay" section that lists accommodations located in the vicinity of each museum village. These accommodations include resorts, inns, bed and breakfast lodgings, motels and hotels, and campgrounds.

In this second edition, we have added a feature entitled "Overview," which provides a brief introduction to each outdoor village. These thumbnail sketches combine historical background and site descriptions and summarize what readers can expect at each museum. The overview is followed by "History," which more extensively tells the story of the village and its residents. Next is "Tour," a detailed description of the village's buildings, furnishings, grounds, and special features.

For added interest and convenience, we've included brief descriptions of side trips to other points of interest in the vicinity of most of the villages.

MAINE

VERMONT

Shelburne
Museum

The Shaker Museum

NEW
HAMPSHIRE

Canterbury
Shaker Village

Hancock
Shaker Village

Historic
Deerfield

Lowell NHP

MASSACHUSETTS

Old Sturbridge Village

Plimoth
Plantation

CONNECTICUT

Mystic Seaport
Museum

NEW ENGLAND

CONNECTICUT
   Mystic Seaport Museum, Mystic

MAINE
   The Shaker Museum, Poland Spring

MASSACHUSETTS
   Historic Deerfield, Deerfield
   Lowell National Historical Park and Heritage State Park,
      Lowell
   Hancock Shaker Village, Pittsfield
   Plimoth Plantation, Plymouth
   Old Sturbridge Village, Sturbridge

NEW HAMPSHIRE
   Canterbury Shaker Village, Canterbury
   Strawbery Banke, Portsmouth

VERMONT
   Shelburne Museum, Shelburne

MYSTIC SEAPORT MUSEUM

Recreation of a nineteenth-century maritime port village

Address: 75 Greenmanville Avenue, P.O. Box 6000, Mystic, CT 06355-0990

Telephone: (203) 572-0711

Location: In southeastern Connecticut, 10 miles east of New London and one mile south of I-95, exit 90

Open: Daily, 10 A.M. to 4 P.M., January through first week in April; 9 A.M. to 5 P.M., second week of April through late June and September through late October; 9 A.M. to 8 P.M., last week of June through August; 9 A.M. to 4 P.M., last week of October through December

Admission: Adults, $15.00; children 6 to 15, $7.50. Group rates available.

Restaurants: The Galley; The Seamen's Inne Restaurant

Shops: Variety Store; Mystic Seaport Museum Stores (including bookstore and maritime gallery)

Facilities: Historic ships and boats; 22 historic buildings on 17 acres on Mystic River; preservation shipyard; crafts demonstrations; steamboat rides; horse and carriage rides; children's museum; youth sail education courses on historic ships; planetarium; educational programs; research library; Archives of American Yachting and Boating; handicapped accessible

WHERE TO STAY

Inns/Bed & Breakfasts: Old Mystic Inn, 58 Main St., P.O. Box 634, Old Mystic 06372, (203) 572-9422; Palmer Inn, 25 Church St., Noank 06340, (203) 572-9000; Red Brook Inn, P.O. Box 237, Old Mystic 06372, (203) 572-0349; Randall's Ordinary, P.O. Box 243, North Stonington 06359, (203) 599-4540

Motels/Hotels: Days Inn, 26 Michelle Lane, Mystic 06355, (203) 572-0574; Inn at Mystic, US 1 at jct. CT 27, Mystic 06355, (203) 536-9604, (800) 237-2415, FAX: (203) 536-9604, ext 290; Hilton, 20 Coogan Blvd., Mystic 06355, (203) 572-0731, FAX: (203) 572-0328; Norwich Inn, Spa & Villas, 607 W. Thames St., Norwich 06360, (800) 275-4772, FAX: (203) 886-9483

Camping: Rocky Neck State Park, Niantic 06357, (203) 739-5471; Camp Niantic by the Atlantic, P.O. Drawer 806, Niantic 06357, (203) 739-9308; Seaport Campground, Box 104, Rt. 184, Old Mystic 06372,

Mystic Seaport, Mystic, Connecticut
The *Charles W. Morgan*, launched in 1841, is the last surviving wooden whaleship
in the United States. It is docked at Mystic Seaport Museum, Mystic, CN.
Photo by Patricia A. Gutek

(203) 536-4044; Highland Orchards Resort Park, P.O. Box 222, Rt.
49, North Stonington 06359, (203) 599-5101, (800) 624-0829

OVERVIEW

Outdoor museums come in all shapes and sizes. Because agriculture
was the predominant occupation among early American settlers, most outdoor museums feature farm life complete with fields, barns, and animals,
as well as the rural businesses that support an agricultural lifestyle. However, along the Atlantic coast, the sea provided a major source of livelihood and was often the determining factor in the lifestyle of coastal
residents.

Mystic Seaport Museum is unique in that it focuses on the country's
Atlantic maritime heritage which includes shipbuilding, shipping, whaling, fishing, and shoreside maritime trades. The historic and recreated

buildings on the Mystic River are typical of those found in a nineteenth-century coastal New England village. Mystic Seaport Museum has done an extraordinary job of gathering exhibits illuminating the development of New England's shipbuilding, shipping, whaling, and fishing industries as well as the lives of the people engaged in those occupations. There are twenty-two historic buildings, four restored ships, more than 400 boats, a working shipyard, a research library, and a large collection of maritime artifacts.

HISTORY

The town of Mystic is actually composed of sections of two other towns, Groton and Stonington, which lie on either side of the Mystic River, and has been jointly governed by them since 1705.

Shipbuilding began on the Mystic River as early as the seventeenth century. A five-mile stretch along the river several miles inland from the Atlantic Ocean provided Mystic with excellent shipbuilding sites. After the War of 1812, sealing and whaling and the increase in southern trade stimulated rapid growth at Mystic, which was becoming the home of shipbuilders and whaling captains.

George Greenman and Company and Charles Mallory & Sons were two of the most famous Mystic shipbuilders, and their shipyards are now the site of Mystic Seaport Museum. The Greenman Company built many of America's renowned packets and clipper ships, and its shipyards launched nearly 100 vessels between 1838 and 1878. One of them, the *David Crockett*, regularly traveled the difficult Cape Horn route to San Francisco. The *Crockett* was one of the fastest clippers, and its average performance on more than twenty-five runs around Cape Horn was never equaled. Mystic shipbuilder Charles Mallory, who began his maritime career as an apprentice sailmaker in the 1830s, produced a fleet of nine whalers that was used in the lucrative whale oil business. Exhibits describing the story of Mystic's shipbuilding industry are housed in the Seaport's **Mallory Building.**

During the Civil War, the demand for ships increased, and Mystic's shipyards received numerous contracts for steam transports and gunboats. The *Galena*, the navy's first seagoing ironclad, was built at the Maxson and Fish shipyards. By the end of the war, Mystic shipyards had built fifty-six steamers for the Union war effort, many of which measured 230 feet or more in length. Mystic shipyards launched 30,000 tons of shipping in the nineteenth century.

Toward the end of the nineteenth century, shipbuilding at Mystic declined because of decreased demand for wooden ships. Also, the Mystic River was not deep enough for construction of modern, steel-hulled ships. Shipbuilding was revived briefly during the early twentieth century. Since then, however, only small numbers of yachts and fishing craft have been produced at Mystic.

In 1929, the Marine Historical Association, Inc., was founded by Mystic residents Dr. Charles K. Stillman, Edward E. Bradley, and Carl C. Cutler. The purpose of the association was to establish a museum of the U.S. maritime past. In 1978, the Marine Historical Association changed its name to Mystic Seaport.

TOUR

Mystic Seaport, the nation's largest maritime museum, occupies seventeen acres along the Mystic River. There are so many ships, boats, museum buildings, and village sites that you should plan to spend the whole day, if possible.

The feature that truly sets Mystic Seaport apart from other historic villages is the opportunity to board four restored major vessels from another era. Reading is no substitute for stepping on board one of these great sailing ships or whalers. It's only then that you begin to understand the experiences of their crews. Board the *Joseph Conrad,* built in Copenhagen in 1882. It served as a training ship for the Danish merchant service until 1934 and was also used by the U.S. Maritime Commission during World War II. Before it was berthed at Mystic Seaport, Alan Villiers, the Australian sea captain who brought Plymouth's *Mayflower II* to America, sailed the *Conrad* on a 58,000-mile, two-year voyage around the world.

Visitors may also board the *L. A. Dunton,* a Gloucester fishing schooner built in 1921 at Essex, Massachusetts. One of the last large, engineless wooden fishing schooners, it was used for halibut and haddock fishing near Boston. The whaleship, the *Charles W. Morgan,* was built by the Hillman brothers of New Bedford, Massachusetts, for the Quaker whaling merchant Charles W. Morgan. The ship, launched July 21, 1841, is the last surviving wooden whaleship in the United States. It has been designated a National Historic Landmark.

Seeing Mystic Seaport from the water is a special treat. The *Sabino,* a 1908 steamboat built in East Boothbay, Maine, makes passenger runs on the Mystic River from mid-May to mid-October; there is a small fee. The *Sabino* originally served the islands of Casco Bay, Maine, and is believed to be the last operating coal-fired passenger steamer in the United States and is a National Historic Landmark.

All the vessels in Mystic Seaport's collection are maintained by the **Henry B. duPont Preservation Shipyard.** This unique facility has the equipment and craftsmen needed to restore and preserve wooden vessels. Visitors may observe the restoration work from the gallery that overlooks the main shop, carpenters' shops, an eighty-five-foot spar lathe, and a rigging loft. There is also a 375-ton-capacity lift dock, which is used to lift ships out of the water for repair.

Exhibited near the shipyard is the ninety-two-foot keel assembly from the whaleship *Thames*, built in 1818, as well as an exhibit on shipbuilding.

Many of the more than 400 small craft in the museum's collection are displayed in the **Small Boats Exhibit** and the **North Boat Shed,** and some are afloat at the docks. Replicas of historically significant small craft are built by the staff for use on the Mystic River.

The village area is a recreation of a nineteenth-century shipbuilding seacoast village primarily composed of original New England buildings moved to the site. However, some buildings that belonged to the Greenman family, who owned a mill after shipbuilding declined, were on the property and have been restored.

The **Thomas Greenman House** is a two-and-a-half-story Greek Revival home built in the mid-1800s.

One of the textile mill buildings, the three-story, 1865 **Stillman Building,** is now used to exhibit ship models, marine paintings, and scrimshaw.

The 1890 **Wendell Building,** a former machine shop, houses an exhibit of ship figureheads and wood carvings. The **Mallory Building** tells the story of the Mallory family's shipping business during the nineteenth and twentieth centuries, as well as that of the shipbuilding industry in Mystic.

Demonstrations by skilled craftspeople take place in the village. Ironwork is forged at the 1885 **Shipsmith,** while at the **Cooperage,** barrels for shipping goods are made. Wood-carvers work at the **Shipcarver's Shop,** and nineteenth-century printing methods are employed at the **Mystic Press.** Maritime skills are demonstrated at the **Clam Shack.** The **Small Boat Shop** is used to build replicas of historically significant small craft and to teach boatbuilding techniques. Other demonstrations on the museum grounds or on the Mystic River include sail setting and furling, whaleboat rowing and sailing, chantey singing, fish splitting, salting and drying, and a breeches buoy rescue drill.

The **Ship Chandlery** carries the vast array of supplies needed for a voyage. The fishing industry is represented by the 1840 **Salmon Shack,** containing fishing gear; the 1874 **Oyster House,** where oysters are sorted; the **Oystering,** which has oyster boats and fishing gear; and the **Whaleboat Exhibit,** which features a fully equipped whaleboat.

The **Lobster Shack** displays lobster fishing gear; the **Hoop Shop** has equipment to make wooden mast hoops and the **Nautical Instruments** building houses clocks, chronometers, and navigational aids. An interesting exhibit is the scale model of Mystic during the decades between 1850 and 1870.

Maritime properties moved to Mystic include the 1845 **New York Yacht Club Building** from Hoboken, New Jersey, and the 1874 **New Shoreham Life-Saving Station** from Block Island. The longest building at Mystic Seaport is the 1824 **Plymouth Cordage Company's Ropewalk,** a gray-shingled building that was part of a rope-making facility.

The village also contains buildings found in most New England towns, including an 1833 **bank** with a shipping office upstairs, an 1889 **chapel,** an 1870 **drugstore** with a doctor's office, an 1880s one-room **schoolhouse,** an 1890s **dry goods store,** and a **tavern.**

The **Children's Museum** is located in the 1860 Edmundson House. In this hands-on museum, children can swab the deck, move cargo, cook in the galley, dress in sailors' garb, and sleep in sailors' bunks.

Mystic Seaport has a **planetarium** that offers daily programs explaining how navigators used the stars to determine their position at sea. A small admission fee is charged.

There are many special events held annually at Mystic Seaport. They include Lobsterfest in May, Sea Music Festival and Small Craft Weekend in June, an Independence Day celebration and the Antique and Classic Boat Rendezvous in July, Photo Weekend in September, Chowderfest in October, and Thanksgiving and Christmas celebrations. Sailing classes and a day camp for children ages twelve to nineteen are also available.

SIDE TRIPS

The **Mystic Marinelife Aquarium** displays over 6,000 specimens of undersea life. Especially appealing to children are the hourly demonstrations with whales, dolphins, and sea lions. In Mystic, 55 Coogan Boulevard, 1-95 Exit 90. (203) 536-9631. Open daily. Admission charged.

Had enough of ships and maritime life? If not, take the *River Queen* or *River Queen II* sightseeing cruises. The cruises pass the submarine USS *Nautilus*, the U.S. Naval submarine base, and the U.S. Coast Guard Academy. The cruises depart daily from Memorial Day to Labor Day from 193 Thames St., Groton, (203) 445-9516. Fee charged.

New London's historic district has buildings dating from the late eighteenth to the twentieth centuries, including the **Lawrence Hospital Building** (1790), **New London Customhouse** (1833), **New London Railroad Station** (1886), and the restored **Nathan Hale Schoolhouse** (1774), which is open Monday to Friday, 10:00 A.M. to 3:00 P.M., Memorial Day to Labor Day. Free. (203) 447-3106.

The **Joshua Hempstead House,** at 11 Hempstead Street, has also been restored. Built in 1678, it is one of the oldest dwellings in Connecticut. (203) 247-8896. Open Tuesday to Sunday, 1:00 P.M. to 5:00 P.M., mid-May to mid-October. Admission charged. **Monte Cristo Cottage** (1888) was the childhood home of playwright Eugene O'Neill. 325 Pequot Avenue. (203) 443-0051. Open Monday to Friday, 1:00 P.M. to 4:00 P.M. Admission charged.

Old Lyme, Stonington, and Norwich also offer opportunities for leisurely strolls through their charming historic districts.

THE SHAKER MUSEUM

Restoration of an eighteenth- and nineteenth-century Shaker community; NR, NHL, HABS

Address: R.R. #1, Box 640, Poland Spring, ME 04274
Telephone: (207) 926-4597
Location: In south central Maine, between Portland and Lewiston, on Rt. 26; 8 miles north of Gray, ME Turnpike, exit 11; 8 miles south of Auburn, ME Turnpike, exit 12
Open: Monday to Saturday, 10:00 A.M. to 4:30 P.M., Memorial Day to Columbus Day
Admission: Guided introductory tour: adults, $4.00; children 6 to 12, $2.00; guided extended tour: adults, $5.50; children 6 to 12, $2.50
Shops: Museum Shop; Shaker Store
Facilities: Active Shaker community; seventeen original buildings; craft demonstrations; workshops; special events; library and archives

WHERE TO STAY

Motels/Hotels: Days Inn, Auburn 04210, (207) 783-1454; Ledgewood, RFD 2, P.O. Box 30, Norway 04268, (207) 743-6347; Ramada Inn, 490 Pleasant St., Lewiston, 04240, (207) 784-2331, FAX: (207) 784-2332; Howard Johnson Hotel, 155 Riverside, Portland 04103, (207) 774-5861; Quality Suites Jetport Hotel, 1050 Westbrook St., Portland 04102, (207) 775-2200
Resorts: Poland Spring Inn, Poland Spring 04274, (207) 998-4351
Camping: Poland Spring Campground, Rt. 26, Box 407, Poland Spring 04274, (207) 998-2151

OVERVIEW

1994 marks the bicentennial of the founding of the Sabbathday Lake Shaker Village, still an active, though quite small, Shaker community today. The Shaker Museum, founded in 1931, and the 200-year-old living Shaker religious community share a picturesque site in rural Maine. "Chosen Land" is the return address on a letter we recently received from a Sabbathday Lake brother. The phrase seems apt when you come upon a cluster of white frame buildings, pine woods, the shining lake from which the village takes its name, sheep grazing in the pasture, apple orchards on the hill, and carefully tended herb gardens.

More than a dozen original Shaker structures, some of which are museum buildings and others that are occupied by the eight sisters and brothers, remain at Sabbathday Lake. As with all the Shaker villages we have seen, the impressive architecture, pastoral setting, well-done preservation and restoration, and elegant furniture are worth any detour necessary to make the visit. The fact that it is a living community adds a special dimension to this historic site. When you meet a Shaker sister or brother who patiently answers your questions, it is a totally different experience from dealing with a museum guide whose job requires dressing in a Shaker costume.

In addition to the historic buildings, the Museum has fine collections of Shaker furniture, folk and decorative arts, tin and woodenware, textiles, early American tools and farm implements.

HISTORY

On April 19, 1794, the Sabbathday Lake community, or New Gloucester United Society of Believers in Christ's Second Coming, was founded under Trustees Nathan Merrill and Barnabus Briggs. (See the Appendix for a brief history of the Shakers.) It was one of three Shaker societies in Maine (Alfred and Gorham were the other two).

Initially, Sabbathday Lake converts met at Gohan Wilson's farmhouse; but before long, the work of building the community was started. The first order of business was a meetinghouse, the place of worship. Moses Johnson, a Shaker brother and architect, designed, framed, and built the meetinghouse at Sabbathday Lake. Gradually, other buildings were added, forming three parallel rows on both sides of what is now Route 26.

A three-and-a-half-story central dwelling house, built in 1795, faced the meetinghouse. When it was no longer large enough for its family, the central dwelling house was moved sixty-five feet northeast and replaced with a five-story brick dwelling house, completed in 1884.

To achieve its goal of self-sufficiency, the New Gloucester community became involved in many businesses, including tannery and cooper shops; herb and garden seeds; lumber; and flour, carding, and spinning mills. These were in addition to the crafts, such as furniture, basketmaking, and textiles, for which the Shakers are so well known.

Despite prosperity, membership in Shaker communities declined. The Gorham community ended in 1819; in 1931, the Alfred community merged with Sabbathday Lake, which remains an active Shaker community with eight members. They raise sheep for wool and harvest herbs for culinary use. The Shaker Museum, founded by Sister Ethel Peacock in

1931, exhibits artifacts made and used at the community over the past three centuries.

TOUR

There are seventeen original buildings remaining on the site. All the buildings are eighteenth- and nineteenth-century frame except the **Dwelling House,** which is brick. Originally, the Shakers owned 2,700 acres; now, they have 1,900.

The Introductory Tour is a guided tour of the 1794 Meetinghouse and the 1839 Ministry's Shop while the Extended Tour includes those two buildings and the 1821 Sisters' Shop and the 1816 Spin House.

The **Boy's Shop** now serves as the **Reception Center.** It is a white, two-story building built in 1850; and although it was partially destroyed by fire in 1965, the facade is original. The building was used to house young Shaker boys until they reached their midteens, along with the brothers who took care of them.

The first floor houses a **bookstore** with a good collection of Shaker books and some reproduction Shaker items. The four rooms on the second floor are furnished with original Shaker furniture, most of it from Sabbath-day Lake.

The 1794 **Meetinghouse,** which now serves as the **Shaker Museum,** was the first building on this site. It was one of ten Shaker meetinghouses built by Moses Johnson, all with gambrel roofs. Chimney bricks were made by brethren near the Sabbathday Pond, and the nails were handmade by Joseph Briggs. In 1839, an ell was added to the north side.

Religious services still take place in the first-floor meeting room; on Sundays, they are open to the public. A divided stairway leads to the second floor, where Shaker costumes are on display. The four rooms on the second floor originally housed the two elders and two eldresses who headed the community. Among the notable items contained in the rooms are a weasel, the Shaker invention used to measure a skein of yarn; chair tilters (one of the few Shaker inventions ever patented); and a sewing desk made by Joshua Bussell. One of the rooms displays a rare Shaker quilt, which is quilted but not pieced. The three rooms on the third floor were used as guest rooms for visiting ministers. All the rooms have built-in cupboards.

Because the lack of insulation made the meetinghouse extremely cold to live in, the elders moved into the **Ministry's Shop,** which was built in 1839 and has insulated walls. This building was used by the two elders and two eldresses as both home and workplace. As the spiritual leaders, they governed the community. In addition to their administrative duties, they were required to do physical labor or craftwork, so the building contains a sewing room and a tailor's room, as well as offices.

The three back rooms of the Ministry's Shop are used for temporary exhibits that have included displays about Shaker food, important leaders, and Victorian Shaker craftsmanship.

The **Sisters' Shop,** originally used as a laundry, houses a mail-order herb business on its second floor. From barrels of herbs, sisters fill small metal cans. Herb can labels are printed in the community **printshop.** This is only one of the businesses operating here; being self-supporting is a Shaker principle.

In your tour of the Sisters' Shop, you will see the original washing machine, invented by the Shakers, and a large press that chemically treated material. Permanent-press material is also a Shaker invention.

In the 1816 **Spin House** is an exhibit on the village's sawmill, called the Great Mill. The Sabbathday Lake Shakers began their lumbering business as early as 1796. The Great Mill, built in 1853 and operated until 1941, was sixty feet long, twenty-one feet wide, and three stories high. On exhibit are more than 100 mill production items and artifacts.

The 1880 New Gloucester Shaker **Schoolhouse** has been restored and houses the Shaker Library and Archives. Designed by Brother Hewitt Chandler and staffed by Shakers, the school served both Shaker and New Gloucester children until 1950. Sold by the town and moved by the purchaser, the school was acquired by the United Society of Shakers at Sabbathday Lake in 1986 and returned to its original site. Library collections focus on the Shakers, especially those in Maine, and include material on other American religious sects and communal groups. The Shaker Library and Archives is open year round. Appointments are preferred.

There are orchards and herb gardens at the village as well as a cemetery. There are no individual markers, just the inscription "Shakers."

Workshops are offered each summer on topics such as planting herb gardens, rug braiding, patchwork, loom weaving, basket making, oval box-making, and architectural photography.

HISTORIC DEERFIELD

Restoration of eighteenth- and nineteenth-century houses in a seventeenth-century colonial frontier village; NR, NHL, HABS

Address: Box 321, Deerfield, MA 01342

Telephone: (413) 774-5581

Location: In north central Massachusetts, in the Connecticut River Valley, 90 miles west of Boston; 6 miles north on Rts. 5 and 10 from I-91 exit 24 or 25

Open: Daily, 9:30 A.M. to 4:30 P.M.; closed Thanksgiving, Christmas Eve, and Christmas Day

Admission: Tickets valid for all houses for two consecutive days: adults, $10.00; children, $5.00; single house admission: adults, $5.00; children, $3.00

Restaurants: Deerfield Inn dining room and coffee shop

Shops: J. G. Pratt Museum Store

Facilities: 13 museum buildings; information center with orientation program; guided tours; hotel; Memorial Libraries; special events; picnic area; summer fellow programs in Early American History and Material Culture affiliated with the Five Colleges; partially handicapped accessible

WHERE TO STAY

Inns/Bed & Breakfasts: Deerfield Inn, The Street, Deerfield, MA 01342, (413) 774-5587; The Yellow Gabled House, South Deerfield 01373, (413) 665-4922; The Brandt House, 29 Highland Ave., Greenfield 01301, (413) 774-3329; Orchard House, Shelburne 01370, (413) 625-9087; Parson Hubbard House, Shelburne 01370, (413) 625-9730

Motels/Hotels: Howard Johnson, 125 Mohawk Trail, Greenfield 01301, (413) 774-2211, FAX: (413) 772-2637

Camping: Erving State Forest, Millers Falls, (617) 544-3939; Northfield Mountain Recreation and Environmental Center, Northfield 01301, (413) 659-3714; White Birch Campground, North St., Whately 01093, (413) 665-4941

OVERVIEW

A New England colonial frontier town is frozen in time at Historic Deerfield. In a small Massachusetts town founded in the seventeenth century, more than a dozen elegant early American homes along a one-mile street have been meticulously restored and furnished with fine American furniture and decorative arts. For the connoisseur of American antiques or architecture, Historic Deerfield is a must. This exceptional restoration is particularly noted for the expertise of its guides regarding antique furniture and artifacts. At Historic Deerfield, special tours can be prearranged around specific interests, i.e., silver, pewter, etc.

The museum houses, which date from 1720 to 1850, are located on what has been called "the most beautiful street in America" in the town of Deerfield. The other stately early Federal and Greek Revival houses located on The Street are occupied by some of the town's 5,000 residents. Deerfield retains its original village design, a colonial agricultural arrangement in which houses were arranged in a linear fashion on a rise surrounded by fields and meadows. Only a small number of places remain that preserve this pattern of strip fields, a medieval English land system used by early settlers but no longer found in England.

The Deerfield Inn, the hotel and restaurant on The Street, is also a property of Historic Deerfield. Visitors can eat, sleep, and sightsee at this historic site, thus totally immersing themselves in the past.

History

Deerfield's history goes back more than 300 years to 1667, when 8,000 acres in the Connecticut River Valley were purchased from the Pocumtuck Indians for four pence an acre. The first settler, Samuel Hinsdell, arrived in the spring of 1669. By 1673, twenty families occupied the town, which for a brief time was called Pocumtuck. Residents laid out its village street and apportioned its house lots essentially as they are now.

An Indian attack in September 1675 left so many Deerfield men dead that the demoralized survivors decided to abandon the town. By 1682, however, people had returned, and the town was rebuilt. Because of its vulnerable geographic location, Deerfield was attacked by Indians several times. In February 1704, a company of Indians and Frenchmen led by Governor de Vaudreuil of Canada attacked Deerfield. Of the town's 291 inhabitants, 48 were killed, and 111 were taken prisoner and forced to march to Canada in winter. Many did not survive the ordeal.

Most of the town was burned during the attack, although several houses including the Ensign Sheldon House remained standing. Many of the Deerfield residents who survived the attack left the town. Deerfield was rebuilt beginning in 1707 by returnees.

Deerfield became a prosperous center for wheat and cattle. Many fine houses were built and furnished with handsome furniture made by Connecticut Valley craftsmen. In 1782, Rev. William Bentley of Salem wrote of Deerfield in his diary: "The street is one measured mile, running north and south, about 60 houses in the street in better style than in any towns I saw" (*The Diary of William Bentley, D.D.*, vol. 1 [Salem, Mass., 1905; reprinted Gloucester, Mass., 1962, p. 92]). Twenty-four of the houses viewed by Bentley are still standing, and there are thirteen others that date from the first quarter of the nineteenth century.

After the Revolution, Deerfield became less agricultural; and with the establishment of Deerfield Academy in 1797, it became a center for learning. A sense of history among Deerfield residents was evident early on. The Memorial Hall Museum was opened by the Pocumtuck Valley Memorial Association in 1880. Preservation was begun in the 1890s, when Charlotte Alice Baker restored the Frary House as a historic house museum.

Many Deerfield homes were in decrepit condition when Henry and Helen Flynt enrolled their son in Deerfield Academy in 1936. They purchased the Allen House and began restoring it. Subsequently, they bought and renovated the Deerfield Inn and six more houses, thus saving these historic houses from certain destruction. They furnished the houses with pieces from their outstanding collection of early American decorative arts. In 1952, the Flynts organized the Heritage Foundation, which was renamed Historic Deerfield, Inc., in 1971.

TOUR

Allow sufficient time to visit Historic Deerfield's 13 house museums. Viewing is by guided tour only, and each tour lasts half an hour. General admission tickets are good for two successive days. An orientation film is shown in the **Hall Tavern Information Center.** In good weather, walking tours of The Street leave from Hall Tavern.

The houses lining Deerfield's mile-long street, known earlier as Old Deerfield Street and now simply called The Street, reflect the prosperity of their owners. They are large, elegant, and well furnished with locally made or imported furniture. There are no log cabins, mud floors, or crude furnishings in this pioneer town.

The Hall Tavern was moved to Deerfield from Charlemont, Massachusetts, where it had been a stagecoach stop. This frame building in the elongated saltbox style was built in 1760; a wing containing a ballroom was added in 1807. The barroom features a fine cage bar. Upstairs, the large, low-ceilinged ballroom is striking because of the extensive wall stenciling, which was done by an anonymous artist and has been restored.

The **Wright House,** a large, two-story, Federal-style brick house, displays the George Alfred Cluett Collection of American Furniture and Clocks of the Chippendale and Federal periods, as well as an extensive collection of Chinese export porcelain.

The **Ebenezer Hinsdale Williams House** has recently been restored to its early-nineteenth-century appearance. It is furnished to show the household of a well-to-do farming and landholding family of the Jacksonian period.

The **Helen Greier Flynt Textile Museum** (1872) is a Victorian barn that holds an overwhelming collection of textiles and exquisite handmade clothing from the sixteenth to nineteenth centuries. Included are hand-embroidered French and English costumes displayed on mannequins; a large number of early bed rugs; handmade and embroidered quilts; hand-stenciled Indian cotton; rare eighteenth-century fabrics from England and India; jacquard coverlets; rugs; needlepoint and flame-stitch upholstered furniture; and a marvelous collection of our favorites, samplers.

The **Henry Needham Flynt Silver & Metalware Collection** is in a small, two-story, gambrel-roofed frame house that was built in Deerfield in 1814. It was moved to Greenfield in 1872 and returned to its original site in 1960. Historic Deerfield added a fireproof cinder-block wing, camouflaged with old boards, to hold the village's extensive silver collection. Glass cabinets display English and American silver pieces by Paul Revere, Jeremiah Dummer, and Isaac Parker and John Russell. A collection of New England pewter is displayed here.

The **Allen House** was the home of Henry and Helen Flynt, the founders of Historic Deerfield, Inc. It was the first house they purchased and restored. Allen House was built by Simon Beaman, a garrison soldier, and Hannah Beaman, the first schoolteacher in Deerfield. During the Indian massacre of 1704, the Beamans were captured. Though they were forced to march to Canada, they survived and returned in 1705 to build their home. Pieces from the Flynts' collections of American furniture and decorative arts are used to furnish the house.

The **Stebbins House,** built in 1799, was the first brick house in Deerfield. This Federal-style house had a gambrel-roofed ell with dormer windows in back that was changed in 1879 to a pitched-roofed ell with a full second story. Asa Stebbins was the son of a prosperous tanner and operated a very successful gristmill with his brother, Joseph. This lavishly furnished house reflects the wealth of its owner. The French wallpaper in the south bedroom and hall, depicting Captain Cook's voyage, was originally in the Ruel Williams' mansion in Augusta, Maine. Designed and made in France in 1804, the paper was brought to Williams by James Bowdoin, U.S. ambassador to France. When the Williams house was demolished, the paper was moved to the Stebbins House.

The **Frary House/Barnard Tavern** was built in the mid-eighteenth century and, around 1795, a tavern wing which included a ballroom was added. The Frary House passed through many hands and was in a neglected state when Charlotte Alice Baker, a Frary descendant, purchased it in 1890. Miss Baker carefully restored the house and eventually willed it to the **Pocumtuck Valley Memorial Association** as the first of Deerfield's house museums.

Ebenezer Wells built the central section of the **Wells-Thorn House** in 1717. It consisted of two rooms: a keeping room and several steps below, following the slope of the land, a kitchen. In 1751, Wells added the two-story, frame front section that now forms the major part of the house. The earlier section has exposed beam ceilings and is furnished with simple seventeenth- and eighteenth-century furniture. The newer part of the house is elegant and decorated with oriental rugs, chandeliers, and draperies.

The **Dwight House** was built in Springfield, Massachusetts, around 1725. It was moved to Deerfield in 1954 by the Flynts and is furnished with Connecticut River Valley and Boston area furniture.

The **Sheldon-Hawks House,** a two-story, timber frame that has weathered to a tobacco brown hue, was built in 1743, and a rear wing was added in 1802. George Sheldon, who was the founder of the Pocumtuck Valley Memorial Association and author of *History of Deerfield,* was born here. The furnishings include many eighteenth-century pieces made in Deerfield.

Ashley House, located at the northern end of The Street, was built around 1730. It is a two-story house with unpainted clapboards, narrow windows, and a double-door entrance. It has a gambrel roof in front and saltbox sweep behind. Jonathan Ashley, a preacher who had graduated from Yale, purchased the house in 1733 for £251. Having strong Tory sympathies, he was often involved in political controversy during the Revolution and religious controversy with Preacher Jonathan Edwards, a fellow Yaleman. The British coat of arms is displayed above the fireplace and on the fireback. Many of Ashley's belongings and pieces of furniture are displayed throughout the house; among them is a portrait of King George III.

Deerfield has a restoration-in-progress exhibit at the **Reverend John**

Farwell Moors House. Visitors are invited to watch the restoration process at this derelict 1848 Gothic cottage as workers carefully search for architectural clues to the original state of the building. An archaeological excavation at the site helps in solving the puzzle.

SIDE TRIPS

Deerfield is the home of several famous prep schools, including **Deerfield Academy,** which was founded in 1797.

Memorial Hall Museum, built in 1798, was the academy's first building. Since 1880, the Pocumtuck Valley Association has maintained the museum, which contains colonial and Indian artifacts. Phone (413) 774-7476. Open daily, May to October. Admission charged.

LOWELL NATIONAL HISTORICAL PARK AND HERITAGE STATE PARK

Restoration of nineteenth- and twentieth-century industrial urban area; NR

Address: 246 Market Street, Lowell, MA 01852

Telephone: (508) 970-5000

Location: In northeastern Massachusetts, just south of the New Hampshire border, 33 miles northwest of Boston; take the Lowell Connector from either I-495 or U.S. 3 (Exit 30N) to Thorndike St. N (Exit 5N), then follow signs

Open: Visitor Center at Market Mills: daily, 8:30 A.M. to 5:00 P.M.; Boott Cotton Mills Museum: daily, 9:00 A.M. to 5:00 P.M.; Working People Exhibit: Tuesday–Saturday, 10:00 A.M. to 4:00 P.M.; Park closed Thanksgiving, Christmas, and New Year's Days

Admission: Market Mills and Working People Exhibit: free; Boott Cotton Mills Museum: adults, $3.00; seniors and Golden Passport Holders, $2.00; children 6 to 16, $1.00

Restaurants: Melting Pot Food Court

Shops: Museum Stores in Visitor Center and Boott Cotton Mills Museum; Brush Art Gallery

Facilities: Guided tours; Visitor Center at Market Mills and Visitor Center at Boott Cotton Mills; trolley transportation; canal boat tours; musical programs; Brush Art Gallery; Sheraton Inn on trolley and canal routes

WHERE TO STAY

Motels/Hotels: Sheraton Lowell Inn, 50 Warren St., Lowell 01852, (508) 452-1200; Radisson Heritage Hotel, 10 Independence Dr., Chelmsford 01824, (508) 256-0800; Lowell Courtyard by Marriott, 30 Industrial Ave. East, Lowell 01852, (508) 458-7575

Camping: KOA Minuteman Campground, Box 2122, Littleton 01460, (508) 772-0042, (800) 822-6746; Wyman's Beach Family Campground, Dunstable Rd., Westford 01886, (508) 692-6287

**Lowell National Historical Park and Heritage State Park,
Lowell, Massachusetts**
A Boott Cotton Mills building, part of a mill complex constructed in the mid-
1830s, is reflected in the Pawtucket Canal at Lowell National Historical Park and
Heritage State Park in Lowell, MA.

Photo by Patricia A. Gutek

OVERVIEW

Lowell National Historical Park is a national park but not a traditional one. Most American national parks contain vast acres of undeveloped land of striking natural beauty preserved as public recreational facilities. Lowell is a developed urban site whose attraction is its nineteenth-century industrial heritage. In this park, which focuses on America's Industrial Revolution, attention is given to five interpretive themes: labor, capital, machinery, power, and the industrial city.

American frontier farming communities are well represented in the museum village genre. While agriculture was a powerful force in early American history, the Industrial Revolution of the nineteenth century was significant in transforming the United States from a rural to an urban nation. Many young people left their farm and village homes for employment in the early factories in this country. Later, immigrants from southern and eastern Europe came to cities to supply the huge labor force industry required. The story of these industrial employees is portrayed at Lowell.

An industrial site, Lowell National Historical Park is an open-air museum encompassing a canal system, mill complexes, worker housing, and nineteenth-century commercial buildings. A trolley system has been provided to move visitors within the park. Because of their large size, only portions of the factory and mill buildings still on their original sites have been restored as museums. Other parts have been remodeled for contemporary usage as apartments, retail stores, and businesses. Over five miles of canals were dug which supplied the water power to ten huge textile mill complexes and a machine-building factory. These canals have been cleaned up and are a significant feature in the industrial park.

HISTORY

The city of Lowell is named for Francis Cabot Lowell, a Boston merchant interested in textile manufacturing. In 1811, he visited textile factories in England and Scotland, seeking to copy the design of their power looms which were essential to factory-produced cotton. With the aid of this remarkable mechanical loom, raw cotton could be manufactured into finished cloth in a single factory. The English and Scottish textile manufacturers, in an effort to restrict competition, refused to sell either the looms or the loom design. Lowell memorized the design of English power looms. He then designed his own model of the power loom which was constructed by mechanic Paul Moody in 1813.

Now, Lowell and his business partners, known as the "Boston Associates," were ready to build textile mills. Their next problem was selecting an appropriate location which could generate a great deal of water power to operate mill machinery. They chose a small rural Massachusetts town called East Chelmsford, acquiring four hundred acres located between the Pawtucket Canal and the Merrimack and Concord rivers.

Originating in New Hampshire, the Merrimack River is one hundred ten miles long and drops ninety feet in elevation over its final forty-eight mile course through northern Massachusetts to the Atlantic port of Newburyport. At its junction with the Concord River was the raging Pawtucket Falls with a drop of thirty-two feet. The Pawtucket Canal, completed in 1796, was built by shipbuilders and merchants who incorporated as the Proprietors of Locks and Canals on Merrimack River. The Merrimack River was used to float timber to shipbuilding yards at Newburyport. Because the steep drop at Pawtucket Falls was hazardous to their cargo, the corporation had a canal dug around the falls to ensure the safety of shipping their timber.

The Boston Associates, a corporation, purchased the controlling stock of the Proprietors of Locks and Canals on Merrimack River, thus acquiring ownership of the canal. In 1822, they formed the Merrimack Manufacturing Company and expanded the Pawtucket Canal and constructed additional canals to power their huge textile mills along the Merrimack River banks. The town, renamed Lowell, expanded rapidly from a population of 2,500 in 1826 to 17,000 a decade later.

The operation of the huge mills required a large labor force. Although Francis Cabot Lowell had been impressed by the factories he visited in England, he was distressed by the miserable living conditions of the English industrial workers. Determined to create a model industrial community with high moral and cultural standards, the Boston Associates recruited as workers the unmarried daughters of New England farmers. Lowell's "mill girls" were Yankee women of English stock and Protestant background.

Corporate paternalism led to strict control over the mill girls' lives. So that they and their families would be assured of a proper environment, lodging was provided for these young, single women in company boarding houses near the mills. Mill girls worked six days a week, twelve hours a day for wages between $2.25 and $4.25 per week, with $1.25 per week deducted for room and board. Along with saving for their dowries and sending money back home, the women's religious and cultural development was provided for in churches, schools, lyceums, concerts, and libraries. The women published a literary magazine. To encourage thrift, banks were opened where they could deposit part of their earnings.

Lowell became known as a model industrial city during the 1820s and 1830s. The textile mills were an economic success, and working conditions were considered very good. A major visitor attraction, distinguished visitors to Lowell's factories included Charles Dickens, Andrew Jackson, and Davy Crockett.

When the second generation of mill owners faced stiffer competition and falling profits, they increased workers' hours in an effort to be more productive. As working conditions deteriorated and wages were cut, a shift in the composition of the work force occurred. Rural women employees formed employee organizations to voice their complaints and waged some unsuccessful strikes. They were replaced by an almost inexhaustible supply of immigrants who came to the United States in the latter half of the nineteenth century. There were Irish, French Canadians, Greeks, Portuguese, African Americans, European Jews, Poles, and Armenians who were willing to take unskilled jobs for low wages. These men and women were the breadwinners for whole families, so they did not live in boarding houses. Tenements sprang up in the industrial area to house these immigrant families. During the post–Civil War period and early twentieth century, the model town turned into an uninviting milltown characterized by exploitation and misery.

The textile business declined in the early twentieth century, and many businesses moved to the South in the 1920s. Industrial buildings stood empty and residents left Lowell to find work elsewhere. What had been a prosperous milltown became an economically depressed town. During the late 1960s and early 1970s, several citizens of Lowell conceived of a historical park which would culturally revitalize the city and rescue it from a fifty-year economic slump. On June 5, 1978, Lowell National Historical Park and the Lowell Historic Preservation District were established. The National Park Service administers the Park.

Tour

Visitors may take self-guided tours or guided tours. Guided tours led by park rangers leave from the Market Mills Visitor Center. Advance reservations are required for guided tours. Both self-guided tourists and those on guided tours may ride the free trolleys which operate daily year-round.

Park Ranger guided tours include The Mill Girls and Immigrants Tour, the Mill Experience Tour, and the Tour Du Jour which focuses on a variety of topics from environmental issues, Native Americans and the Merrimack River, African American history in Lowell, to Women's History.

Lowell National Historical Park tours start at the **Visitor Center** located in the ground level of Market Mills. Market Mills is comprised of two three-story, red brick industrial buildings built in 1882 and 1902 by Lowell Manufacturing Company. In addition to an audio-visual presentation called *Lowell: The Industrial Revelation,* there are exhibits on labor and water power. Also at Market Mills is the **Brush Art Gallery,** an artists' cooperative, and the **Melting Pot Food Court.** Across Market Street is **Mack Plaza** where visitors can catch the trolley.

Housed in the Suffolk Manufacturing Company building which was built in 1831 is the **Suffolk Mill Turbine Exhibit,** which may only be visited on a guided tour. This massive factory houses an original nineteenth-century operating turbine powered by the Western Canal which was dug in 1832. Watching the turbine, you get a sense of the enormous power it generates. Visitors also see the machinery that operates the turbine. Also displayed in Suffolk Mill are a series of hydraulic pumps and an operating cotton power loom.

The restored Boott Mills boarding house, known as the **Working People Exhibit** in the Mogan Cultural Center, provides insight into the lives of the young rural women who comprised the initial Lowell factory laborers. Restored to 1837, the boarding house has a dining room with a long table at which the residents ate their meals. Boarding houses, owned by the textile companies, were often run by widows whose job included buying food for the three meals a day prepared for the young women residents. Exhibits describe typical menus and the meals served. Upstairs, four women shared each small bedroom. On display are some of their letters which tell of their adjustment or lack of it to leaving home and working in the factory. Other exhibits focus on the cultural activities the young women enjoyed, the advertisements that attracted country girls to Lowell, and biographical sketches of several mill girls.

Boarding houses disappeared around 1860 after the labor force changed to European immigrants. The Working People Exhibit displays photographs of immigrants who lived in Lowell from the 1860s to the present. The exhibits identify and portray their churches and fraternal, cultural, and recreational associations.

Boott Cotton Mills Museum is located in Boott Mills, the most architecturally significant of the surviving mill complexes. Named for Kirk Boott, who laid out the designs for Lowell's first mills, canals, and worker housing, Boott Cotton Mills was started in 1835. Originally consisting of four mill buildings, the complex grew in the next eighty years and eventually included eight boarding houses. In 1893, Boott employed more than

2,200 workers of whom three quarters were female. The eight-foot-deep, 2,037-foot-long Eastern Canal was the source of Boott Mills' water power. The factory ceased production in 1954.

The most remarkable sight in Boott Cotton Mills Museum is the recreated 1920s weave room with eighty-eight operating power looms. Several of the looms are actually producing cotton products like dish towels which are sold in the museum shop. The Model E looms were built by the Draper Corporation of Hopedale, Massachusetts, and were used by Borden Mills of Fall River, Massachusetts, from 1913 to 1986. The overhead line shafting and the electric motors powering the lines are from the Appleton Mills in Lowell. Earplugs are provided for visitors as the noise from these machines is deafening. Although conditions in today's weave room are better than they would have been for nineteenth-century workers who would have experienced more heat, humidity, and cotton dust, you still get a feel for what workers had to endure during their twelve-hour work days.

The second floor of the Boott Museum uses multi-image, interactive, oral history, audio-visual programs, mill models, historic machines, and photographs in exhibits on the impact of industrialization on rural New England, the growth and decline of Lowell's mills, and textile production. The oral histories are particularly moving. One former mill worker tells the story of a fatal industrial accident she witnessed.

The Mack Building, constructed in 1886, holds the Lowell Heritage State Park's **Water Power Exhibit.** It is a hands-on museum on the history of water power in Lowell. Its eight-ton, red drive pulley wheel was built by the Lowell Machine Shop around 1908. It transferred about 1,500 horsepower from the turbines to all the textile machines in the mill building via a series of leather belts, shafts, and smaller pulleys.

Both a walking path and the trolley ride will take you along the more than five miles of canals in Lowell National Historical Park. In addition to the museum sites mentioned above, you will pass the Lower Locks, St. Anne's Church (1825), Boarding House Park, and Eastern Canal Park/Kerouac Commemorative dedicated to the author, Jack Kerouac, who was a Lowell native.

HANCOCK SHAKER VILLAGE

Restoration of a Shaker community, 1790–1959; NR, NHL

Address: P.O. Box 898, Pittsfield, MA 01202

Telephone: (413) 443-0188

Location: In the Berkshire Hills of western Massachusetts, five miles west of Pittsfield, at the junction of Rts. 20 and 41

Open: Daily, 9:30 A.M. to 5:00 P.M., May 1 to October 31; 10:00 A.M. to 3:00 P.M., April and November; tours by appointment only from December through March

Admission: Adults, $10.00; children 6 to 17, $5.00; families, $25.00

Restaurants: Village Cafe; Saturday evening candlelight dinner in Believers' Dining Room from mid-July through mid-October

Shops: Village Shop: reproduction Shaker furniture and furniture kits, crafts, books, herb products

Facilities: 1,200 acres; craft demonstrations; historic farm and gardens; orientation films; children's summertime discovery room; special events; craft workshops; twice yearly tours for sight- and hearing-impaired persons

WHERE TO STAY

Inns/Bed & Breakfasts: Inn at Stockbridge, Box 618, Stockbridge 01262, (413) 298-3337; Red Lion Inn, Main St., Stockbridge 01262, (413) 298-5545, FAX: (413) 298-5130; Williamsville Inn, MA 41, West Stockbridge 01262, (413) 274-6118; Apple Tree Inn, Box 699, 224 West St., Lenox 01240, (413) 637-1477; Blantyre, Rt. 20, Lenox 01240, (413) 637-3556, (413) 298-3806

Motels/Hotels: Cranwell Hotel, 55 Lee Rd., Lenox 01240, (413) 637-1364, (800) 272-6935, FAX: (413) 637-4364; Berkshire Hilton Inn, Berkshire Common at West St., Pittsfield 01201, (413) 499-2000, FAX: (413) 442-0449; Best Western Springs Motor Inn, US 7, New Ashford 01237, (413) 458-5945; Jiminy Peak Resort, Corey Rd., Hancock 01237, (413) 738-5500, FAX: (413) 738-5513

Camping: October Mountain State Forest, Woodland Rd., Lee 01238, (413) 243-1778; Pittsfield State Forest, Cascade St., Pittsfield 01201, (413) 442-8992

OVERVIEW

Hancock Shaker Village is the site of a Shaker community founded more than 200 years ago—one of eighteen American communities founded by the communal religious group. About 300 believers lived, worked, and worshipped at Hancock during its 170 years of existence, 1790 to 1959. Twenty original Shaker buildings have been restored at this museum village situated on 1,200 acres in western Massachusetts' picturesque Berkshire Hills. Hancock has an impressive collection of original Shaker furniture, tools and equipment, household objects, textiles, and spirit drawings displayed in room settings or in gallery exhibits. Since the Shakers at Hancock were engaged primarily in agriculture, farming activities and gardens are also a significant aspect of this outdoor museum of Shaker life, crafts, and farming.

HISTORY

In August 1783, Mother Ann Lee, founder of the Shakers, conducted a meeting at the home of Daniel Goodrick, Sr., in Hancock. (See the Appendix for a brief history of the Shakers.) As a result of Mother Ann's visit, several families in the area accepted the Shaker creed and joined their lands and possessions to form a new Shaker settlement.

In 1790, Elder Joseph Meacham, the first American-born leader of the United Society of Believers in Christ's First and Second Appearing, or Shakers, dispatched several brethren to Hancock to bring the believers there into gospel order. This marked the official beginning of the Hancock community, the third of the eighteen main communities founded by the Shakers.

Agriculture was the major pursuit with 2,000 acres under cultivation. Calvin Harlow became the first elder of Hancock, and, in 1791, Sarah Harrison was appointed eldress of the Hancock community sisters.

In 1796, the members of the Hancock community drew up their first written covenant, pledging to "devote themselves and services, with all they possess, to the Service of God and the support of the Gospel forever, solemnly promising never to bring debt nor damage, claims nor demand, against the Society, nor against any member thereof, for any property or service which they have devoted to the uses and purposes of the institution" (John Harlow Ott, *Hancock Shaker Village, A Guidebook and History* [Hancock, Mass.: Shaker Community, Inc., 1976, p. 25]).

The early decades of the nineteenth century brought an increase to the ranks and prosperity of the Hancock Shakers. In 1803, the community's 142 members were engaged in farming, blacksmithing, milling, and

Hancock Shaker Village, Pittsfield, Massachusetts
The Round Stone Barn at Hancock, a 1968 reconstruction of the 1826 daily barn,
lends architectural testimony to the efficient labor techniques developed by the
Shakers. It has become the symbol of Hancock Shaker Village in
Pittsfield, MA.

Photo by Patricia A. Gutek

manufacturing items for sale. Shaker garden seeds, medicinal herbs, and
flat brooms were well-known items produced there.

During the Shakers' period of spiritual renewal in the early 1840s,
Hancock Village was renamed the City of Peace, and a mountain near the
settlement was called Mount Sinai and used for religious services. Hancock
residents received spirit communications in the form of songs or drawings
(see the Appendix for a description of Shaker spirit drawings and songs).
After the period of spiritualism ended, the drawings were placed in drawers
and forgotten. It has been said that they were discovered by Edward Dem-
ing Andrews, a Shaker scholar and collector who lived near Hancock,
when he noticed a sister lighting a fire with a rolled-up spirit drawing.
Andrews's rescue of Shaker drawings was a valuable addition to American

folk art, and this extensive collection is one of the outstanding features of the Hancock restoration.

The population at Hancock reached a peak of between 250 and 300 members organized into six families in the 1830s. In 1853, it had dropped to under 200. Membership gradually declined until only 3 sisters remained in 1959, and the Central Ministry at Canterbury, New Hampshire (see page 00) closed the community. In 1960, the remaining 900 acres and 17 buildings were sold to Shaker Community, Inc., a group of local citizens who wanted to develop the site for an outdoor museum interpreting the Shaker way of life. Restoration of the buildings started soon after.

TOUR

At Hancock Shaker Village, twenty of the approximately sixty buildings that once made up the community have been restored. These buildings belonged to the Church family, one of the six families living at Hancock in its heyday.

The **Visitors' Center,** where tickets are sold and tour information is available, is housed in a modern wooden building. Visitors are advised to allow at least two hours for touring the village; we spent an enjoyable five and a half hours, including a lunch break. The **lunchroom** is located in the Visitors' Center, which also houses the **village shop,** which sells books, Shaker crafts, some needlework kits, herbs, and furniture.

The six-story **Brick Dwelling,** built in 1830, was home for the 100 members of the Church family, who slept, cooked, ate, and worshiped here. On the lowest floor, you'll find the kitchen, a very large room with a brick oven capable of baking fifty loaves of bread at a time. The kitchen had running water and wood-fired appliances for boiling, steaming, deep frying, and grilling which are still used today by interpreters to prepare food from Shaker recipes.

The Brick Dwelling housed both men and women who used separate entrances and staircases. At meals, men sat on the east side of the dining room and women on the west at long tables. They ate their hearty meals in silence. The small dining room was for elders and eldresses, who always ate apart from the others.

Today, visitors can enjoy Saturday evening candlelight dinners in the summer and fall, which are served in the Believers' Dining Room of the Brick Dwelling.

Some of the retiring rooms on the upper floors in the dwelling house are furnished to portray rooms in other buildings that have since been demolished. Consequently, there is a deacon's office, a deaconess's sewing room, an infirmary (which contains cradles for sick adults), and a pharmacy. All the furniture in the Hancock restoration is Shaker, and much of it was made in Hancock.

One of the highlights of Hancock Shaker Village is the imposing **Round Stone Barn.** The three-story dairy barn, built in 1826, was twice destroyed by fire and faithfully reconstructed, the last time in 1968. Inside, the scope of the barn is majestic. The soaring ceiling, with its cupola, and the huge open space gives it the feeling of a cathedral, not a barn. However, the Shakers built it this way for functional reasons: one man could easily feed fifty-two head of cattle working the circular area. The hay was stored in a central area. All three levels are ramped, which enabled wagons pulled by teams of horses to reach the highest level for unloading hay. Still considered an architectural treasure, the round barn alone justifies a visit to Hancock.

The **Meetinghouse,** designed and built by Moses Johnson in 1793, was originally located in Shirley, Massachusetts, but was moved to Hancock in 1962. It replaced the original Hancock meetinghouse, also built by Johnson, which had been dismantled by the Shakers in 1938 because it had fallen into disuse. Like Johnson's other meetinghouses, it is a two-story, white frame building with a gambrel roof and two front entrances, one for men and one for women. Its built-in benches, where visitors sat while observing the Shakers at worship, are original. Docents discuss Shaker religious practices and music in the Meetinghouse. (See the Appendix for a description of Shaker services.)

The **Ministry Shop,** constructed around 1874, was where the two elders and two eldresses, who constituted the ministry, carried out their administrative duties. Like the other members of the community, the ministry was required to do manual labor, so the building had both administration offices and craft workshops.

Many Shaker crafts are demonstrated at Hancock. Visitors can watch the making of oval boxes, brooms, and chairs at the 1795 **Brethren's Workshop** and weaving and spinning in the 1795 **Sisters' Dairy and Weave Shop.** There is a blacksmith's shop and a cabinetmaker in the 1835 **Tan House,** which also has equipment for making apple cider. A printing office is in the **Hired Men's Shop and Print Shop.**

The **Machine Shop and Laundry** is the oldest building at Hancock; it was built in 1790. It contains early water-powered machinery and institution-size facilities for washing. Its ironing room has a conical stove that warmed twenty-five irons at a time. There is an herb and seed exhibit upstairs.

The Shakers established a school in 1791; and by 1817, it had become a public school. The **Schoolhouse** is a reconstruction on the original foundation. The original schoolhouse still exists, but it was moved to nearby Route 41 in the late 1920s.

The **Trustees' Office and Store** was the site of the offices of the trustees, who were charged with regulating trade and administering the lands, monies, and property of the family, as well as with conducting business with all visitors to Hancock. The Trustees' Office, built in 1830, was remodeled in 1895, and the austere Shaker building was converted into a High-Victorian structure with a tower, bay windows, bracketed porches, and awnings and was decorated inside with wallpaper. Victorian furniture, lace curtains, and machine-turned woodwork reflect the changing tastes of the Shakers.

The brick **Poultry House** (1878) now houses a research library on its second floor while the first floor is used for changing exhibits and an orientation program.

Increasing emphasis has been placed on recreating agrarian activities at Hancock during recent years. Hancock was a self-sustaining agricultural village. Farming and raising livestock, rather than furniture making or crafts, were the major activities. An herb garden, an heirloom vegetable garden, and historic breeds of livestock represent Hancock's agricultural heritage. The vegetable garden is planted with many documented Shaker seed varieties. Gardeners use cultivation techniques from the mid-1800s. There are 120 varieties of herbs, both culinary and medicinal, in the herb garden. The Shakers were well known for their high-quality seeds and herbs, and both industries flourished at Hancock. Museum animals include a flock of Merino sheep, striped Dominique and white Wyandotte chickens, work horses, Brown Swiss oxen, and short horn cows. Garden tours and farm animal talks are given daily.

During July and August, the **Village's Discovery Room** has hands-on activities which introduce visitors of all ages to nineteenth-century life. Visitors may try spinning, weaving on a loom, writing with a quill pen on a slate, or weaving a basket. Shaker-style clothing can be tried on, and there are toys and games for youngsters.

Annual special events include Shearing Days with sheep shearing and other spring farm activities at the end of May; an Americana Artisans' Crafts Show in mid-July; an Antiques Show the last weekend in August; Autumn Weekend the first weekend in October; Christmas Festival the first weekend in December; Winter Week in February; craft workshops for adults and children several times a year; tours for sight- or hearing-impaired visitors twice a year; and candlelight Shaker dinners on Saturday nights from mid-July through mid-October.

SIDE TRIPS

Hancock Shaker Village is located near Pittsfield in the Berkshire Hills vacation area, which is rich in natural beauty, cultural activities, and historic attractions. Pittsfield, known as a winter ski area, was home to Herman Melville from 1850 to 1863. He completed *Moby-Dick* at **Arrowhead,** his home, 780 Holmes Road, (413) 442-1793. Arrowhead is open for guided tours daily, from June 1 to Labor Day, Thursday to Monday in September and October. Admission charged.

Norman Rockwell lived the last twenty-five years of his life in nearby Stockbridge. A new **Norman Rockwell Museum** has opened on Route 183 outside of Stockbridge. In its 7,500 square feet of exhibition space are displayed original paintings, drawings, and illustrations from the museum's holdings which include 500 Rockwell works. Rockwell's studio is also located on the property. Admission charged.

On Main Street is the **Berkshire Playhouse,** site of the annual summer Berkshire Theater Festival, which features American drama; (413) 298-5536.

Chesterwood, the summer residence and studio of Daniel Chester French, is near Stockbridge. French was the sculptor of the Lincoln Memorial and the Minuteman statue in Concord. The buildings and gardens are open daily, May to October; P.O. Box 827, Stockbridge 01262, (413) 298-3579. Admission charged.

The town of Lenox is famous for its annual **Tanglewood Music Festival,** with Boston Symphony Orchestra concerts running from early June to late August, Thursdays through Sundays; (413) 637-1940. The festival is held at **Tanglewood,** Nathaniel Hawthorne's 210-acre estate. Most of Tanglewood's formal gardens are open daily and can be visited free except during the festival. The estate contains a replica of Hawthorne's **Little Red House;** (413) 637-1940.

A third important summer cultural event is the **Jacob's Pillow Dance Festival,** held at the **Ted Shawn Theater,** 9 miles east of Lee, on George Carter Rd. in Becket; (413) 243-0745. The festival features celebrated dancers and classic ballet.

Twenty miles southwest of Hancock Shaker Village, in Old Chatham, New York, is the highly acclaimed **Shaker Museum and Library.** Set in a secluded country setting, the museum has a comprehensive collection of Shaker artifacts gathered from many Shaker communities. In addition to a wide-ranging collection of furniture, there are oval boxes, baskets, buckets, stoves, tools, farm equipment, sewing implements, looms, and machinery. Open daily, May through October. Admission charged. Old Chatham, New York 12136, (518) 794-9100.

Eleven miles west of Pittsfield, off Rt. 20, is **Mount Lebanon Shaker Village,** a Shaker community from 1785 to 1947 and the nineteenth-century home of the Central Ministry of the Shakers. Although twenty-six of the original 125 Shaker buildings remain at this impressive site, Mount Lebanon is only in the beginning stages of restoration. The few buildings that have been restored are used for museum exhibits or as a visitor center. Many buildings at the site are occupied by the Darrow School. Open daily, Memorial Day weekend through Labor Day weekend. Admission charged. P.O. Box 628, New Lebanon, NY 12125, (518) 794-9500.

PLIMOTH PLANTATION

Recreation of the 1627 Pilgrim colony; reconstruction of the *Mayflower II*

Address: P.O. Box 1620, Plymouth MA 02362

Telephone: (508) 746-1622

Location: On the Massachusetts coast, 45 miles south of Boston and 20 minutes north of Cape Cod on U.S. 3; take U.S. 3's Plimoth Plantation Highway exit and follow signs; *Mayflower II* is at the State Pier on the downtown Plymouth waterfront, three miles north of Plimoth Plantation on Route 3A

Open: Daily, 9:00 A.M. to 5:00 P.M., April to November at Plimoth Plantation's 1627 Pilgrim Village, Hobbamock's Homesite and *Mayflower II*

Admission: Pilgrim Village and *Mayflower II*: Adults, $18.50; children 5 to 11, $11.00; seniors, $17.50; *Mayflower II*: adults, $5.75; children 5 to 11, $3.75

Restaurants: Visitor Center cafeteria and dining courtyard

Shops: Crafts Center Shop; museum shops in Visitor Center and the ship; J. Barnes Bake Shop at waterfront

Facilities: The Eel River Site includes the 1627 Pilgrim Village, Hobbamock's Homesite, the Carriage House Crafts Center, and the Visitor Center with two orientation theatres and an exhibit gallery; the Waterfront Site at State Pier in Plymouth Harbor has *Mayflower II*, a reproduction of the original *Mayflower*; special events, concerts, and workshops; a Victorian Thanksgiving dinner; seventeenth-century dinners; conference facilities

WHERE TO STAY

Motels/Hotels: Pilgrim Sands Motel, 150 Warren Ave., Plymouth 02360, (508) 747-0900; Sheraton Inn Plymouth at Village Landing, 180 Water St., Plymouth 02360, (508) 747-4900, FAX: (508) 746-2609; John Carver Inn, 25 Summer St. at Market St., Plymouth 02360, (508) 746-7100, (800) 447-7778, FAX: (508) 746-8299; Governor Bradford Motor Inn, 98 Water St., Plymouth 02360, (508) 746-6200, (800) 332-1620

Camping: Myles Standish State Forest, Cranberry Rd., Rt. 3, 44 & 58, South Carver, (508) 866-2526; Scusset Beach State Reservation,

Scusset Beach Rd., Sandwich, (508) 888-0859; Indianhead Resort, 1929 State Rd., Plymouth 02360, (508) 888-3688

OVERVIEW

Plimoth Plantation is a recreation of the first permanent English colony in New England in the seventeenth century. The Pilgrims who settled at Plymouth are inextricably associated with the history and myths surrounding America's forefathers. Important elements of the story include Plymouth Rock, the *Mayflower*, the Mayflower Compact, relations with the indigenous Wampanoag, and our Thanksgiving holiday. Plimoth Plantation tells the story of the 102 English settlers who in 1620 sailed on the *Mayflower* to North America, and those people who joined the colony during the next several years. Pilgrim Village is set in 1627, seven years after the first arrival, and depicts the daily life of the colonists along with that of their Native American neighbors, the Wampanoag Indians. To recreate the atmosphere of some 365 years ago, first-person narration, in which museum interpreters play the roles of actual historical residents, is used at both Pilgrim Village and *Mayflower II*. The staff at Hobbamock's Homesite speak as twentieth-century people because of linguistic difficulties in recreating seventeenth-century Native American roles.

HISTORY

North America was the turf on which European powers' expansionist ambitions were played during the sixteenth, seventeenth, and eighteenth centuries. The major contestants were Spain, France, and England, although Holland, Russia, and Sweden also established colonies. The vast new continent was viewed as a source of gold, silver, and raw materials which would add to the wealth and prestige of the mother European nation. Inter-European rivalry for power stimulated the exploration and colonization of the newly discovered land. Colonies were needed to protect each country's claims to the new land. Needless to say, European nations found no problem in asserting possession of land inhabited by other people. Ethnocentric European colonists did not respect the claims of the indigenous Native American nations who had inhabited North America for centuries. The European colonists, appropriating huge tracts of territory as their own, restricted Native Americans to smaller tracts of their homelands.

In contrast to the economic and power interests of the European monarchies in the New World, individual colonists usually ventured across the ocean for personal reasons. They often were dissatisfied with their lives

Plimoth Plantation, Plymouth, Massachusetts
Native American crafts are demonstrated by interpreters at Hobbamock's
Homesite, a recreation of a Wampanoag family's 1620 New Plymouth summer
encampment near Plymouth Colony. At Plimoth Plantation, Plymouth, MA.
Photo courtesy of Plimoth Plantation

in the Old World and wanted to make a new beginning even at the risk of
privation and death. Colonists' motives were religious and political as well
as economic. This was true of the 102 people who sailed from Plymouth,
England, on the *Mayflower* in the fall of 1620.

Among those on the *Mayflower* were people who were part of a
strong religious reform movement that occurred in England early in the
seventeenth century. Many of these religious reformers, or dissenters, believed that the Church of England, the official state church, needed to be
reformed because it retained unscriptural elements and too many "popish"
vestiges of Roman Catholicism. Those who strove for reform within the
Church of England were known as Puritans while those who formally left
the Church of England to form their own church were called Separatists.

According to English law, the Church of England, or Anglican

Church, was the officially approved state religion. In 1608, an Anglican congregation of small English farmers from Scrooby Manor, Nottinghamshire, formally left the Church of England and established their own congregation. To avoid criminal prosecution and to practice religion freely in their own way, these Separatists emigrated to Holland. Although they found religious freedom in the city of Leiden, the English farm families had a difficult adjustment to urban life. They also felt that their children were being assimilated into the Dutch culture and language and were losing their own ethnic identity.

In 1617, some members of the Scrooby congregation began exploring the idea of sailing to America where they would have both religious freedom and the ability to preserve their ethnic identity. They petitioned for a land patent from the Virginia Company of London, and sought investors who would underwrite the expenses of the voyage. They were joined by a group, recruited by Thomas Weston and other merchants, who were seeking economic prosperity. After obtaining a Virginia land patent and investors, 102 people including about half of the Leiden Separatists, set sail from Plymouth on the *Mayflower* September 6. Due to a navigational error, the *Mayflower* landed at Provincetown at Cape Cod, not in Virginia, on November 11, 1620.

The Pilgrims faced many serious problems. It was winter and they had no shelter. Also, their land patent from a Virginia company was worthless in New England. Thus, the group had no authority to form a civil government. The *Mayflower* passengers reached a decision to govern themselves by mutual agreement—to covenant and combine themselves into a civil body politic. Now known as the Mayflower Compact, the document, signed by forty-one men, established the ideal of voluntary obedience to lawful majority rule in America.

An advance party chose Plymouth, twenty-six miles west of Provincetown, as a good place to settle because of its harbor, defensible high ground, and fresh water. In December, the Pilgrims dropped anchor in Plymouth harbor. The colonists lived on the *Mayflower* while they built their houses. Disease ravaged their numbers and fifty people died during the first winter. However, in the following years other English people arrived to join the Plymouth Colony which became an English farming community transplanted to the northeastern American coast. In 1627, there were more than 150 people living in the colony.

Agriculture and raising livestock were the primary occupations. A Native American named Squanto showed the colonists how to plant corn which became their most successful crop. Surplus corn was traded for beaver skins which were then sent back to England as payment of their debt. A Harvest Home celebration after a bountiful harvest in 1621 became the basis for our American Thanksgiving tradition. Fifty Pilgrims and ninety Wampanoag men were present at the three-day feast.

The Native Americans who lived in what is now southeastern Massachusetts were the Wampanoag. Although each community spent the winters together, they divided into family groups and planted crops in the spring. They hunted deer year round and fished in the warmer months.

Plymouth Colony lasted from 1620 to 1692. In 1945, Henry Hornblower II founded Plimoth Plantation, an educational, not-for-profit organization dedicated to recreating the Pilgrim village. Continuous historical research has been undertaken to ensure the accuracy of the recreated seventeenth-century village, its artifacts and interpretation.

TOUR

The 1627 Pilgrim Village, Hobbamock's Homesite, and the Visitor Center are located at Plimoth Plantation's Eel River Site. The *Mayflower II* is docked at the downtown Plymouth waterfront, three miles north of the Eel River Site, off Route 3A.

Begin your tour at the **Visitor Center** where an orientation film is shown. The exhibition galleries showcase seventeenth-century colonial furniture, tools, and cooking utensils. The Visitor Center has museum shops with reproduction items, a cafeteria, and a dining courtyard.

The **1627 Pilgrim Village** is a fortified town enclosed by a palisade or fence made of eight-feet-high split white oak logs. Inside the palisade is a small town of twenty-one structures with a main street which runs through the middle and is intersected at the center by a cross street. None of the buildings at Plimoth Plantation is original, nor is the village on its original site. However, reproduction period tools and seventeenth-century construction methods were used in building village structures. Designs were based on archaeological digs of early houses in Plymouth and field research in England and Wales. Historical research was also used to accurately reproduce fences, tools, furnishings, costumes, agricultural procedures, crops, and animals that would have been present in the early-seventeenth-century village.

Plimoth Plantation has an amazingly realistic feel which successfully conveys the hard, unglamorous life of the Pilgrims more than 365 years ago. First-person interpretation contributes to transporting visitors back more than three centuries. Each museum guide has assumed the identity of an original resident of 1627 Plymouth and plays only that role. In Jacobean accents, they introduce themselves and talk about their experiences, problems, or their work in New Plymouth. We encounter familiar names like Myles and Barbara Standish, John and Priscilla Alden, William and Alice Bradford, William Brewster, and John and Elinor Billington. Interpreters, who are dressed in reproduction seventeenth-century clothing, carry out the daily chores of the colonists including cooking, baking in the communal oven, tending herb and vegetable gardens, feeding animals, conducting musket drills, shearing sheep, and working in the fields.

Houses, each with a small garden in the rear, line both sides of the main street. The houses are small, dark, cramped, and smoke-filled as fires are lit and cooking is done indoors even in the heat of August. Most are one-room structures with a half loft above for storage. Exteriors are made of unpainted hand-riven clapboards, some with thatched roofs. Chimneys have a wooden framework filled with wattlework (rods and twigs woven together) and daubed with clay. Tiny windows are covered with oiled paper and linen to keep out the cold, or are of wooden lattice or upright wooden bars to keep birds from entering. Another house design is the hovel in which the first floor is dug into the ground.

The **Fort/Meetinghouse,** the dominant village structure, is a timber-framed blockhouse with a ground floor meeting area and an upper gundeck. The original seafront fort, built in 1622 after the Plymouth colonists received news of an American Indian massacre of Jamestown, Virginia, settlers, was intended to provide protection from American Indian assaults or attacks by Spanish or French ships. Plymouth Colony never needed to use the fort for defense. The large structure was primarily used for religious services conducted by Elder William Brewster, and as a courthouse. Other village structures include a **Cow House,** a **Dutch Barn,** a **Storehouse**, and the **Old Common House.**

In its continuing effort to make all details of Plimoth Plantation accurate, animals in the village were selected because they represented or resembled breeds that would have been found in the original Plymouth colony. In February 1992, when the village was closed for the winter, a fire swept the animal barn killing seventy-seven rare breed animals. Raised by hand, these animals were pets of the staff and had been trained to inhabit an environment filled with hundreds of tourists daily.

Hobbamock's Homesite is a recreation of one Wampanoag family's 1620 New Plymouth summer encampment. The Wampanoag were the native people who inhabited southeastern Massachusetts and eastern Rhode Island when the Pilgrims arrived. Hobbamock was the native ally, Massasoit's, representative to Plymouth. He lived with the colonists from 1621 to 1641, serving as a guide and interpreter. The recreation of Hobbamock's residence has four structures in the homesite. One house is a twenty-by-twelve-foot, bark-covered, bent-sapling framed, rectangular house, with two fireplaces in the center and a bed platform along three walls. A small round house is interpreted as the home of a second wife. Hobbamock had at least two wives. Women were isolated during their menstrual cycles in another small house. In hot weather, outdoor work was done in the **Arbor,** a shelter made of saplings and boughs. Houses are furnished with baskets and pottery, as well as Native American and European stone tools. Nearby is a field planted with native New England varieties of corn, beans, squashes, sun flowers, and tobacco. Native Americans dressed in period clothing describe the family's life and demonstrate some of their skills.

If you would like to see seventeenth-century crafts, visit the **Carriage House Crafts Center** which is entered through an exhibit on seventeenth-century trade. Weavers, potters, basket makers, and joiners use their skills to make reproduction seventeenth-century products using traditional methods and tools. A shop in the Crafts Center sells some of their products.

Travel to the Plymouth Harbor to board the *Mayflower II*, a full-scale reproduction of the type of early-seventeenth-century vessel used by the Pilgrims. It was constructed in Brixham, England, and sailed to Plymouth, Massachusetts, in 1957. You'll hear stories about the sixty-six-day voyage in 1620 from the guides who have assumed the identities of the 1620 crew who are preparing the three-masted ship for its return to England. You may also talk to those passengers who have been lucky enough to survive the first winter at New Plymouth, much of it spent aboard ship. Dockside exhibits inform you about the backgrounds of the original *Mayflower's* passengers, and the building and 1957 ocean crossing of *Mayflower II*.

Plimoth Plantation has frequent special events including seventeenth-century weddings, funerals, court sessions, Muster Day, and concerts. The museum also runs workshops on such topics as carving, dyeing with natural materials, doll making, shoemaking, hearth cooking, butter and cheese making, children's archaeology, doublet and waistcoat making, and half model ship building. A mid-nineteenth-century Victorian Thanksgiving Day dinner and celebration is presented annually. Another annual event is the visit by Dutch colonists from Fort Amsterdam which occurs on Columbus Day weekend.

SIDE TRIPS

A must when visiting Plymouth is **Plymouth Rock,** located on the harbor at Water Street and protected by a Greek temple-like colonnade. It is considered the site where the Pilgrims landed.

Plymouth is a treasure chest of historic houses, ranging from the very early **Richard Sparrow House** (1640), 42 Summer St., (508) 747-1240, to the **Antiquarian House** (1809), 126 Water Street, (508) 746-9697.

Pilgrim Hall Museum, 75 Court Street, Plymouth, is the oldest public museum in the country. It was built in 1824 by the Pilgrim Society to house its collection of Pilgrim possessions which includes firearms, furniture, housewares, portraits, manuscripts, and books. The Bibles of John Alden and Governor Bradford are also exhibited. Open daily 9:30 A.M. to 4:30 P.M., (508) 746-1620. Admission.

For a change of pace, take a **Whale Watch Cruise** which will take you to Stellwagen Bank, the mammals' feeding grounds. The full or half-day cruises leave from Plymouth's Town Wharf daily during summer and fall, and on weekends starting in mid-April, (508) 746-2643. Fee.

OLD STURBRIDGE VILLAGE

Recreation of an early-nineteenth-century New England village

Address: One Old Sturbridge Village Road, Sturbridge, MA 01566

Telephone: (508) 347-3362, TDD: (508) 347-5383

Location: In south central Massachusetts, about 45 miles southwest of Boston; on Rt. 20, at the jct. of I-84 (exit 2) and MA Turnpike, (exit 9)

Open: Daily, 9:00 A.M. to 5:00 P.M., April through October; Tuesday to Sunday, 10:00 A.M. to 4:00 P.M., November through March; closed Christmas and New Year's Day

Admission: Adults, $15.00; children 6 to 15, $7.50; admission valid for two consecutive days

Restaurants: Bullard Tavern; Grant Store & Bake Shop

Shops: Museum Gift Shop and New England Book Store; Grant Store & Bake Shop

Facilities: Visitors' Center; picnic area; craft demonstrations; wagon rides; special events; elderhostel program; research library, conference center; Old Sturbridge Village Lodges and Oliver Wight House; handicapped accessible

WHERE TO STAY

Inns/Bed & Breakfasts: Oliver Wight House, US 20, Sturbridge 01566, (508) 347-3327, FAX: (508) 347-3018, TDD: (508) 347-2235; Publick House, Box 187, Sturbridge 01566, (508) 347-3313

Motels/Hotels: Old Sturbridge Village Lodges, US 20, Sturbridge 01566, (508) 347-3327, FAX: (508) 347-3018, TDD: (508) 347-2235; Sturbridge Coach Motor Lodge, US 20, Sturbridge 01566, (508) 347-7327; Sturbridge Host Hotel & Conference Center, 366 Main St., Sturbridge 01566, (800) 582-3232, (508) 347-7393, FAX: (508) 347-3944

Camping: Wells State Park, Rt. 49, Mountain Rd., Sturbridge 01566, (508) 347-9257; The Old Sawmill Campgrounds, Longhill Rd., Box 377, West Brookfield 01585, (508) 867-2427; Wood Lot Campground, Stafford St., Box 968, Charlton City 01508, (508) 248-5141, (800) 255-4153

OVERVIEW

One of the most popular museum villages, Old Sturbridge Village is not old nor was it ever a village. It is an outdoor museum that authentically recreates a typical New England rural town of the 1830s. Characterized by a charming rural setting, original New England buildings arranged around a village common, fine antique furnishings, good historical interpretation, costumed staff, plenty of craft demonstrations and animals, Old Sturbridge Village successfully transmits the feel of a New England town 160 years ago. The village is well suited to family recreation; half a million people a year spend a day or two at this living history museum. The staff makes exceptional efforts to accommodate visitors with disabilities.

HISTORY

Old Sturbridge was founded by Albert B. and J. Cheney Wells, two brothers from Southbridge, Massachusetts, who collected New England antiques during the early 1920s. They accumulated a wide variety of tables, chairs, beds, china, clocks, paper weights, glass, brassware, tools, and pottery. After amassing a sizable collection that quickly outgrew their houses and barns, the Wells brothers decided to share their collection by placing it in a museum. And because they wanted it to be displayed in appropriate settings, they decided to recreate a small New England rural village.

For the museum, the Wells brothers purchased the 167-acre Wight Ballard farm in Sturbridge. It had the geographic characteristics of a New England village, including fields, arable land, woodland, a stream and mill-pond, hills, and ravines. There were two buildings on the property, the Wight House and the Gate House.

Among the first projects that the brothers tackled was moving a barn and two houses onto the green. Next came a gristmill, blacksmith shop, country store, school, meetinghouse, and tavern. Including recent building acquisitions, Sturbridge Village has more than forty buildings which are furnished with the Wellses' collection.

The Wellses succeeded in recreating a typical rural New England town of the early nineteenth century. Unlike the coastal cities, Old Sturbridge is representative of interior New England. It is located in south central Massachusetts and has an agricultural as well as an industrial base, using its own source of waterpower. Daily activities at Sturbridge relate to the agricultural, social, political, religious, commercial, and industrial activities of a typical New England community.

Old Sturbridge is also outstanding for its demonstrations of handicrafts that were common in early-nineteenth-century New England. Visi-

Old Sturbridge Village, Sturbridge, Massachusetts
A costumed interpreter walks in center village during fall
at Old Sturbridge Village, Sturbridge, MA.
Photo by Robert S. Arnold, courtesy of Old Sturbridge Village

tors can see more than eighteen working crafts including weaving, tinsmithing, broom making, coopering, pottery making, candle dipping, and cooking.

Old Sturbridge Village opened officially to the public in 1946, although it had been chartered by the state of Massachusetts as early as 1936 as an independent, nonprofit, educational institution. The village is now administered by an independent board of trustees representing all sections of New England.

TOUR

Old Sturbridge Village is set along the Quinebaug River and is complete with **covered bridge.** The **village common** is particularly picturesque, with historic buildings carefully arranged among trees, shrubs, and gardens containing nineteenth-century varieties of plants and flowers. Only horse-drawn vehicles are allowed on the dirt roads.

Old Sturbridge Village tours begin at the **Visitors' Center** which has a captioned orientation slide show along with information about special activities. The Visitors' Center also holds the J. Cheney Wells Clock Gallery, which displays more than 100 early American clocks and timepieces, and formal galleries with changing exhibitions.

At the **Center Village,** the common is surrounded by the **Meetinghouse,** a **parsonage,** a **law office,** a **tavern,** a **bank,** a **store,** and several homes. The **Meetinghouse,** which faces the Village Common, is a classic white New England church with a tall spire. It was built in 1832 and served Fiskdale, Massachusetts, for over a century.

The **Fenno House,** which also faces the Village Common, is the oldest dwelling at Sturbridge; it was built in 1704 near Canton, Massachusetts. Each home in the village has its own story, and historically costumed staff take the roles of residents. Fenno House is inhabited by an elderly widow and her unmarried daughter. They support themselves by sewing bonnets, taking in a boarder, and maintaining a large vegetable garden. Behind the house is a reproduction nineteenth-century barn.

The **Fitch House,** the second-oldest structure in the village, began as a one-room cabin built in 1737 in Willimantic, Connecticut. Additions were made, and finally, in 1880, the roof was raised to its present half-gambrel appearance. The kitchen has wide-paneled, painted wainscoting and a paneled fireplace wall. The Fitch House is occupied by a country printer and his family.

The small **Village Bank,** in country Greek Revival style, was built in Thompson, Connecticut, in 1835. No community would be complete without a general store, and **Miner Grant's Store & Bake Shop,** built in 1780, served Stafford, Connecticut, from 1802 until it was moved to the village in 1939. The benches on the covered porch still provide visitors with relief for tired feet after an examination of the store's well-stocked shelves.

The fully equipped **Print Shop** is housed in a small gray building nearby. The shop, built in the 1780s, belonged to Isaiah Thomas of Worcester, Massachusetts, author of A *History of Printing in America* (1810). Broadsides are produced on an Acorn Frame press by a printer, who sets the type by hand. Folding and sewing of pamphlets and preparation of books for binding in leather and cloth are done in the **Bookstore,** which is also stocked with early-nineteenth-century books, papers, ink, slates, and almanacs.

The **Salem Towne House** stands at the east end of the common, facing the meetinghouse. A two-story, white, Federal building, it was the home of Salem Towne, a prosperous farmer, Revolutionary War major general, member of the Constitutional Convention of 1780, and Massachusetts state legislator. This elegant home, built in Charlton, Massachusetts, in 1796, has finely detailed woodwork, including wainscoting, window and door moldings, overmantels, and cornices. The sitting room is furnished with a set of mid-eighteenth-century cherry Chippendale chairs from Connecticut and an early-nineteenth-century Massachusetts secretary. The dining room, where one of several Towne portraits hangs, is furnished with New England Empire chairs.

The second-floor ballroom extends across the front of the house. Towne held Masonic meetings here, and the walls have cedars of Lebanon, a Masonic symbol, painted on them. The "all-seeing eye of God," another Masonic symbol, looks down from the ceiling. The ballroom also served as sleeping quarters for the Towne children.

The **Bullard Tavern** is still filling two of its original functions: providing food and drink to tired travelers. The **Taproom** on the main floor serves beer, wine, and cocktails. The Tavern also serves seasonal buffets specializing in chicken pie, baked ham, baked Indian pudding, and deep-dish apple pie. On the lower level is a **cafeteria.**

A white saltbox built in East Brookfield, Massachusetts, about 1748 is known as the **Richardson Parsonage,** home of a Congregational minister and his family. This is a "touch it" house, where visitors are allowed to sit in the reproduction chairs and touch the furnishings.

You can also visit a small **Law Office,** which once belonged to John McClellan of Woodstock, Connecticut, a **Shoe Shop** with a shoemaker hard at work, a one-room **District School,** built in Candia, New Hampshire, about 1800–1810, a **Friends Meetinghouse** built in Bolton, Massachusetts, in 1796, and the **Asa Knight Store,** built in 1810 in Dummerston, Vermont, stocked with fabrics, china, hardware, tea, molasses, and books.

Craft demonstrations are an important feature of Old Sturbridge Village. Demonstrators have been carefully trained in traditional methods and use the same tools as their 1830 counterparts. In many cases, original tools are on exhibit, but the craftspeople use reproductions. Children, especially, appreciate the willingness of the demonstrators to explain their work and answer questions.

Women's work was carefully separated from men's work in New England rural villages. Women will be found throughout the village giving cooking demonstrations, spinning and weaving, making candles, and milking cows. Men can be seen plowing fields, shearing sheep, blacksmithing, and running the mills.

Wooden barrels are still being made at the c. 1840 **Cooper Shop,** and pottery is still being fired in the Goshen, Connecticut, **Pottery.** Every mid-nineteenth-century village had a blacksmith, and the **Blacksmith Shop** still uses the original double forge, built for father and son, in Bolton, Massachusetts, around 1810 by Moses Wilder.

The **Mill Neighborhood,** with its weathered buildings and big waterwheels, is the industrial area of the town. Water supplied the power to most New England mills, and three kinds of waterpower can be seen at work here. The reconstructed **Gristmill** uses the breast wheel, a seventeenth-century invention, to move the heavy millstones that grind rye, corn, and other grains into flour. The **Carding Mill** came from South Waterford, Maine, where it was built around 1840. The water-powered machines separate, comb, and roll the wool, replacing tedious hand carding. The carding machines are powered by a tub wheel, a small, vertically mounted wheel, encased in a wooden tub. The **Sawmill** is a reconstruction of an 1838 New Hampshire up-and-down saw mill. A water-powered turbine operates the mechanism, in which a reciprocating saw cuts logs into boards and planks.

At the early-nineteenth-century **Cider Mill** from Brookfield, New Hampshire, cider making is demonstrated on October weekends. Apples are crushed into pomace at the horse-powered mill, and then pressed to extract the juice.

The **Pliny Freeman Farm,** which originated in Sturbridge c. 1810–1815, will delight children because of its animals. Like most farmers in the mid nineteenth century, Freeman kept oxen as work animals and cattle, sheep, pigs, and chickens for food. Rye, corn, oats, barley, potatoes, pumpkins, and squash were all grown here. Crops not needed to feed the family were traded for needed goods.

The Pliny Freeman Farm is a working farm where agricultural methods of the 1830s are used. Crops grown are 1830s varieties, not modern hybrids, and animals have been back-bred to produce specimens of the same size and appearance as in the mid nineteenth century. This is typical of the careful research done at Sturbridge Village. A three-tiered **herb garden** grows household, culinary, and medicinal plants.

The **Museum Gift Shop and New England Book Store** sells good reproductions, many produced in the village, along with books relating to the period. Special events at Old Sturbridge include town meetings, militia days, an agricultural fair, antiquarian book fair, harvest weekends, maple sugaring, vacation week activities, wool days, elderhostels, holiday workshops, and summershops for children.

Frequent *Crafts at Close Range* programs allow visitors to spend a day learning a traditional craft such as tinsmithing or coopering. On the Fourth of July and Thanksgiving Day, 1830s celebrations are reenacted.

CANTERBURY SHAKER VILLAGE

Restoration of an eighteenth- to twentieth-century Shaker community; NR, NHL

Address: 288 Shaker Rd., Canterbury NH 03224

Telephone: (603) 783-9511

Location: In south central New Hampshire, 15 miles north of Concord; follow signs from I-93, exit 18

Open: Monday through Saturday, 10:00 A.M. to 5:00 P.M., and Sunday, 12:00 noon to 5:00 P.M., May through October; Friday and Saturday, 10:00 A.M. to 5:00 P.M., and Sunday, 12:00 noon to 5:00 P.M., April, November, and December

Admission: Adults, $7.50; children 6 to 16, $3.75; family (2 adults and children under 16), $20.00; Candlelight Dinner & Tour: $32.00 per person; Special Events: adults, $6.00; children 6 to 16, $3.00

Restaurants: Creamery Restaurant open daily for lunch, Sunday brunch, and candlelight dinners on Friday and Saturday evenings; Summer Kitchen

Shops: Carriage House Gift Shop

Facilities: Special events; picnic area; workshops on Shaker crafts; guided tours; nature trails; weekend candlelight dinners

WHERE TO STAY

Inns/Bed & Breakfasts: Wyman Farm, RFD 13, Box 163, Concord 03301, (603) 783-4467; Canterbury Hall, Baptist Rd., Canterbury 03224, (603) 783-9822; Colby Hill, Box 778, The Oaks, Henniker 03242, (603) 428-3281, (800) 531-0330, FAX: (603) 428-9218; Lake Shore Farm, Jenness Pond Rd., Northwood 03261, (603) 942-5921

Motels/Hotels: Brick Tower Motor Inn, 414 S. Main St., Concord 03301, (603) 224-9565; Days Inn, 406 S. Main St., Concord 03301, (603) 224-2511; Hampton Inn, 515 South St., Bow 03304, (603) 224-5322, FAX: (603) 224-4282; Ramada Inn, 172 N. Main St., Concord 03301, (603) 224-9534, FAX: (603) 224-8266

Camping: Silver Lake Park, Lochmere 03252, (603) 524-6289; Thousand Acres, Route 3, W. Franklin 03236, (603) 934-4440; Cascade Park Camping Ground, Rt. 106, Loudon 03301, (603) 224-3212

OVERVIEW

A village of twenty-four original Shaker buildings on a hill surrounded by woods and fields remains as a symbol of peace and tranquility in rural New Hampshire. All Shaker villages are unique, wonderful places to visit, but Canterbury is special because it was, until very recently, one of only two Shaker communities that existed to the present day. During the early 1970s, the remaining handful of sisters decided to turn their property over to a non-profit organization for a museum in which they would share control. Thus, preservation efforts began before the Shakers actually ended their tenure at Canterbury, and the sisters were active participants in the historic interpretation of the site. During the next two decades, fortunate museum visitors were routinely welcomed by Shaker sisters who had been members of the community since childhood. For 200 years, until 1992 when the last Shaker sister died, Canterbury Shaker Village was an active Shaker community. Now, it is a fine museum village where restored original buildings are on their original site. Guided tours are given of selected buildings, and restoration is ongoing. In 1993, Canterbury Shaker Village was designated a National Historic Landmark.

HISTORY

Canterbury Village, chartered in 1792, was the seventh Shaker community founded in America (see the Appendix for a brief history of the Shakers). Since Canterbury was founded in 1792, approximately 2,500 people lived in the village, some for a short time, others for most of their lives. It was an active Shaker community for 200 years. In 1965, Canterbury closed the covenant and accepted no new members. When the last Canterbury Shaker, Sister Ethel Hudson, died in 1992 at age ninety-six, the Canterbury community of Shakers ended.

The Canterbury community began with meetings held at Benjamin Whitcher's home in the 1780s. Eventually, he donated his 100-acre farm as the communal site for the Church Family. Canterbury's meetinghouse was built in 1792 by the Shaker architect Moses Johnson. By 1850, the village consisted of 100 buildings on 4,000 acres.

The 300 residents were divided into four families: Church, Second, West, and North. In addition to farming, they produced wooden boxes and washing tubs, maple sugar, seeds, and herbs; had fine orchards; tended large herds of cattle; and ran a printshop that served the entire Shaker movement. One of Canterbury's most successful products was the Dorothy cloak, designed by Eldress Dorothy Durgin and worn by Frances Cleveland,

President Grover Cleveland's wife, at the 1893 inaugural ball. The cape became the rage among Victorian women.

Like all Shaker communities, Canterbury began a steady decline about the time of the Civil War. In 1972, the three remaining Shakers turned over their twenty-four buildings and 694 acres to Shaker Village, Inc., a nonprofit organization.

Tour

Canterbury is situated on a hilltop surrounded by 694 acres of pastoral land. Its twenty-four buildings, many of which are New England-style, white frame structures, form a serene cluster. These remaining buildings originally belonged to the Church Family. Knowledgeable guides take visitors through the buildings on guided tours.

The **Moses Johnson Meetinghouse,** the village's first building, was completed on September 22, 1792. Like many other Johnson meetinghouses, it is a Federal-style, white frame meetinghouse with a gambrel roof. Initially, all interior woodwork was painted a dark blue, as prescribed by the Millennial Laws, and the woodwork in the upstairs rooms still retains its almost-200-year-old paint. Woodwork in the meeting room was repainted light blue in 1878. It houses exhibits of Shaker-made furniture, baskets, medicines, and stoves.

The **Ministry's Shop** was built in 1848. Traditionally, the elders and eldresses lived on the upper floors of the meetinghouse; but as time passed, they occupied a separate building in which they worked, slept, and carried out their administrative duties. Today, the building's sleeping rooms, workrooms, and offices are furnished with Shaker furniture, much of it made at Canterbury. Elder Henry Blinn, who was a beekeeper, dentist, and carpenter, made the bookcase desk displayed in his office.

The **Sisters' Shop,** a white frame, two-story building, dates from 1817. Shakers made their own clothing, and much of the sewing was handled in the Sisters' Shop. Many sisters were involved in cutting and sewing the extremely popular broadcloth Dorothy cloaks. The room in which the cloaks were made features built-in cupboards and a tailoring bench, a combination tailor's table and chest of drawers designed especially for this work.

Doing laundry was another task assigned to the sisters. In the 1795 **Laundry** at Canterbury, clothes, cleaned in a mechanical washing machine, a Shaker invention, were brought upstairs in a laundry elevator and hung on wooden racks. A steam-operated boiler was used for heating the building and drying the clothes. The Laundry has its original soapstone sinks, washing machines, mangle, extractor, laundry elevator, and steam drying cabinet. The building also contains the original steam-powered woodworking shop.

School was first taught at Canterbury in 1801 by Hannah Bronsen; she used a room in the Blacksmith's Shop. A one-room **Schoolhouse** was built in 1823. The traditional Shaker curriculum was expanded to include agriculture, history, geography, botany, physiology, music, drawing, and elocution.

In 1863, the schoolhouse became a two-story building. Because it was too far from the Church family, it was moved, and a new first floor was added *under* the original building. It was considered easier to add four walls than to replace the roof. Therefore, the second floor of the schoolhouse is forty years older than the first. Moving or adding to buildings was a common practice among the Shakers, along with recycling buildings for other uses. Structures no longer being used were usually torn down.

The restored 1806 **Carpenter Shop** houses woodcrafts such as dovetailing demonstrations, oval box making, and ash basket making. Shaker-inspired furniture and accessories displayed in the Carpenter Shop Gallery are for sale.

The 1819 **Horse Barn,** which has been restored to the 1910 period, is used to exhibit horse-drawn equipment including Shaker sleighs and carriages, and a Concord Coach.

Canterbury's **Infirmary** was built in 1811 and remodeled in 1849 and 1892. It is said to be the oldest extant community healthcare facility in New Hampshire. Patient rooms reflect 1848 and 1892 periods. There is a pharmacy with shelves lined with bottles containing extracts, oils, and powders. In the dental care area are a dental chair, dental tools, and a foot-pedalled drill. There is an original kitchen and nurses' quarters. The Canterbury Shakers were known for their patent medicines, particularly brother Thomas Corbett's Syrup of Sarsaparilla which was prepared from roots, herbs, and berries grown, selected, and discovered by the Shakers. Advertised as a great purifier of the blood and other fluids of the body, it was said to have beneficial effects on cases of dyspepsia, indigestion, thin watery blood, malaria and liver complaint, weak nerves, lungs, kidneys and urinary organs, consumption, emaciation, exhaustion of delicate females, nursing mothers, sickly children, and the aged. Sounds like it could do anything but set broken bones.

The production garden and Physician's Botanical Garden have been moved to their original terraced setting, and all the plants are identified. There is a self-guided nature trail around Turning Mill Pond. A self-guiding pamphlet describes the archaeological mill ruins, a series of dams and sluiceways and the flora and fauna. Another nature trail to Carding Mill Pond passes additional mill ruins.

Canterbury has also been particularly known for Shaker crafts. Workshops given by fine craftspeople are offered in broom making, herbal arts, basket making, woodworking, and weaving.

In the restored **Carriage House,** craftspeople demonstrate basket-making, tinsmithing, woodworking, and sewing. These products are among the items sold in the **gift shop,** which is located in the carriage house. An herbalist has cultivated sixty-two varieties of medicinal and culinary herbs, and some of these are sold in the shop.

Annual special events at Canterbury include Wood Day and Herb Day in May, Mother Ann Day and the Antique Show and Sale in August, Wool Day in September, and Harvest Day in October.

SIDE TRIPS

Canterbury is about twelve miles from **Concord,** the state capital. The **State Capitol Building,** a neoclassical structure of Concord granite and Vermont marble, is the nation's oldest state capitol in which a legislature still meets in its original chambers. Main Street, Concord 03301, (603) 271-2154. Open daily.

Concord's historic district is predominantly residential, with brick and frame houses dating from the 1730s to mid twentieth century. A pleasant way to spend an afternoon is to walk through this district, which is bounded by North State Street, Horse Shoe Pond, the B & M railroad tracks, and Church Street.

Don't miss the **League of New Hampshire Craftsmen** at 36 North Main Street. This is one of several locations throughout the state where jewelry, pottery, needlework, and wooden objects by the finest New Hampshire craftspeople are sold in state-run stores. Open Monday to Saturday, 10:00 A.M. to 5:00 P.M., (603) 228-8171.

The **Christa McAuliffe Planetarium** is dedicated to the memory of Christa McAuliffe who was the nation's first teacher in space. Tuesday through Sunday. I-93 exit 14, 3 Institute Drive, Concord 03301, (603) 271-7827. Admission charged.

STRAWBERY BANKE

Restoration of a seaport town from the seventeenth century to the 1950s; NR

Address: P.O. Box 300, Portsmouth, NH 03802-0300

Telephone: (603) 433-1100

Location: In Portsmouth, on the Piscataqua River, off the New Hampshire coast, about 60 miles north of Boston and 50 miles south of Portland, Maine; I-95 exit 7

Open: Daily, 10:00 A.M. to 5:00 P.M., May to October; 3:30 P.M.–8:30 P.M., first two weekends in December

Admission: Adults, $10.00; children 6 to 17, $7.00; families, $25.00; group rates available

Restaurants: Washington Street Eatery in Conant House

Shops: Dunaway Store; Peacock House

Facilities: Visitors' Center; guided tours; special events; education center; craft shops; picnic area; Thayer Cumings Memorial Reference Library

WHERE TO STAY

Inns/Bed & Breakfasts: Bow Street Inn, 125 Bow St., Portsmouth 03801, (603) 431-7760; Sise Inn, 40 Court Street, Portsmouth 03801, (603) 403-1200; Martin Hill Inn, 404 Islington St., Portsmouth 03801, (603) 436-2287

Motels/Hotels: Port Motor Inn, US 1 bypass at Portsmouth Circle, Portsmouth 03801, (603) 436-4378, (800) 282-7678; Holiday Inn, 300 Woodbury Ave., Portsmouth 03801, (603) 431-8000, FAX: (603) 427-0104; Howard Johnson, jct. US 1, 4 & NH 16, Portsmouth 03801, (603) 436-7600, FAX: (603) 436-7600, ext 199

Camping: Pawtuckaway State Park, Nottingham, (603) 895-3031; Bear Brook State Park, Suncook, (603) 485-9869; Exeter Elms, RFD 3 Court St., Exeter 03833, (603) 778-7631; Pine Acres, Prescott Rd., Raymond 03077, (603) 895-2519

OVERVIEW

Life in Portsmouth, New Hampshire, a New England seacoast village, during a three hundred year period from colonial days to the 1950s is the story told at Strawbery Banke. Unique among museum villages which are usually restored to a single historical era, Strawbery Banke's 300 years

Strawbery Banke, Portsmouth, New Hampshire
The restored Captain John Sherburne House, built in 1695, features leaded
diamond-paned casement windows and twin front gables. It is the oldest structure
at Strawbery Banke in Portsmouth, NH.

Photo by Patricia A. Gutek

of social and architectural history illustrate preservation and change. The tale of the New Hampshire town began in the 1630s when the English first settled New England. It grew into an active seacoast trading port during the eighteenth century, an immigrant neighborhood in the nineteenth century, and a historic restoration in the twentieth century. Nine furnished houses depict the lifestyles of actual residents, while other buildings are used for exhibits on archaeology and architecture. Although most museum villages are found in rural areas, Strawbery Banke is located in the city of Portsmouth, combining the features of an urban historic district and an outdoor museum.

HISTORY

The English who first settled Strawbery Banke in 1630 were sent by the Laconia Company, a group of London merchants headed by Captain John Mason who had a large grant of land in North America. These settlers founded a community on the Piscataqua River and engaged in hunting, fishing, farming, and lumbering. Joined by their wives and families, the community grew to 170 people by the next decade.

In 1638, the Laconia Company went bankrupt, and three years later, the Massachusetts Bay Colony extended its jurisdiction over the town. Soon, Massachusetts Puritans joined the settlement. In addition to their religious orientation, many Puritans were able businesspeople who developed Portsmouth into a thriving trading and shipping center. In 1653, Strawbery Banke received permission from the Massachusetts General Court to change its name to Portsmouth.

Portsmouth was a trading town and the leading port north of Boston during the second half of the seventeenth century. In addition to trade with England, trading in basic commodities took place along the coast from Newfoundland to Virginia, while a lumbering trade was maintained with the West Indian Islands, Spain, and Portugal.

In 1679, heirs of John Mason succeeded in wresting New Hampshire away from Massachusetts. New Hampshire became a royal colony with Portsmouth its capital. By 1700, Portsmouth was a city with much of its land subdivided into house lots, including the Strawbery Banke neighborhood. Artists, merchants, and mariners began building residences and commercial structures. As commerce flourished, the elegant mansions, large taverns, and prosperous shops reflected Portsmouth's accumulating wealth.

A sophisticated town, shipbuilding, trade, and lumbering were the dominant businesses in Portsmouth during the eighteenth century.

Wealthy merchants built imposing homes and their families engaged in an active social life in the royal colony. America's Revolutionary War brought many changes. Trading was disrupted, shops were seized, the British fort was attacked, and the royal governor fled. When New Hampshire became part of the new nation, Portsmouth was no longer its capital.

The shipping trade recovered after the Revolutionary War. However, the War of 1812 again disrupted commerce when President Jefferson placed a general embargo on foreign trade. Lumbering also declined because, by the early 1800s, timber in the Piscataqua region was depleted. Shipbuilding and manufacturing became the backbone of the economy during the nineteenth century. John Paul Jones's famous ship *Ranger* and the USS *Constitution* were built here.

As Portsmouth became secondary to other Eastern seaports and prosperity waned, descendants of the original artisans and mariners began to move away. Their homes were converted to multifamily rental dwellings. The waterfront Strawbery Banke area known as Puddle Dock deteriorated throughout the late nineteenth and early twentieth centuries, but in the 1950s, a local group of preservationists decided to restore the area. In September 1964, Strawbery Banke Inc., a private, nonprofit educational institution, purchased ten acres of land and thirty-five buildings, all but five of which are on their original foundations. The buildings reflect architectural changes in the neighborhood over a period of 350 years. Nine buildings have been fully restored and furnished to reflect the period between 1766 and 1954.

TOUR

A visit to Strawbery Banke provides exhibits on the architecture, furnishing, and crafts of the nation's early maritime period.

On a ten-acre site, there are forty-two historic houses, thirty-seven of which are on their original foundations. Eight houses are furnished, five others have exhibits on architecture and archaeology, and several others are used as craft shops. The remaining houses may only be viewed from the exterior. The **Visitors' Center** has an orientation film and exhibits. There is also a working potter, craft shops, and period gardens.

The **Captain John Sherburne House,** built in 1695, is the oldest structure at Strawbery Banke. It has leaded diamond-paned casement windows and twin front gables. Inside, there are exhibits on the early architecture and settlement of Portsmouth.

The two-story **Drisco House** was built in 1795 and owned by James Drisco, a sea captain and merchant who operated several stores. The house was continuously occupied until the late 1950s, and its furnishings reflect that relatively recent era.

The **Peter Lowd House** dates from 1810. Lowd was a cooper, and his house contains exhibits of nineteenth-century tools used by seacoast builders of houses and dories.

The **Joshua Jackson House,** built in 1790, was the home of a blacksmith who worked for the shipbuilding industry. This house has not been restored because it is meant to show the changes and remodeling added by successive residents during the 160 years it was occupied. An exhibit in the house relates to the lives of twentieth-century residents when the neighborhood was known as Puddle Dock.

The **Captain John Wheelwright House** (1780) was built in the Georgian style prevalent in New Hampshire from 1725 to 1780. The exterior is painted according to a formula used in the late eighteenth century; it combines linseed oil, turpentine, and iron oxide to produce a deep rust tone. The interior of this furnished house is noted for its excellent wood paneling.

A twentieth-century restoration is the Abbott family's 1940s **Little Corner Grocery Store** in the 1720s **Marden House.** Depicting life in the Puddle Dock neighborhood during World War II, the shop and accompanying exhibition, "The Home Front Battlefield," focuses on civilian efforts to support the war. Puddle Dock, as the neighborhood was called then, had many deteriorated houses which had been carved into multifamily dwellings for a newly arrived immigrant population, many of whom were employed at the Portsmouth Naval Shipyard.

A working cooper occupies the **Dinsmore Shop,** located on the site where a small smithy once stood. However, this building, which dates from 1800, came from the Dinsmore Farm in Dundee, New Hampshire.

The **Joshua Jones House** was built in 1790 and purchased by Joshua Jones, a farmer and trader, in 1796.

An **archaeology exhibit** displays artifacts found in digs at Strawbery Banke and in the greater Portsmouth area. There is redware and stoneware from the Marshall Pottery Site which operated from 1736 to 1749.

In one of the **Leonard Cotton Tenant Houses,** built in 1835, a skilled potter demonstrates his craft, explaining his work and answering questions. His fine traditional works are for sale.

The **Winn-Yeaton Houses** were built simultaneously around 1795 by traders Timothy Winn and Thales Yeaton. These dwellings are examples of the compact design necessitated by the space limitations of the urban area. The Winn House contains a thorough exhibit on house construction covering the methods used in four major building styles, three of which are represented at Strawbery Banke: medieval (Sherburne), 1600 to 1700; Georgian (Wheelwright), 1710 to 1800; Federal (Winn and Pierce), 1790 to 1830; and Greek Revival, 1820 to 1860. Exhibits cover windows, plaster, doors, hardware, and decoration, including wallpaper and painting appropriate to each period. The Yeaton house is for exterior viewing only.

The three-story frame **William Pitt Tavern** was built in 1766, and designed to house a Masonic Lodge on its third floor. The tavern was originally named The Earl of Halifax by its loyalist owner, John Stavers. The site of loyalist meetings, the tavern was attacked by a patriot mob in 1775 and Stavers was arrested. Stavers prudently decided to change sides in the conflict between England and its American colonies and renamed his tavern after a pro-American Englishman. Many Revolutionary War figures visited the Pitt Tavern including the Marquis de Lafayette, John Hancock, and George Washington.

The **Chase House** dates from 1762. The Chases, who were in the import-export business, lived there from 1799 to 1881. It then became the Chase Home for Orphans until 1916. The classic Georgian house boasts rich architectural detail both inside and out, as well as the Wendell Collection of Portsmouth furniture.

The **Aldrich House** (1797) was owned by Thomas D. Bailey, the grandfather of Thomas Bailey Aldrich, editor of *The Atlantic Monthly* and a Portsmouth literary figure. Aldrich lived with his grandfather from 1849 to 1852, from ages 13 to 16. His novel, *The Story of a Bad Boy*, is a barely fictionalized account of his childhood years in Portsmouth. After Aldrich's death in 1907, his widow purchased the house, which had been immortalized by Aldrich's book, and restored it to 1850 based on his reminiscences in *The Story of a Bad Boy*. It has been a house museum since 1909. The adjacent **Aldrich Museum** contains Aldrich's books, manuscripts, and other memorabilia.

The two-story frame **Rider-Wood House,** 1800, was the home of Mary and John Rider who purchased it in 1809. A shop was probably operated in the addition on the west side of the house. The furnished house has been restored to the 1830s.

Space limitations dictated the design of the **Walsh House** (1796). Because the house was squeezed on a lot shaped like a pie wedge, it has no square corners. Notable for the unusual painted graining and marbling of its interior woodwork, the Walsh House is furnished with Chippendale and Federal furniture.

The **Goodwin Mansion** was moved from its original site on Islington

Street. Goodwin was governor of New Hampshire during the Civil War. His Federal-style house, with its balustraded hipped roof, has some Greek Revival touches. It was built in 1811 but is furnished as it would have been when the Goodwins lived here from 1832 to 1882. Among the furnishings are many family pieces.

Strawbery Banke's restored gardens reflect a variety of plantings and time periods. The **Sherburne Garden** is a recreated vegetable and herb garden of 1720 while the Herb Garden contains over 100 herbs used for medicinal and cooking purposes during the eighteenth and nineteenth centuries. The **Aldrich Garden** is a colonial revival flower garden complete with a sundial, brick paths, and colonial urns. The **Goodwin Mansion Garden** presents a mid-Victorian floral display based on an 1862 landscape plan found in Sarah Goodwin's diary. The **Rider-Wood Garden** is a utilitarian urban work yard, shed, and garden of the 1830s with heirloom plant varieties.

Special events include New England Gardening Day, Boat Builders Day, the Christmas Candlelight Stroll, the fall festival, July 4th Celebration, and Market Square Day. Demonstrations on boat building, theorum painting, calligraphy, lacemaking, and gardening are offered at the museum.

SHELBURNE MUSEUM

Restored nineteenth-century New England buildings;
important collections of American folk art, transportation,
fine art; SS *Ticonderoga*

Address: P.O. Box 10, Shelburne, VT 05482

Telephone: (802) 985-3346; (802) 985-3344

Location: In northwestern Vermont, on Lake Champlain, 8 miles south of Burlington, on U.S. 7, 7 miles south of I-89 exit 13

Open: Daily, 10:00 A.M. to 5:00 P.M., late May to late October; daily, 1:00 P.M. guided tour only, late October to late May; Children's Tours, Saturday, 11:00 A.M. and 1:00 P.M., late October to late May; closed winter holidays

Admission: Summer: adults, $15.00, children 6 to 14, $6.00; winter guided tours: adults, $6.00, children 6 to 14, $2.50

Restaurants: Tuckaway Cafeteria; Covered Bridge Snack Bar

Shops: Museum store, books, gifts, and reproductions; Diamond Barn Store, candy, toys, souvenirs

Facilities: Visitor Center with audio-visual orientation program; jitney service; picnic areas; partially handicapped accessible; festivals; workshops; lectures

WHERE TO STAY

Inns/Bed & Breakfasts: Shelburne Farms, Harbor and Bay Rds., 05482, (802) 985-8686; Middlebury Inn, Box 798, Middlebury 05753, (802) 388-4961, (800) 842-4666; Swift House, 25 Stewart Ln., Middlebury 05753, (802) 388-9925

Motels/Hotels: Days Inn, 1976 Shelburne Road, Shelburne 05482, (802) 985-3334; T-Bird, Shelburne Rd., Shelburne 05482, (802) 985-3663; Howard Johnson, 1720 Shelburne Rd., S. Burlington 05403, (802) 860-6000, FAX: (802) 864-9919; Holiday Inn, 1068 Williston Rd., S. Burlington 05403, (802) 863-6363, FAX: (802) 863-3061; Sheraton Hotel & Conference Center, 870 Williston Rd., S. Burlington 05403, (802) 862-6576, FAX: (802) 862-5137

Camping: Mt. Philo State Park, Shelburne 05482, 5 miles south of Shelburne on US 7, (802) 425-2390, (802) 483-2314; Little River State Park, Waterbury 05676, (802) 244-7103, (802) 479-3241; Shelburne Camp Area, 44 Webster Rd., Shelburne 05482, (802) 985-2540

OVERVIEW

Shelburne Museum is an outdoor museum which displays extraordinary collections of eighteenth- and nineteenth-century American folk art, artifacts, and architecture. The 80,000 objects in the collections, which represent the life's work of its founder, Electra Havemeyer Webb, can be categorized as folk art, transportation, fine and decorative arts, childhood, New England home life, and tools and trades. The folk art at Shelburne is widely regarded as the best collection of Americana in New England. Not a museum village per se, Shelburne Museum is a collection of collections, one of which is historic buildings including houses, shops, a school, a church, and barns. Of its thirty-seven structures, twenty-four are historic while the remainder of the exhibit buildings have been constructed on site. Buildings are distributed informally in a forty-five-acre park of fruit trees, ornamental shrubs, roses, and formal gardens. Paved paths are a boon to handicapped visitors.

HISTORY

The Shelburne Museum was founded in 1947 and opened to the public in 1952. Most of the objects on display, as well as the twenty-four historic structures, date from the early to late nineteenth century.

Electra Havemeyer Webb is the person responsible for Shelburne Museum. Born in 1889, she was the daughter of Henry Havemeyer, president of the American Sugar Refining Company. Mr. Havemeyer and his wife, Louisine, were avid collectors of European Impressionist and old master paintings. Under the guidance of their friend, the artist Mary Cassatt, they assembled a fine collection that now hangs in New York's Metropolitan Museum of Art.

The Havemeyers were dismayed when they learned that their daughter was collecting folk art and Americana, terms that had not even been coined in 1907, when Electra bought her first cigar-store Indian. She collected quilts, weather vanes, merchants' trade signs, ships' figureheads, dolls, carousel animals, carved eagles, decoys, pewter, toys, hatboxes, carriages, sleighs, covered bridges, and, believe it or not, the steamboat *Ticonderoga*. Electra's early interest in folk art is supposed to have stimulated others, leading to important collections by Abby Aldrich Rockefeller, Henry Ford, and Henry du Pont.

In 1910, Electra Havemeyer married J. Watson Webb, whose family owned a large estate in Shelburne on Lake Champlain. The Webbs had five children, but Mrs. Webb still found time to add to her extensive folk art collection.

Shelburne Museum, Shelburne, Vermont
The restored steamboat SS *Ticonderoga*, a steel-hulled sidepaddle-wheel vessel 220
feet long, was an excursion boat on Lake Champlain from 1906 to 1963. The only
extant ship of its kind, it is at Shelburne Museum, Shelburne, VT.
Photo courtesy of Shelburne Museum

After decades of voluminous collecting, Electra wanted to display
her acquisitions. Her husband, a great-grandson of Commodore Vanderbilt, was interested in local architecture, so the Webbs began acquiring
New England buildings in Shelburne for the purpose of displaying the collections.

Although all the buildings of a typical New England town can be
found at Shelburne, they are not arranged in a village setting. Apparently,
Mrs. Webb saw recreated villages as less than honest. She was more interested in preserving the past than in recreating it. Both Mr. and Mrs. Webb
died in 1960. The museum is now a public, nonprofit educational organization.

TOUR
Shelburne, a small town chartered in 1763, borders Lake Champlain
and is nestled between the Adirondack Mountains to the west and the

Green Mountains to the east. Shelburne Museum has a distinctive flavor, different from that of any of the other sites covered in this guide.

It contains vast and important collections of folk art and other Americana which are eclectic, if not eccentric. The collections are massive rather than representative and total 80,000 items. No matter what category of folk art you are interested in, you will find Mrs. Webb's acquisitions overwhelming. The samplers and quilts, for instance, are outstanding, as is the New England painted furniture.

All of Shelburne Museum's collections are unique, including the collection of buildings. In addition to typical New England homes, barns, churches, and shops, there is a railroad station complete with train, a lighthouse, a covered bridge, a sawmill, a steamboat, and specially designed buildings housing a miniature circus parade and the Webbs' Park Avenue apartment.

The **McClure Visitor Center** is in the **Round Barn** which was built by Fred Quimby in East Passumpsic, Vermont, in 1901. Considered a labor-saving design as a herd of cows could be fed by one person in a half hour, the barn is eighty feet in diameter with a central silo twenty-five feet in diameter. In addition to an orientation slide show, there are videos about the collections. Farm tools and vehicles are displayed in the **Round Barn.**

The **Shelburne Railroad Depot** is a Victorian structure built in 1890 for Dr. W. Seward Webb, president of the Rutland Railroad and Electra Webb's father-in-law. The restored station displays all manner of railroadiana. Outside the station sit a 1915 **Baldwin steam locomotive** and the **Grand Isle,** a sumptuous private car built around 1890 as a gift from Dr. Webb to Governor Edward C. Smith of Vermont.

The SS *Ticonderoga,* a steamboat listed in the National Register and a National Historic Landmark, is the most unusual item found at Shelburne. This 1906 steel-hulled, 220-foot-long, side-paddle-wheel vessel served as an excursion boat on Lake Champlain from 1906 to 1953. The *Ticonderoga* is the only extant ship of its kind. A film about the arduous overland journey to get it to Shelburne is shown aboard. Prints, paintings, broadsides, and photographs related to the steam transportation era are displayed inside the ship.

For many years, the *Ticonderoga* sailed past the **Colchester Reef Lighthouse** on Lake Champlain, and now they are located next to each other at the museum. The small, white frame lighthouse was built in 1871 to warn ships about treacherous Colchester Reef near Grand Isle. It was decommissioned in 1933 and sold by the Coast Guard in 1952 and brought piece by piece to Shelburne. It now houses a display of maritime and whaling paintings and prints, ships' figureheads, scrimshaw, early maps and charts, and Currier and Ives prints.

The **Circus Building** displays a hand-carved miniature circus parade, complete with sixty bandwagons, cage wagons, animals, riders, clowns, and musicians created by contemporary artist Roy Arnold. It stretches 518 feet in the horseshoe-shaped building custom-made for it. The Circus Building also displays forty hand-carved, full-sized carousel figures and a collection of circus posters.

The first building moved to Shelburne in 1947 was the **Vergennes Schoolhouse,** a one-room brick structure resembling a meetinghouse. It was built in 1830 at Vergennes, Vermont, by General Samuel Strong, who rented the school to the town for an annual fee of one kernel of American Indian maize. Today, it is furnished with school desks, blackboards, stove, and copybooks.

The 1782 **Stagecoach Inn** comes from Charlotte, Vermont, where it was on the stage route between Canada and southern New England. Hezakiah Barnes's spacious inn, complete with ten fireplaces, now exhibits folk art, including carved eagles, cigar-store Indians, trade signs, and weather vanes.

Wildfowl decoys, another part of the Webb folk art collection, fill the **Dorset House,** a Greek Revival structure built in 1840 in East Dorset, Vermont.

Textile arts are displayed in the **Hat and Fragrance Unit.** Quilts, coverlets, hooked and bed rugs, samplers, homespun cloth, and lace from the eighteenth century to the present are exhibited in tremendous quantities. The quilt collection has 400 pieced, appliqued, crazy and embroidered quilts. Rooms filled with dollhouses and miniature furniture also abound.

Electra Havemeyer Webb began collecting dolls when she was a child. Her 1,500 dolls are displayed in the **Variety Unit,** a red brick two-story house built in 1835. Originally known as the Weed House, it, along with the Toy Shop, are the only buildings at Shelburne still on original sites.

The **Toy Shop** also commemorates a child's world with handmade wooden toys, banks, trains, and music boxes, just to name a few of the playthings on display.

Over 200 carriages, sleighs, farm wagons, Conestoga wagons, stagecoaches, and trade wagons occupy the **Horseshoe Barn and Annex.** This newly constructed building is based on a horseshoe-shaped barn near Georgia, Vermont. Many of the vehicles were from the Shelburne estate of Electra Webb's father-in-law, Dr. William Seward Webb, where they had been maintained and stored in a coach house until 1946. At that time, they were offered to Electra just as she was founding her museum. Although not arranged as a village, Shelburne has assembled and restored many original New England buildings. There is the well-stocked 1840 **general store** from Shelburne; the **Charlotte Meeting House,** a brick 1840 church from Charlotte, Vermont; the **Castleton State Jail,** a solid brick and slate 1890 structure from Castleton, Vermont; a **sawmill;** a **smokehouse;** an 1800 hand-hewn log cabin called **Sawyer's Cabin** from East Charlotte, Vermont; and the 1840 **Little Stone Cottage** from South Burlington, Vermont.

Period houses that have been restored and furnished with American furniture are the **Prentis House,** the oldest house at Shelburne, a saltbox built in 1733 by the Dickenson family of Hadley, Massachusetts; the **Dutton House,** a red saltbox built in 1782 at Cavendish, Vermont; and the charming 1790 Cape Cod cottage from Columbus, New York, known as **Stencil House** because of its beautifully stenciled walls done by an itinerant artist, possibly Moses Eaton.

The **Shaker Shed** is from the Shaker village in Canterbury, New Hampshire (see page 55). Built in 1834 for horses and carriages, this large, two-and-a-half-story building houses a display of tools and household implements built around the extensive Frank H. Wildung collection of woodworking tools.

The children of J. Watson and Electra Webb built an unusual memorial to their parents at Shelburne: a Greek Revival building that contains six of the seventeen rooms from their **Park Avenue apartment.** Faithfully reconstructed in every detail, the rooms are decorated with the couple's fine furnishings and filled with art inherited by Mrs. Webb from her parents, Henry and Louisine Havemeyer. Paintings by Monet, Degas, Cassatt, Goya, and Rembrandt hang throughout the apartment.

Three centuries of American artwork, including primitive folk art and early portraits, are displayed in the **Webb Gallery.**

The **Tuckaway Barn,** an 1835 structure from Shelburne, houses the cafeteria.

Craftspeople demonstrate traditional skills at the Blacksmith, Printing, and Weaving Shops. Special events are held throughout the year and include Children's Tours, Craft Fair, and Christmas at Shelburne.

SIDE TRIPS

Shelburne Farms, the summer estate of Dr. William Seward Webb and his wife, Lila Vanderbilt, was established in 1885 on 4,000 acres along the shore of Lake Champlain. Tours of the 110-room Shelburne House, which is now operated as an inn, the farm barn, coach barn, Gate House Visitor Center, and 1,000 remaining acres, landscaped by Frederick Law Olmsted, are available daily, Memorial Day to mid-October. Located on Harbor Road, 1 mile west of Shelburne. Admission fee. (802) 985-8442; Inn: (802) 985-8686.

The Shelburne Museum is only a few miles away from beautiful **Lake Champlain,** a popular recreation area. Ferries cross the lake to New York from Charlotte and Burlington. For information, call (802) 864-9804. You can take a paddle-wheeler cruise on the *Spirit of Ethan Allen,* which also has dinner cruises. For information, call (802) 862-9685.

NEW YORK

Genesee Coutry Village

The Farmer's Museum
and Village Crossroads

PENNSYLVANIA

Old Economy Village

Landis Valley
Museum

Hopewell
Furnace

Ephrata Cloister

Hagley Museum
and Library

DELAWARE

MIDDLE ATLANTIC

DELAWARE
  Hagley Museum and Library, Wilmington

NEW YORK
  The Farmers' Museum and Village Crossroads,
    Cooperstown
  Genesee Country Village, Mumford

PENNSYLVANIA
  Old Economy Village, Ambridge
  Hopewell Furnace, Elverson
  Ephrata Cloister, Ephrata
  Landis Valley Museum, Lancaster

HAGLEY MUSEUM AND LIBRARY

Restoration of the early-nineteenth-century Du Pont estate and black powder mills; NHL, NR

Address: P.O. Box 3630, Wilmington, DE 19807
Telephone: (302) 658-2400
Location: On Rt. 141; from I-95, take exit 5N to Rt. 141 south
Open: Daily, 9:30 A.M. to 4:30 P.M., March 15 to December; January to March 14: Saturday and Sunday, 9:30 A.M. to 4:30 P.M., and Monday to Friday, 1:30 P.M. guided tour only; closed Thanksgiving, Christmas, and New Year's Eve
Admission: Adults, $9.75; senior citizens and students, $7.50; children 6 to 14, $3.50; families, $26.50; group rates available
Restaurants: Belin House Coffee Shop
Shops: Hagley Store sells gifts and books
Facilities: Research library of American business and technology; visitors' center and museum; visitor buses; guided tours; picnic areas; special events; partially handicapped accessible; National Recreational Trail

WHERE TO STAY

Inns/Bed & Breakfasts: Brandywine River Hotel, Rts. 1 & 100, P.O. Box 1058, Chadds Ford, PA 19317, (215) 388-1200; The Boulevard B&B, 1909 Baynard Blvd., Wilmington 19802, (302) 656-9700; Meadow Spring Farm, 201 E. Street Rd. (Rt. 926), Kennett Square, PA 19348, (215) 444-3903; Fairville Inn, Rt. 52, Box 219, Mendenhall, PA 19357, (215) 388-5900; B&B of Chester Co. (a reservation service), Kennett Square, PA 19348, (215) 444-1367
Motels/Hotels: Best Western Brandywine Valley Inn, 1807 Concord Pike, Wilmington 19803, (302) 656-9436; Hotel du Pont, 11th & Market Sts., Wilmington 19801, (302) 594-3100, (800) 441-9019; Holiday Inn Downtown, 700 King St., Wilmington 19801, (302) 655-0400, FAX: (302) 655-5488
Camping: Odessa Campground, 801 Blackbird Landing Rd., Townsend, DE 19734, (302) 378-4111; West Chester KOA Campground, Box 502, Unionville, PA 19375, (215) 486-0447; Chester Co. Parks & Recreation, 235 W. Market, West Chester, PA 19375, (215) 344-6415

Overview

Hagley Museum tells two stories: the history of nineteenth-century industrialization and the history of the du Pont family of Delaware, founders of E. I. du Pont de Nemours & Company, today one of the world's largest corporations. Almost two hundred years ago Eleuthère Irénée du Pont began manufacturing black powder for ammunition and explosives, a trade learned in his native France. On Delaware's Brandywine River banks stood the black powder mill, the first home of the du Pont family in America, and the rowhouse dwellings of the mill workers. Restoration of this very early nineteenth-century industrial site and community includes the du Pont mansion, garden and company office, many powder mill buildings, and some workers' dwellings on a 240-acre wooded site.

History

During the eighteenth and early nineteenth centuries, economic development was closely tied to water power. Small-scale industries, such as the Du Pont black powder mills, were located on the banks of rivers.

Eleuthère Irénée du Pont, his brother Victor, and their father, Pierre Samuel du Pont de Nemours, emigrated to America from France in 1800. E. I. du Pont, who had worked in black powder manufacturing in France, decided to establish a black powder mill in America. Upon arriving in Delaware, he purchased property along the Brandywine River.

The sixty-mile-long Brandywine River was the site of flour, cotton, paper, saw, snuff, and black powder mills. Originating in the Welsh Mountains of Pennsylvania, the Brandywine has a daily volume of 600,000 tons of water and drops 125 feet in its last five miles. Moreover, it was surrounded by fertile land and close to well-traveled trade routes. Du Pont chose a site along the Brandywine not only because of good water power but also because ingredients needed to make black powder (sulphur from Italy and saltpeter from Bengal) could be shipped to nearby Wilmington. Another ingredient, charcoal, was produced from willow trees that grew on or near du Pont's property.

In 1802, E. I. du Pont began construction of powder mills, a home, and a garden. The home, now known as Eleutherian Mills, was built on the hillside overlooking the mills so that du Pont could direct operations from his home. Business was conducted from the house until 1837, when the first office of the Du Pont Company was built near the northwest corner of the family dwelling. It served as the company office until 1891.

Hagley Museum and Library, Wilmington, Delaware
Exhibits in the Millwright Shop, a restored machine shop built in 1858, explain
the black powder manufacturing process developed by Eleuthère Irénée du Pont,
the founder of the Du Pont Corporation. At Hagley Museum and Library,
Wilmington, DE.

Photo by Patricia A. Gutek

Thus, both the du Pont family and its business were based at Eleutherian
Mills for almost a century.

Although du Pont had the advantage of being able to see and direct
his mills' operations from home, there was a serious disadvantage in that
he and his family shared with workers the danger of their business. When
the inevitable accidental explosion occurred in the mills, the home usually
sustained damage. A particularly severe blast in 1890 drove Louisa du
Pont, widow of E.I.'s son Henry, and their daughter, Evelina, from their
home permanently.

Du Pont's use of the finest ingredients and manufacturing methods
learned in France produced black powder superior to any made in

America. His business was so successful that in 1810, he purchased additional land along the Brandywine previously named Hagley. The Hagley property allowed du Pont to expand the powder yard and increase his business significantly. Du Pont black powder was used in mining, canal construction, land-clearing, hunting, and war.

Du Pont's first powder mills were powered by water wheels. However, other energy sources were adopted as they became available. In the 1840s, waterwheels started to be replaced with more efficient water turbines; and by the 1880s, turbines had replaced all the company's waterwheels. Because turbines also relied on the sometimes inadequate water power, steam engines were purchased beginning in 1855. By the late 1880s, electrical power provided current for lighting the mills. In 1900, the New Century Power House, a hydroelectric plant, was built. The mills themselves continued to be operated by water power most of the time.

The Du Pont Company became the largest powder manufacturer in America under the leadership of E. I. du Pont's son Henry and was incorporated in the early 1900s. Expansion led to the production of other chemical products. The company supplied forty percent of all the explosives used by the Allied forces in World War I.

In 1921, powder manufacturing was discontinued along the Brandywine River. The Du Pont Company sold the land to several members of the du Pont family. Some of those, in turn, later donated portions of that property to make possible today's Hagley Museum and Library.

TOUR

Though during its 120 years of operation, the Du Pont black powder mills undoubtedly created a noisy, smoke-filled environment, the atmosphere at today's restoration is positively idyllic. The former industrial site is now a 240-acre wooded site filled with flowering shrubs and formal gardens on the banks of a cascading river; it is also a wildlife preserve and home to Canada geese. Most buildings at Hagley Museum, and indeed countless buildings in the Brandywine River valley, are of locally quarried granite, which blend naturally into the peaceful landscape.

Tours start at the **Henry Clay Mill** building, a three-story Delaware stone building constructed in 1814 as a cotton-spinning mill. In 1884 it was converted by the Du Pont Co. to the production of metal powder kegs. Now a **visitors' center and museum,** the building has exhibits on the first floor relating to the harnessing of Brandywine water power for industrial use. Dioramas of mill operations, along with tools and items relating to company history are displayed. Additional exhibits focus on the Delaware Indians, the du Pont family in France during the French Revolution, and the industries of the Brandywine area. The second floor of the museum is used for changing exhibits. Guided tours leave from the Henry Clay Mill.

In the restored industrial site are three areas: the **Powder Yard** which focuses on the black powder making process through working models and machinery demonstrations. The Millwright Shop, powder mills, a water wheel, turbine, and stone quarry are in the Powder Yard. The Eleutherian Mills area has Eleutherian Mills, the E. I. du Pont residence, the restored French garden, the first Du Pont Company office building, and a barn. Blacksmith Hill, the workers' community, has the Gibbons House, the Brandywine Manufacturers' Sunday School, and the Belin House.

The **Millwright Shop,** a restored machine shop, was built in 1858 and used for repairing power yard machinery. Exhibits explain E. I. du Pont's superior process of black powder manufacture. From here, visitors can follow the steps in manufacturing black powder as they visit other restored buildings, and see a working 1870s **machine shop.**

Twenty-one **powder mills** still stand at Hagley, but only some have been restored. They are constructed of three heavy stone walls with the fourth wall and roof of lighter material. They were designed to channel the force of an explosion toward the river rather than toward nearby powder-filled structures.

Black powder was originally mixed in stamping mills; by 1822, these were replaced by roll mills, where huge cast-iron wheels ground the three ingredients: sulphur, saltpeter, and charcoal. Demonstrations of turbine-powered roll mills are given throughout the day at the **Eagle Roll Mills,** which was constructed in 1839 and rebuilt in 1886. The powder was then pressed hydraulically in the **press house** and reduced to grains at the **graining mills.** The next step was to tumble the powder in glazing barrels at the **glaze mill** to round the grains. Then powder was either dried in the **dry house,** which was heated by the **steam engine house,** or spread on dry tables outdoors in the sun. Demonstrations are conducted at the engine house and the dry table area. Powder was then packaged in wrappers, metal canisters, and wooden kegs at the **pack house** and shipped by Conestoga wagon or ship and, later, railroad.

Opposite the Millwright Shop is a **stone quarry** where demonstrations of drilling, cutting, and transporting stone are conducted.

Blacksmith Hill, a recently restored area, includes the Gibbons House, Belin House, and the Brandywine Manufacturers' Sunday School, some of the few buildings that remain of the workers' communities that once covered the hillsides on both sides of the river. The focus of Blacksmith Hill is on the lives of the employees who worked, lived, and raised their families on the mill property.

The restored **Gibbons House** was the home of the family of John Gibbons, a powder yard foreman from the late 1850s to the 1880s. Like many of his fellow employees, Gibbons was Irish. A restored garden is planted with historically authentic vegetables which provided many of the ingredients of Irish stew often prepared on the wood-burning stove.

The **Belin House** was the home of a succession of company book-keepers. It is now used as a coffee shop.

The **Brandywine Manufacturers' Sunday School** is a one-story stone building dating from 1817. Many children worked in the area mills, though not in the powder mills, and their day off was Sunday. The only education offered to them was this Sunday School, which at its height was attended by 200 children. The interior of the one-room school has rows of desks and benches. Quill pens and black slates sit on the desks. Heat was provided by a wood-burning stove.

The Eleutherian Mills area is dominated by the 1802 two-and-a-half-story residence, which was renovated in the colonial revival style by E. I. du Pont's great-granddaughter, Louise Crowinshield, in 1923.

The first floor of **Eleutherian Mills** reflects Louise Crowinshield's decor. A morning room is furnished with Queen Anne and Chippendale antiques, a dining room has French wallpaper, and there is a nineteenth-century pianoforte in the parlor. The rooms on the second floor are deco-rated in a variety of furniture styles, each of which reflects the taste of a particular generation of du Ponts. The blue room is furnished with Federal pieces dating from about 1800 to 1830, some of which belonged to E. I. du Pont. Among them are a Philadelphia desk, a black windsor chair, a rush-bottom rocker, and a mahogany sleigh bed. Sophie and E. I. du Pont's bedroom contains a mahogany bed they purchased from a Philadelphia cabinetmaker around 1808, and their mahogany crib. The daughters' room reflects the empire period while the library is Victorian.

The small **First Office** has been restored to its appearance in 1850, when Henry du Pont, E.I.'s son, was director of the company. There are several Bob Cratchett-type desks and stools for the bookkeepers and a large vault where money and company papers would be safe from an explosion. During the company's 120 years on the Brandywine, 230 persons lost their lives in explosions.

The du Pont family also engaged in farming, raising corn, oats, rye, and fodder crops to feed workhorses, mules, and oxen. The **Stone Barn** was built in 1802 and enlarged and reconstructed in 1844, with stone buttresses added to resist the force of explosions. The most impressive of the vehicles on display is the man-dwarfing Conestoga wagon. Several teams of oxen or horses were needed to haul its load of explosives to market.

E. I. du Pont's gardens and orchards were planted in 1802 and designed in the French manner, with vegetables and flowers side by side. The lovely restored garden is composed of four quadrants, each bordered by dwarf fruit trees. It also contains a reconstructed pump, a summerhouse, and an arbor.

The **Hagley Library** is housed in a modern granite building nearby. A research library, its extensive holdings include printed, graphic, and manuscript sources relating to more than 1,000 firms, as well as major business organizations. The library is an internationally known center for the study of business, economic, and technological history.

SIDE TRIPS

The Brandywine Valley is an area of natural beauty, historical significance, and cultural attractions. Because of its proximity to Philadelphia and Wilmington, it is a busy area, with fairly heavily traveled roads. Consequently, reservations are a must at hotels, motels, popular restaurants, and some of the sights.

The Hagley Museum is not the only property associated with the du Pont family that is open to visitors. **Winterthur Museum and Gardens** is a museum of American decorative arts in a house built in 1839 for James Antoine and Evelina Gabrielle du Pont Bidermann, E. I. du Pont's daughter and son-in-law. In 1927, it was inherited by Henry Francis du Pont, a grandnephew of the Bidermanns and a collector. He greatly enlarged the house to a sprawling nine-story building with 196 rooms and display areas.

The collection of Americana housed in Winterthur is considered one of the finest and largest in the world. Not content simply to collect furnishings, Henry Francis also collected entire rooms, complete with such architectural elements as fireplaces, walls, floors, and ceilings, so that the furnishings would be displayed in appropriate settings. Therefore, the house is really a collection of rooms that have been moved and installed in their entirety, representing the history of American furnishings and interior architecture. There are even some building facades arranged around a courtyard.

Henry Francis du Pont was also a gardener and a landscape artist. There are 60 acres of display gardens in addition to 900 acres of woods and farmland.

A 35,000-square-foot exhibition center in which permanent and changing exhibits are displayed is the newest addition to Winterthur.

Winterthur is located on Rt. 52, six miles northwest of Wilmington. Open Tuesday to Saturday, 9:30 A.M. to 5:00 P.M.; Sunday, 12:00 noon to 5:00 P.M.; closed Mondays and holidays. Admission tickets which include the garden, the exhibition center, and two guided museum tours are: adults, $9.00; seniors and children 12 to 18, $7.50; children 5 to 11, $4.50. Museum specialty tours are available for an additional admission. For information, call (302) 888-4600 or (800) 448-3883.

Nemours, the chateau of Alfred I. du Pont, great-grandson of E. I. du Pont, contains fine examples of European antique furniture, oriental rugs, tapestries, and paintings dating to the fifteenth century. Fine French-style gardens surround the chateau. On Rockland Road, off Route 141, Wilmington. Tours available Tuesday to Sunday, May to November. Admission: $6.00 (visitors must be over 16 years old). For information, call (302) 651-6912.

Longwood Gardens is a 1,000-acre property; some 350 acres are gardens open to the public. Some of the property was originally owned by William Penn, who sold it to a Quaker family named Peirce in 1700. The Peirces created one of America's first tree parks. Pierre S. du Pont, a great-grandson of E. I. du Pont, was deeply interested in horticulture and landscape design. He purchased the property in 1906 and began designing gardens and building conservatories. There are twenty indoor gardens in glass conservatories; they are magnificent in their color, quantity, and design. Outdoors, carefully laid-out gardens feature the seasonal foliage. In addition, tours of the **Peirce–du Pont House** are available.

Longwood Gardens is on U.S. 1 in Kennett Square, Pennsylvania. The outdoor gardens are open daily from 9:00 A.M. to 6:00 P.M., April to October, and from 9:00 A.M. to 5:00 P.M., November to March; the conservatories are open daily from 10:00 A.M. to 5:00 P.M. Admission charged. For information, call (215) 388-6741.

The **Brandywine River Museum,** Chadds Ford, Pennsylvania, has one of the largest public collections of paintings by Andrew Wyeth, a resident of Chadds Ford, as well as works by his father, N.C. Wyeth, and his son, Jamie Wyeth. Open daily, 9:30 A.M. to 4:30 P.M. Admission charged. Handicapped accessible. On U.S. 1, Chadds Ford, PA 19317, (215) 388-7601 or (215) 459-1900.

Brandywine Battlefield Park commemorates the Revolutionary War Battle of Brandywine which occurred here September 11, 1777. This defeat for George Washington led to the capture of Philadelphia by the British. Visitors can tour the reconstructed Washington's Headquarters, the restored Lafayette's Quarters, Birmingham Hill and the Visitor Center. Open Tuesday to Saturday, 9:00 A.M. to 5:00 P.M., Sunday, 12:00 noon to 5:00 P.M. Admission charged. P.O. Box 202, Chadds Ford, PA 19317, (215) 459-3342.

THE FARMERS' MUSEUM AND VILLAGE CROSSROADS

Recreation of an early-nineteenth-century upstate farming village

Address: Lake Rd., P.O. Box 800, Cooperstown, NY 13326
Telephone: (607) 547-2593
Location: In central New York state, 70 miles west of Albany and 30 miles south of the New York Thruway
Open: Daily, 9:00 A.M. to 6:00 P.M., May to October; Tuesday to Sunday, 10:00 A.M. to 4:00 P.M., April, November, and December
Admission: Farmers' Museum: adults, $8.00; children 7 to 12, $3.00. Combination ticket with Fenimore House: adults, $6.00; children 7 to 12, $2.50. Combination ticket with Fenimore House and Baseball Hall of Fame: adults, $15.00; children 7 to 12, $6.00
Restaurants: Snack bar
Shops: The Farmers' Museum Gift Shop; General Store; Fenimore House Bookstore
Facilities: Twelve restored buildings; main barn exhibition center; working craftspeople; workshops; seminars; lectures; special events; partially handicapped accessible

WHERE TO STAY

Inns/Bed & Breakfasts: Cooper Motor Inn, Cooperstown 13326, (607) 547-9931, (800) 334-0114; Inn at Cooperstown, 16 Chestnut St., Cooperstown 13326, (607) 547-5756; Tunnicliff, 36 Pioneer St., Cooperstown 13326, (607) 547-9611, (800) 446-8466
Resorts: Otesaga Hotel, Cooperstown 13326, (607) 547-9931, (800) 334-0114
Motels/Hotels: Deer Run, Box 722, RD 2, Cooperstown 13326, (607) 547-8600, (607) 547-8644; Hickory Grove Motor Inn, Box 896, RD 2, Lake Rd., Cooperstown 13326, (607) 547-9874; Lake 'N Pines, Box 784, RD 2, Cooperstown 13326, (607) 547-2790
Camping: Glimmerglass State Park, East Lake Rd., Cooperstown 13326, (607) 547-9662; Gilbert Lake State Park, Oneonta, (607) 432-2114; Beaver Valley Campground, Box 704, Cooperstown 13326, (607) 293-7324; Cooperstown Shadow Brook Campground, RD 2, Box

646, East Lake Rd., Country Rd. 31, Cooperstown 13326, (607) 264-8431; Meadow Vale Campsites, RD 1, Mt. Vision 13810, (607) 293-8802; Cooperstown Famous Family T & T, RD 3, Box 281, Cooperstown 13326, (607) 293-7766

OVERVIEW

Known primarily as the birthplace of baseball and the home of the National Baseball Hall of Fame, Cooperstown, New York, is a two-hundred-year-old picturesque resort village with a historic district of large old homes on tree-lined streets on the shore of Lake Otsego. Surrounded by rolling, wooded hills, Lake Otsego was dubbed "Glimmerglass" by James Fenimore Cooper, the early nineteenth-century American novelist from Cooperstown, who wrote about the American frontier.

Today, Cooperstown proudly calls itself the "Village of Museums" because it is home not only to the National Baseball Hall of Fame but also to The Farmers' Museum and Village Crossroads, Fenimore House, which has an outstanding folk art collection and an American Indian Art collection, and the New York State Historical Association. The area's tranquil natural setting contributes to The Farmers' Museum's mission to be an educational center for the study of the rural past through historic nineteenth-century buildings, exhibitions of agricultural tools and artifacts, and working craftspeople plying traditional crafts.

Cooperstown is a something for everyone kind of town—the baseball fan, the history buff, the art lover, and the naturalist.

HISTORY

The village of Cooperstown, on the southern shore of Otsego Lake, was founded by William Cooper in 1786. In 1790, he and his wife, Elizabeth Fenimore, moved their family from Burlington, New Jersey, to Cooperstown. Fourteen-month-old James was the youngest of the Coopers' seven children. Later in life, he added his mother's name, and the world knew him as the famous novelist, James Fenimore Cooper.

In his well-known *Leather-Stocking Tales*, such as *The Last of the Mohicans*, Cooper wrote about the American wilderness and civilization on the frontier. Our visit to Cooperstown conjured up images of the long rifle, Natty Bumppo, Chingagook, and other characters of Cooper's tales of frontiersmen, American Indians, and fur trappers during the French and Indian wars.

Although Cooperstown was prosperous, it was bypassed by the Erie Canal, and later, the interstate highways. It remained primarily agricultural. In 1943, Stephen C. Clark, a local philanthropist, proposed the creation of a museum of agricultural and rural life at Cooperstown. Clark wished to preserve craft and agricultural tools, as well as the skills and techniques needed to use them. The museum was designed to depict the life of the average farmer from 1776 to 1860, the decades from the Revolutionary War to the Civil War. Buildings were acquired and moved to Cooperstown to form a recreated crossroads village. The buildings, all from upstate New York, were carefully restored and decorated.

The museum is located on the former estate of Edward Severin Clark, Stephen Clark's brother. His home, Fenimore House, on the shore of Lake Otsego, one mile north of Cooperstown, became the Art Museum; his barn now houses The Farmers' Museum.

TOUR

Arranged as a main street, the **Village Crossroads** is a collection of about a dozen original nineteenth-century structures that recreates a typical upstate New York preindustrial village during the period from 1820 to 1850. In almost every building is a person at work using early-nineteenth-century methods and equipment.

The **General Store,** dating from 1828, was moved from Toddsville. It is stocked with spices, patent medicines, coffee, tea, candy, shoes, cloth, dishes, and tin pans—items that farmers and their families were unable to produce themselves. The store also served as the post office.

The 1827 **Blacksmith Shop,** moved from New Berlin, is loaded with tools and has a working forge. Blacksmithing is demonstrated regularly, and items made here are for sale.

Handbills and broadsides are still being produced on the Washington flatbed press in the **Printing Office** (1829), which served as the newspaper office of George Shafer of Middlefield.

Used by physicians in Westford for over a century, the **Doctor's Office** dates from 1825 and is fully furnished and equipped with medical instruments. The **Druggist Shop** (1832), originally a Hartwich doctor's office, contains herbal medicines and perfumes.

Samuel Nelson, a country lawyer who later became a U.S. Supreme Court justice, practiced in Cooperstown's small, white frame, two-room **Lawyer's Office** (1830). The small, white **New England Church** was built in Durham in 1791 and later moved to Cornwallville.

The **Lippitt Homestead** was a pioneer home built in Hinman Hollow by Joseph Lippitt in 1800. Food is cooked in the kitchen's fireplace and beehive oven; butter and cheese are made in the buttery. Located behind the house is the **Brooks Barn** (1795), from South New Berlin. It is built of logs sheathed in hemlock and is home to geese, chickens, and cows.

The 1830 **Schoolhouse** from Filers' Corners was considered a model of school design because it was warmer and lighter than others of that time. It has a small library and a cloakroom.

The **Bump Tavern,** built in Windham in 1795 by Jehiel Tuttle, is a typical turnpike tavern, complete with barroom, ladies' parlor, gentlemen's reading room, ballroom, and bedrooms. The walls of the upstairs rooms are beautifully stenciled. The tavern's roof was raised and porches added by E. Bump in 1844.

The **Main Barn Exhibition Center,** housed in Edward Clark's 1918 gambrel-roofed stone dairy barn, features an extensive collection of tools along with craft demonstrations. All the craftspeople, including woodworkers, broom makers, spinners, and weavers, use tools appropriate to the era.

Major exhibits include *Beginnings* which focuses on the origins of agriculture in upstate New York including the clearing of forests, planting of crops, and use of horses.

Happy Times, an exhibit of nineteenth-century rural amusements, includes the Cardiff Giant, a hoax perpetrated by George Hull in 1869 to confound people who believed there had been giants on earth.

On the second floor is the **Spinning and Weaving Loft** where the process of transforming flax, cotton, and wool into cloth is demonstrated. Other exhibits include *Sheltered Nest* which concerns women's domestic chores between 1840 and 1880 and the tools and inventions which impacted them. *The Tradesman's Tool Chest* displays tools and processes used by nineteenth-century craftsmen.

Special events include exceptional week-long Seminars in American Culture in which traditional crafts are taught. There are Wool Days in May; Town Ball and baseball games during the summer; Junior show, a competitive livestock show, in July; an Independence Day celebration on July 4; a September Harvest Festival, along with Halloween, Thanksgiving, Christmas, and New Year's celebrations.

Across the road from the Farmers' Museum and Village Crossroads is **Fenimore House,** an imposing stone mansion fronting Lake Otsego. It was built in the 1930s by Edward Clark on the site of the Fenimore cottage (demolished in 1932) and farm that once belonged to James Fenimore Cooper.

Like the museum, Fenimore House is administered by the New York

State Historical Association, whose headquarters are in the house. It is now a museum featuring a very fine collection of American folk art, American Indian art, and, of course, Cooper memorabilia.

The library displays portraits of Judge William Cooper, the founder of Cooperstown, and James Fenimore Cooper, his famous son. Several paintings illustrate scenes from Cooper's *Leather-Stocking Tales*, such as *The Last of the Mohicans*, *The Spy*, and *The Prairie*.

On the second floor, there is an interesting collection of bronze busts by J. H. I. Browere, who made plaster life masks of leaders of the early Republic. The busts were cast from these masks. Those on exhibit include Thomas Jefferson, John Adams, Alexander Hamilton, James and Dolly Madison, and DeWitt Clinton.

The folk art collection consists of naïve paintings, fireboards, weather vanes, ships' figureheads, embroidered pictures, and samplers. Among the most interesting naïve paintings are those of the local gentry, their families, and, especially, their children done by itinerant painters.

The **Fenimore Bookstore** on the first floor features books on American art and handicrafts and on the history of New York State.

SIDE TRIPS

The other museum to see at Cooperstown is the **National Baseball Hall of Fame and Museum.** According to tradition, Abner Doubleday, a Civil War general and West Point graduate, invented the game of baseball in 1839, and it was first played in Farmer Phinney's Cooperstown pasture. The museum was dedicated in 1939, when baseball was 100 years old.

The Hall of Fame is a high-ceilinged, paneled room hung with bronze plaques for each player, giving his name, team, years of play, and a summary of his career. Another room celebrates the **Great Moments of Baseball** such as pitcher Sandy Koufax's perfect game.

The second floor is devoted to the origins of baseball, the evolution of uniforms, and information on all-star games. The third floor features displays on Casey Stengel and Babe Ruth and much baseball memorabilia. Whether you're a die-hard fan or not, you're sure to enjoy this fine tribute to our national pastime. Located on Main Street. Open daily, 9:00 A.M. to 9:00 P.M., May to October; 9:00 A.M. to 5:00 P.M., November to April. (607) 547-9988. Admission charged.

GENESEE COUNTRY VILLAGE

Recreation of a nineteenth-century western New York country village

Address: P.O. Box 310, Flint Hill Road, Mumford, NY 14511

Telephone: (716) 538-6822; FAX: (716) 538-2887

Location: In western New York state, 20 miles southwest of Rochester; directions and maps at New York Thruway exits 46 and 47

Open: 10:00 A.M. to 5:00 P.M., Saturday, Sunday, and holidays, from the second Sunday in May through the third Sunday in October; 10:00 A.M. to 4:00 P.M., Monday to Friday in July and August, and Tuesday to Friday in May, June, September, and October

Admission: Adults, $10.00; seniors, $8.50; youths 13 to 17, $6.00; children 6 to 12, $5.00

Restaurants: Genesee Junction Cafeteria and Tavern; Victorian Refreshment Pavilion

Shops: P & L Junction Craft Shop; Flint Hill Country Store; The Bookseller; Art Gallery Gift Shop; Nature Center Gift Shop

Facilities: Visitor Center; trolleys for senior citizens and handicapped visitors; handicapped accessible; picnic areas; special events; Gallery of Sporting Art; Nature Center

WHERE TO STAY

Inns/Bed & Breakfasts: Genesee Country Inn, Box 340, 948 George St., Mumford 14511, (716) 538-2500, FAX: (716) 538-4565; Avon Inn, 55 E. Main St., Avon 14414, (716) 226-8181

Motels/Hotels: Hampton Inn, 717 E. Henrietta Rd., Rochester 14623, (716) 272-7800, FAX: (716) 272-1211; Howard Johnson Lodge, 3350 W. Henrietta Rd., Rochester 14623, (716) 475-1661, FAX: (716) 475-1667; Radisson, 175 Jefferson Rd., Rochester 14623, (716) 475-1910, FAX: (716) 475-1910, ext. 199; Red Roof Inn, 4820 W. Henrietta Rd., Rochester 14467, (716) 359-1100, FAX: (716) 359-1121

Camping: Genesee Country Campground, P.O. Box 100, Caledonia 14423, (716) 538-4200; Frost Ridge Campground, Conion Rd., Le Roy 14482, (716) 768-4883, (716) 768-9730; Timberline Lake Park, 8150 Vallance Rd., Le Roy 14482, (716) 768-6635

OVERVIEW

Genesee Country Museum is a recreated village of almost sixty western New York buildings that date to the first three quarters of the nineteenth century. The museum's founder, John L. Wehle, wanted to preserve historic country architecture, the work of creative Genesee Valley carpenters, master builders, and housewrights.

In a well-landscaped setting, this large village features a wide variety of architecturally interesting buildings. An extremely comprehensive village, it includes businesses, craft workshops, services, farm buildings, and homes.

HISTORY

Genesee comes from the Iroquois word *gennishey*, meaning beautiful valley. The Iroquois named the river that flows from Pennsylvania northward to Lake Ontario. The region known as Genesee country, in western New York, is bounded by the Finger Lakes, the Niagara frontier, and Lake Erie.

Genesee country was inhabited by the Senecas, an Iroquois tribe. They rebuffed attempts by French Canadians to settle this area and during the Revolutionary War joined the British in raids on frontier communities. In retaliation, General George Washington sent General John Sullivan and nearly a third of the Continental army in 1779 to attack Iroquois strongholds in the Genesee area. The Iroquois fled, and soon after white settlers from New England started arriving in the fertile valley. They cleared the land for farming, and merchants and tradesmen soon followed.

Although the first half of the nineteenth century was not an easy time for these early New York settlers, the land was rich and especially good for raising wheat. With plenty of hard work, settlers on the Genesee frontier prospered.

The Genesee Country Museum is the realization of a dream of John L. Wehle, chairman of the Genesee Brewing Company. In 1966, Stuart Bolger was hired as museum director to recreate a nineteenth-century Genesee frontier town. The buildings needed to form a village were obtained from the various communities that made up the Genesee frontier and were moved to the 125-acre site near Mumford.

Opened in 1976, the year of the Bicentennial, the museum portrays the everyday life of a rural western New York village in the early nineteenth century. All buildings are original, though not on original sites. Most furnishings and artifacts in the buildings have also been gathered from the Genesee area.

Genesee Country Village, Mumford, New York
Rates of Toll are posted on the Tollhouse wall of the 1850 Rochester and Hemlock
Lake Plank Road Company. "Do" means "ditto," or the same as the line above.
For example, "do. & 2 do." means "Vehicle & 2 animals." At Genesee Country
Village, Mumford, NY.

Photo by Patricia A. Gutek

TOUR

You enter the village through the **Tollhouse.** This 1850 structure
belonged to the Rochester and Hemlock Lake Plank Road Company,
which built some of the almost 3,000 miles of plank road in New York
State. Tolls for passage on the roads were collected here, and the building
was also home to the toll collector and his family.

Facing the **village green** is the 1836 **Foster-Tufts House,** a sophisticated two-story colonial-style frame with a side ell, built by Charles Foster.

The two-story brick-lined Federal-style **McKay House** was built in
1814. Its owner, John McKay, was a wealthy Scot from Pennsylvania. The
house reflects his prosperity in its size, design, and furnishings.

A one-and-a-half-story frame home, **Amherst Humphrey House** was built near the Genesee Turnpike in the 1790s. Humphrey was pathmaster of his road district and, eventually, overseer of highways. The mantels, the house's five fireplaces, and the rest of the interior millwork and trim were intact when the house was acquired for the village.

A printer works in the adjoining small building from Caledonia, dating from 1840.

The village's **Drugstore** is a small Greek Revival building from Tyrone built around 1840. It is equipped with all the ingredients necessary for a pharmacist to measure and mix medicine.

Other village shops include an 1840 **dressmaker's shop** from Roseboom; an 1802 **cooper shop** from Stafford; an 1825 **bookseller shop** from Rush, where books, prints, and stationery may be purchased; an 1830 **blacksmith shop** from Elba; an 1840 **tackle shop** from Mumford, which was famous for its fishing streams (a fly-tying business was unusual for the nineteenth century), and a **wagonmaker and woodwork shop.**

The **Pioneer Farmstead** is representative of a first-generation Genesee Country farmstead. The **log cabin** was built around 1809 in Scottsville, and the 1810 **smokehouse** is also built of logs. The farm includes pastures, cornfields, orchards, gardens, and, of course, animals. Open-hearth cooking is demonstrated here.

An unusual two-story, eight-room log house, **Kieffer's Place,** was built in 1814 in Rush. Not considered a cabin because of its size, this log home had lath and plaster walls and ceilings. Clapboards applied over the outside log walls were removed during restoration.

The **Jones Farmhouse,** a one-and-a-half-story frame home built in Orleans around 1820, has a remarkable stenciled parlor and bedroom. The Jones Heirloom Garden contains hardy crops commonly grown in nineteenth-century kitchen gardens.

Genesee Village recreates all the services needed by its citizens: an 1822 one-room **schoolhouse,** an 1845 **physician's office,** the 1848 **Hasting's Law Office,** and the 1824 **Delancey Stow Insurance Office.** Other village businesses include the 1848 **Altay Store,** a general store; the 1820 **boot and shoemaker's shop;** the 1834 **post office and store;** the 1860 **tinsmith shop;** and the 1870 **gunsmith's shop.**

A well-stocked trading post, **Thompson's Tavern and Store** which also served as an inn for drovers, comes from Riga Center. Its inventory is based on account books from the Tyron Trading Post near Irondequoit Post.

Hosmer's Inn is a Georgian-style 1818 inn that originally stood alongside the Ontario and Genesee Turnpike near Avon, and was known for its good food and pleasant accommodations. A brick-floored kitchen is on the ground floor; the first floor includes a taproom, a public dining room, a ladies' dining room, and a ladies' sitting room.

Not every building at Genesee is a typical small-town building. One exceptional structure is the **Hamilton House,** a fifteen-room Victorian Italianate villa found in Campbell. The villa, which has a two-story carriage house and an icehouse, was built in 1870 by J. D. Hamilton, who was in the tannery business. Another unusual home is the **Octagon House,** built in 1870 and occupied by Erastus Hyde, a physician who also headed a spiritualist colony in Lily Dale.

The **Eastman Birthplace,** the birthplace of George Eastman, the father of modern photography, is a comfortable house built in 1847 in Waterville. The well-furnished Eastman House reflects the success of George's father, a hardworking entrepreneur who died while his son was a child. Several photographs of George Eastman at various phases of his career are displayed.

The **Shaker Trustees' Building** is an 1839 frame structure from the Shaker religious community at Sonyea in Groveland, which lasted from 1836 to 1892. Trustees' Buildings were used to conduct business matters with the "world's people," non-Shakers. Displaying the Shaker sense of symmetry, first floor rooms on either side of the central hall are mirror images of each other. They are used for offices and stores, while on the second floor are the living quarters of the male and female trustees. There are Shaker furnishings and artifacts throughout the large building. A botanic and seed garden nearby attests to the highly successful Shaker seed business.

Something you don't run into in most museum villages is the **Brewery and Hop House.** This is a reconstruction based on drawings and descriptions by Lord Dunkirk, an English nobleman who visited the brewery at Geneva, New York, in 1803. Portions of the old Enright Brewery from Rochester were used in the three-story structure. Nearby is a Hops Drying House, and fields of hop are between the two buildings.

Settlers on the frontier brought their religious beliefs with them, and places of worship were found throughout the Genesee Valley. A simple 1854 **Quaker Meeting House** from Wheatland, the 1854 **St. Feehan's Roman Catholic Church** from Chili, and the 1844 **Brooks Grove Methodist Church** and 1835 **Parsonage** from Brooks Grove reflect the variety of religious denominations.

The **Flint Hill Pottery** is a reconstruction of the Morganville Pottery based on archaeological research and photographs. Working potters reproduce redware and stoneware.

The **Romulus Female Seminary,** a private school where young ladies studied the arts, language, and literature, was built in Romulus in 1855.

The **Great Meadow,** near the entrance to the village, has a Victorian bandstand in its center.

The **Livingston-Backus House** is a mansion built in Rochester in 1827 by entrepreneur James Livingston. Dr. Frederick Backus purchased the house in 1838 and made substantial structural alterations including Greek Revival elements. Interior decorations and furnishings reflect the high style of the 1830s and 1840s. The Livingston-Backus Garden is laid out in a classical style with brick paths edged with boxwood. The 1828 **Garden House** from Cortland has Federal detailing carved by Simeon Rouse.

The **Carriage Barn** houses a collection of horse-drawn vehicles. The **Gallery of Sporting Art** displays John L. Wehle's exceptional international collection of paintings, prints, and bronze sculptures of sporting and wildlife art. Nine galleries feature subjects ranging from fox hunting and wild-fowl shooting to trotting horse races, broncobusting, and North American and African animals.

A free **trolley** makes regular rounds of the village daily during July and August and on weekends in the spring and fall. Of special note among many special events are the Highland Gathering, Horse Competition Weekend, Nineteenth-Century Games Day, the Independence Day Celebration, Civil War Battle Reenactment, Old Time Fiddlers' Fair, Quilt Shows, and Christmas Programs.

Genesee Country Museum operates a **Nature Center** on 175 acres adjacent to the museum. It has over three miles of hiking and interpreted nature trails along with exhibits on local plants and animals in the Nature Center building. Open year-round, 10:00 A.M. to 5:00 P.M., Tuesday to Sunday. Admission charged.

SIDE TRIPS

The Genesee Country Museum is only twenty miles from Rochester, where you'll find the **International Museum of Photography.** This museum has an important collection of photographic art and technology. It is in the mansion of George Eastman, founder of the Eastman Kodak Company, 900 East Avenue, Rochester 14607, (716) 271-3361. Open Tuesday to Sunday, 10:00 A.M. to 4:30 P.M. Admission charged.

The **Susan B. Anthony House** is a National Historic Landmark.

The famous suffragette wrote *The History of Woman Suffrage* in this house, which has been restored to its late-nineteenth-century appearance. 17 West Madison Street, Rochester 14610, (716) 235-6124. Open Saturday and Sunday, 1:00 to 4:00 P.M. Admission charged.

OLD ECONOMY VILLAGE

Restoration of the 1830s Harmony Society Community; NR, NHL

Address: Fourteenth and Church Streets, Ambridge, PA 15003
Telephone: (412) 266-4500
Location: Ambridge is in west central Pennsylvania, 15 miles northwest of Pittsburgh
Open: Tuesday to Saturday, 9:00 A.M. to 3:00 P.M.; Sunday, 12:00 noon to 3:00 P.M.; closed holidays, except Memorial Day, July 4, and Labor Day
Admission: Adults, $5.00; senior citizens, $4.00; children 6 to 17, $3.00
Shops: Gift Shop
Facilities: Special events

WHERE TO STAY
Motels/Hotels: Beaver Valley, Big Beaver Blvd., Beaver Falls 15010, (412) 843-0630; Best Western Conley's Motor Inn, Big Beaver Blvd., Beaver Falls 15010, (412) 843-9300, (800) 345-6819; Holiday Inn, Box 969, PA 18N, Beaver Falls 15010, (412) 846-3700, ext. 290; Hampton Inn Airport, 1420 Beers School Rd., Coraopolis 15108, (412) 264-0020, FAX: 264-0020, ext. 185; Pittsburgh Plaza, 1500 Beers School Rd., Coraopolis 15108, (412) 264-7900, (800) 837-0555, FAX: (412) 262-3229
Camping: Raccoon Creek State Park, Frankfort Springs, (412) 899-2200; KOA Mercer/Grove City, RD 6, Box 6794, Mercer 16137, (412) 748-3160; Rocky Springs Campground, Mercer 16137, (412) 662-4415; Bradys Run Parks, Rt. 51, Beaver 15009, (412) 846-5600

OVERVIEW
Old Economy is a restored village maintained and operated by the Pennsylvania Historical and Museum Commission. It is located in the Pittsburgh suburb of Ambridge.

The museum is well administered, with authenticity the rule; many of the artifacts on display were made or used on the site. Because of the communitarian nature of the society, the buildings are impressively large. It is interesting to compare Economy with its sister community, New Harmony, Indiana (see page 237).

The center of the original 20-acre town has been restored to its

Old Economy Village, Ambridge, Pennsylvania
A typical Harmonist home, the early-nineteenth-century Baker House was the
residence of the Romelius Baker family. Grapevines grow on the outside wall, and
the brick path leads to a garden planted with old varieties of plants and vegetables.
At Old Economy Village, Ambridge, PA.

Photo by Patricia A. Gutek

1830s appearance. Seventeen buildings, many of them two-story brick in the Federal style, have been preserved; they constitute the administrative, cultural, and economic center of the town. Eighty original Rappite buildings stand outside the restored area and are privately owned.

A visit to Economy presents a study in sharp contrasts between the nineteenth-century Rappite community and the industrialism of Pittsburgh and its suburbs. Smoke from steel mills and factories, expressway traffic, and other aspects of modern life seem incongruous with the fenced-in village. You get the sense that the Industrial Revolution surrounded the community site, nearly enveloping it.

HISTORY

Economy was the third and final home of the Harmony Society, a pietistical group of German Protestants founded by George Rapp (1757–1847). After emigrating from Germany, Rapp and his followers first built at Harmony, Pennsylvania, where they lived from 1804 to 1814 and then moved to New Harmony, Indiana, where they lived from 1814 to 1824. They returned to Pennsylvania and established *Oekonomie* in 1825, where they lived until the society dissolved in 1905.

A Lutheran offshoot, the Harmonists were a millennialist sect who considered themselves among the chosen people of God. They expected the imminent return of Jesus Christ who would establish the kingdom of the godly on earth for a thousand-year reign of peace. The group practiced celibacy, were pacifists, and lived communally.

Like other German Pietists, they were a practical group who excelled in agriculture, crafts, and light industry. They sold their products—crops, beer, wine, whiskey, and cloth—and built an economic surplus for the community. They were excellent furniture makers and carpenters.

In 1824, Father Rapp asked David Shields of Pennsylvania to find property suitable for the group which had decided to leave New Harmony Indiana. Shields found a 3,000-acre tract of land on the Ohio River, which the society purchased. Rapp called the village *Oekonomie*, derived from a Greek term that meant living as a family unit. The town was laid out in a grid arrangement of streets with houses at the center. A formal garden was surrounded by the principal buildings. Factories and farm buildings were located on the outskirts, and fields ringed the town.

A schism in 1832 which claimed one-third of the membership was a serious blow to the original group. The schism was caused by Bernard Muller, who called himself Count Leon Maximillan. He arrived in Economy in 1831 and was initially believed by Father Rapp to be the Messiah.

After staying for several months, Count Leon left to form his own, more liberal community, taking many young Harmonists—and their valuable personal property—with him. Leon and his group founded a short-lived communal settlement called Phillipsburg, the present site of Monaca, Pennsylvania.

Despite these losses of people and property, the Harmony Society's cloth mills were very successful. After Rapp's death in 1847, the society became a financial power. It invested in oil and railroads; bought land; developed the town of Beaver Falls; and backed many local businesses.

By 1880, the Harmony Society, like other business enterprises in the region, was experiencing financial difficulties. Their mill operation was becoming outdated by the technological advances of the Industrial Revolution. Simultaneously, the Harmonists were growing older. The average age of the membership was about seventy in 1880. The society liquidated all its capitalist ventures and paid its debts in 1894. In 1905, the last three living members dissolved the 100-year-old group.

In 1919, the Commonwealth of Pennsylvania took over the six acres of land that constitute the present historic site and turned it over to the Historical and Museum Commission. In 1937, architects Charles Stotz and Edward Stotz, Jr., began restoration work; they were later aided by the Works Progress Administration.

TOUR

The **Feast Hall,** built in 1825 and one of the largest buildings in the village, was used for several purposes. It housed a Natural History and Fine Arts Museum, established by the Harmonists in 1826, that contained art, American Indian relics, botanical specimens, and stuffed animals, all used for teaching purposes. Another room has a wooden Franklin printing press that the society used to print six religious books.

The second floor of the building is entirely occupied by a room large enough to hold 500 people that was used for *Liebesmahl* (Last Supper). On most religious holidays, all the members of the society gathered in the room, with men on the right and women on the left, to eat a meal of stew, noodles, bread, fruit, salad, beer, and wine. After the meal, a religious service that included music was held.

Fearing fire, the Harmonists did not permit a kitchen in the Feast Hall. Cooking was done nearby in the **Community Kitchen,** a separate one-story frame building. Meals for as many as 500 people at a time were prepared here; the large-scale functional design of this kitchen includes twelve large kettles sunk in ovens.

A series of shops produced necessities for the community. The **Cabinet Shop** is a one-story building; this is where the furniture, doors, moldings, and mantels for society buildings were made.

The large **Granary** held a year's supply of grain on the upper three and a half floors; the first floor was used for stockpiling food. Although the Harmonists were expecting the millennium, they were well prepared for the fire, disease, and starvation that were to precede it. The granary is constructed of huge chestnut beams, and the first floor is half-timbered.

The first floor of the large two-story brick **Mechanics Building** houses a **shoemaker's shop,** a **tailor's shop** and a **hat shop.** The tailor and the shoemaker were responsible for the appearance of the members who wore clothes supplied by the society. As members filed into church each Sunday, the tailor and shoemaker would check their attire; if they noted signs of wear or shabbiness, the craftsmen would ask that person to come to the shop to be measured for a replacement.

A Ramage Press, acquired by the Society in 1822, is displayed in the **Print Shop** of the Mechanics Building. Dr. Muller, who was also the community's printer, used the press to print several books including the Society's hymns, a speller, a school singing book, a book of pietistic maxims, and George Rapp's *Thoughts on the Destiny of Man* published in German and English.

Underneath the Mechanics Building is a large vaulted stone **wine cellar** where the homemade wine was aged in large casks both for the Harmonists' own use and for sale.

The **Blacksmith Shop** is located in a 1905 auto garage.

The society sold shoes, hats, flour, whiskey, farm products, and cloth to the public. Distribution of goods to the 120 households that made up the Harmony Society was also handled at the 1826 **store.** During the community's most prosperous years, 1825 to 1850, the store took in $100,000—brisk business by nineteenth-century standards.

The store, in addition to several other functional rooms, includes the **doctor's office,** furnished with some pieces that belonged to Dr. Christopher Muller. Dr. Muller was also the town's pharmacist, taught school, conducted the orchestra, was in charge of the museum, operated the printing press, and tended the botanical garden. What a loss when this jack-of-all-trades left in the 1832 schism!

Rappites lived in groups of three to seven people; they ate, cooked, and slept in the houses they shared. Love feasts were the only meals taken communally. The houses followed uniform design. The necessary doors, windows, sashes, precut lumber, and bricks were delivered to each building site and quickly assembled. A man headed each household, and the house was known by his name.

Baker House is a typical Harmonist household. The first floor has a large living room, where the members ate and relaxed. It is simply furnished with Harmonist-made tables, chairs, and a corner cupboard containing Harmonist pottery. It also has a kitchen and bedrooms with rope beds and large wardrobes.

Each house also had a shed. The **Family Shed** has been reconstructed on its original site. Its four rooms were used for food storage, tool and wood storage, as a chicken house, and as an outhouse. All food was drawn from the store except vegetables, which were grown in each household's kitchen garden.

The **Baker House Garden** has been restored with appropriate vegetables, flowers, and herbs based upon a Harmonist girl's list of 1825.

Economy's restored **formal George Rapp garden** at the center of town has boxwood-edged intersecting paths dividing it into quarters. The garden, which has the same kind of flowers as those planted by the Harmonists, has been recreated based on planting lists maintained by the Harmonists. Using historically correct, non-hybrid seeds, the garden display includes a colorful profusion of old-fashioned peonies, lilies, and a large variety of columbines.

The large **pavilion** and **grotto** were designed by Frederick Rapp, George's adopted son. The orchestra played in the pavilion while villagers strolled through the garden admiring the flowers. A thatched-roofed **grotto** made of rough stones stands in the southwest corner. The interior is decorated like a Roman temple, and under a large dome is a gold lily, said to have had religious significance for the Harmonists.

The **George Rapp House** consists of two separate, but connected, structures: The **George Rapp House,** built in 1826 and the **Frederick Rapp House,** which dates from 1828. The central structure and two wings of George Rapp's house have twenty-five rooms. It is furnished more elegantly than other Harmonist homes. Although equality was one of the tenets of the religion, the Rappites wanted their leader, whom they considered a prophet, to live in a house appropriate to his position. The great house faced the main street so that visitors could see "what a united brethren could do," according to George Rapp.

Frederick Rapp's two-story house is a separate structure, but connected. Frederick Rapp, who was born in 1775 as Frederick Reichert, was adopted by George Rapp in 1803. Trained as a stonemason, Frederick was responsible for the planning and architecture of the three Harmonist communities and was also interested in the museum and the orchestra.

Here, too, the furniture and decorations are elegant. There are both American and Harmonist pieces, carpeting, and wallpaper. Some of Frederick Rapp's possessions, including his surveyor's compass, a microscope, musical instruments, and books, are displayed.

The **Carriage House** contains the 1826 fire engine pumper built by the Society, a Seneca Falls, New York, suction-hose engine purchased in 1836, a carriage made for George Rapp in 1843, and the Harmony Society hearse.

Outside the museum grounds are sixteen square blocks containing eighty privately owned Harmonist buildings. Notable is the **Harmonist Church,** built in 1828. Now named **St. John's Lutheran Church,** it is located on Church Street across from the George Rapp House. Six hundred Harmonists are buried in unmarked graves in the **Harmonist Cemetery** at Church and 11th Streets.

Many special events are held annually at Old Economy. There are workshops in textiles, basket making, old-fashioned cooking, and painting. Several dinner-lecture programs are offered by Harmonist specialists. Traditional crafts are demonstrated on summer weekends. A *Kunstfest,* or craft festival, takes place in July; an *Erntefest,* or harvest festival, in October; and candlelight Christmas programs in December.

SIDE TRIPS

Twenty-five miles north of Old Economy is **Harmony,** the site of the first Rappite community in the United States. Harmony is located on Routes 19 and 68. George Rapp purchased 4,000 acres from Dettmar Basse in 1804, and in 1805, the Harmony Society was formed. The Harmonists built a town of over 100 houses along with vineyards and apple orchards. In 1815, they sold Harmony to Abraham Ziegler, a Mennonite, for $127,000 and moved to Indiana. Many of the original Harmonist structures are located around the central square, including the **Frederick Rapp House** and the **church.** The **Harmonist Cemetery** has 100 people buried in it, but there is only one gravestone, that of Johann Rapp, George's son.

The **Harmony Museum** is in an 1809 Harmonist building at Main and Mercer Streets. It contains objects owned and used by the society's members, including a one-handed clock. Open Tuesday to Sunday, 1:00 P.M. to 4:00 P.M., June 1 to October 1, (412) 452-7341.

HOPEWELL FURNACE

Restoration of an 1830s iron-making community; NHS, NR, HABS

Address: 2 Mark Bird Lane, Elverson, PA 19520
Telephone: (215) 582-8773, (215) 582-2093 (TDD)
Location: In southeastern Pennsylvania, about 50 miles northwest of Philadelphia; 15 miles southeast of Reading; 10 miles northeast of PA Tpke. (I-76) exit 22 (Morgantown) via PA 23 east and PA 345 north
Open: Daily, 9:00 A.M. to 5:00 P.M., closed Thanksgiving, Christmas, and New Year's Day
Admission: Adults 17 to 61, $2.00
Shops: Book Shop in Visitor Center
Facilities: Visitor Center with orientation program, craft videos, and exhibits; iron molding and casting demonstrations; craft demonstrations; audio stations and wayside exhibits; special events; apple picking; handicapped accessible

WHERE TO STAY

Motels/Hotels: Ramada Inn, W. King St. & PA 100, Pottstown 19464, (215) 326-6700, FAX: (215) 970-2665; Holiday Inn, Morgantown 19543, (215) 286-3000, FAX: (215) 286-0520; Comfort Inn, 2200 Stacy Dr., Reading 19605, (215) 371-0500, FAX: (215) 478-9421; Dutch Colony Motor Inn, 4635 Perklomen Ave., Reading 19606, (215) 779-2345, (800) 828-2830
Camping: French Creek State Park, Rt. 345, Elverson 19520, (215) 582-9680; Warwick Woods Family Camping Resort, Box 280, St. Peters 19470, (215) 286-9655; Oak Creek Campground, P.O. Box 128PH, Bowmansville 17507, (215) 445-6161, (800) 446-8365

OVERVIEW

Hopewell Furnace National Historic Site is a restored nineteenth-century iron-making community. Like Hagley Museum in Wilmington, Delaware, a single property served as both an industrial location and home for hundreds of employees and their families. You might call it a cross between a company town and a plantation. At any one time, as many as 1,000 people lived in the community, and Hopewell tells their story.

Iron was one of the earliest products made in the American colonies, having been manufactured since the seventeenth century, and Pennsylvania became the most important iron-producing colony. Hopewell Furnace produced pig iron and castings in its cold-blast charcoal furnace for more than 100 years, from 1771 to 1883. Designated a National Historic Site, Hopewell is the nation's most completely restored example of a rural American nineteenth-century iron-making village. It illustrates an important facet of American industrial history. Restoration has been to the 1830s, the furnace's most prosperous period and the one best represented by the preserved community structures.

HISTORY

Pennsylvania had many of the natural resources needed for iron making: iron ore in abundance, large forests from which charcoal fuel could be made, rich deposits of limestone for use in the separation of impurities from the iron, and numerous streams for powering waterwheels.

Operating a furnace and cutting down trees required a large number of workers who lived near their work. Family-owned iron plantations usually consisted of several thousand acres of woodlands, the ironmaster's mansion, tenant homes, a company store, blacksmith shops, barns, and of course, the furnace.

Mark Bird, the son of an ironmaster, owned thousands of acres of land in Berks and Chester counties. In 1771, he built Hopewell Furnace on French Creek in southern Berks County, five miles from a forge he inherited from his father.

The British Iron Act of 1750 limited the American iron industry to the production of pig and bar iron that could be reworked by British forges into finished products and exported again to the colonies. Mark Bird, like most ironmasters, resented the act and British interference in colonial business interests. Prominent in the revolutionary movement, he was elected to the state assembly and served as colonel of the Second Battalion of the Berks County Militia.

During the Revolutionary War, Bird was the deputy quartermaster general of Pennsylvania. His ironworks supplied cannon and shot to the Continental army. After the war, the new government was unable to pay off all its debts, including its debt to Bird. This loss, along with damage to Hopewell by floods and fire, led to Bird's economic ruin.

In 1788, Hopewell Furnace was auctioned off. It passed through several hands and was eventually purchased by Daniel Buckley and his brothers-in-law, Thomas and Matthew Brooke, in 1800. The two families owned and operated the furnace until 1883.

By the mid-1830s, after an unpromising start complicated by eco-

Hopewell Furnace, Elverson, Pennsylvania
The white, barn-like structure consists of the large Cast House and the smaller
Cleaning Shed where castings were cleaned. The early colonial iron casting process
consisted of running molten iron into molds made by pressing patterns into a sand
bed on the Cast House floor. At Hopewell Furnace, Elverson, PA.

Photo by Patricia A. Gutek

nomic slowdowns, natural disasters, and litigation over title to the land,
Hopewell Furnace had become highly profitable. Technological changes
made by the Buckley-Brooke partners improved productivity. According
to an 1832 Treasury Department report, Hopewell Furnace employed 168
men with 800 dependents, owned 84 horses, and produced 1,000 tons of
pig metal and 700 tons of castings.

Furnace workers ranged from the ironmaster at the top of the economic and social hierarchy to woodcutters, miners, and laborers at the
bottom. An owner/ironmaster like Clement Brooke made policy decisions,
was responsible for the successful operation of the business, and took a
paternalistic interest in his employees' lives. He and his family lived like
country gentry in the Big House and had a number of servants. The com-

pany clerk, who held the second most important management position, kept the books. Next in importance was the founder who was in charge of day-to-day furnace operations and was assisted by keepers, fillers, and guttermen. Moulders, who did the casting, were highly skilled workers and received the highest wages. Colliers were responsible for the coaling process in which wood was processed into charcoal. These were skilled craftsmen who received decent wages.

Other employees included miners who dug the ore and woodcutters who supplied the wood that would be made into charcoal. About 5,000 cords of wood were necessary to keep the furnace in blast for a year, and an acre of forest produced from thirty to forty cords of wood. Owners of iron furnaces typically owned thousands of acres of heavily wooded land and built their furnaces nearby. Teamsters were hired to haul ore from the mines, charcoal from the forests, limestone from the quarries, and finished products to markets. Artisans included blacksmiths, wheelwrights, cabinetmakers, carpenters, and masons. Tenant farmers supplied much of the food for the villagers. Virtually all of these jobs were held by men. Women managed their households, took in boarders, raised chickens, did sewing or laundering, or served as maids in the Big House. Some women were hired as seasonal farm laborers during harvest time, and, on rare occasions, worked as miners, woodcutters, or castings cleaners.

Young children were often apprenticed to masters until they were twenty-one or worked at the furnace learning their fathers' trade or doing menial chores. In 1804, a teacher was hired to start an elementary school at Hopewell. Tuition was $1.75 a quarter for each pupil which limited the enrollment to children of the better paid employees. In 1837, a public school was built in compliance with Pennsylvania's Common School Law. Most pupils attended for only one to four years.

On Sunday, most employees' day off, people attended church. Recreational activities included swimming, hunting, fishing, ice-skating, and sleighing. Holiday parties at the Big House revolved around music and dancing.

Clement Brooke, a son of one of the original partners, was resident manager and ironmaster from 1816 until 1848 and is credited with Hopewell Furnace's economic success. He made many improvements to the property and built Hopewell Furnace into a self-contained village, a company town.

Hopewell Furnace produced cast-iron stoves, which had replaced the open fireplaces traditionally used for cooking and heating. Other products included iron housewares, wheels, mill screws, clock weights, hammers, grindstone wheels, and prison bars. Products were shipped overland by wagons until the opening of the Schuylkill Canal in 1825, after which they were shipped by boat. In the early 1840s, shipping by rail began.

The panic of 1837 brought bank failures and depression to American business. Hopewell Furnace's markets shrank, and although the operation remained viable, it began slowing down. Large-scale stove-plate casting ended at Hopewell in 1844. Clement Brooke retired in 1848.

Industry was undergoing rapid changes because of coal and steam. Cold-blast, charcoal-fueled iron furnaces like Hopewell's had to compete with coke and hot-blast anthracite furnaces that were less expensive to run. In an attempt to modernize Hopewell, the company built an anthracite furnace in 1853; but it was a failure, and Hopewell returned to traditional methods. Business generally declined except for a brief resurgence during the Civil War. Hopewell Furnace was shut down permanently on June 15, 1883.

Hopewell was a deserted village until 1935, when the federal government became interested in using the area in a New Deal conservation program. Louise Clingan Brooke, a descendant of the Buckley-Brooke partners, sold 4,000 acres to the government for about $100,000. Two Civilian Conservation Corps camps were established. They were regarded as a recreational park, and trails were built and French Creek dammed to create Hopewell Lake. When National Park Service historian Roy E. Appleman was sent to survey the site, he became interested in restoring the furnace town. Thanks to his efforts, the furnace was restored to its condition during its most prosperous period, from 1820 to 1840.

In 1938, the secretary of the interior designated the area as Hopewell Furnace National Historic Site within the National Park System. In 1946, the federal government separated the historic and scenic areas. About 5,000 acres, including Hopewell Lake, were deeded to Pennsylvania, and 848 acres were set aside for the historic site. In 1985, the National Historic Site's name was changed to Hopewell Furnace, restoring the community's historic name.

Tour

What remains of Hopewell Furnace today is a picturesque village-plantation hidden away along a wooded side road. The huge furnace is no longer lit, but the exhibits help one imagine the around-the-clock heat, noise, and dirt that accompanied the manufacturing of iron.

Begin with the **Visitor Center**'s audiovisual presentation on iron making. Then start your brochure-guided tour at the **Charcoal House** and

Cooling Shed. Colliers hauled the charcoal by wagon to the two-part charcoal house and cooling shed. There it was unloaded, completely cooled, and stored for later use.

The crumbling stone ruins of the 1853 anthracite furnace are all that remains of the failed attempt to modernize Hopewell's operation. Charcoal was made at the **charcoal hearths,** a large circular clearing where from twenty-five to fifty cords of wood were piled in mounds, covered with leaves, and set on fire. *Coaling,* as this process was called, took from ten days to two weeks. The smoldering fire had to be constantly monitored by colliers, who often lived in huts near the hearths.

Hopewell Furnace was built in 1771. Its stack is thirty-two-and-a-half feet high and seven feet wide at its widest point, tapering to one-and-a-half feet at the top. The outside wall is of limestone; the interior is lined with sandstone. Fluid slag and iron ran down and collected on the hearth at the bottom of the furnace. The lighter-weight slag floating on the iron was drawn off, and every twelve hours, the molten iron was tapped for casting.

French Creek provided the fast-flowing water necessary to propel the **waterwheel** that drove the blast machinery to keep the furnace fire hot. The reconstructed twenty-two-foot wheel exudes a feeling of quiet power.

Between the charcoal house and the furnace was the **Connecting Shed** and **Bridgehouse,** where ingredients for charging the furnace for the next few hours were stored. Workers called *fillers* charged the furnace about every half hour with fifteen bushels of charcoal, 400 to 500 pounds of ore, and thirty to forty pounds of limestone.

The restored **Office Store** is a two-story stone building with a wooden lean-to shed on the east side. Workers at Hopewell did not receive cash wages; instead, their accounts at the store were credited with the amount they earned. A worker's credit could be used to make purchases at the store, to pay bills to the company, or to pay for purchases made elsewhere that had been ordered through the store, or could be drawn as cash. Hopewell workers were not required to shop at the store, and prices were competitive. The store was viewed as a convenience rather than a monopoly.

Hopewell Furnace's products—finished cast-iron goods and bars of pig iron that were sold to other foundries—were made in the **Cast House.** Summer programs in the Cast House describe the progression of casting technology. Other buildings related to iron production are the **blacksmith shop,** which is completely equipped and functioning, and the **barn,** which now houses a collection of horse-drawn vehicles.

Because Hopewell Furnace was in a fairly isolated location, the company built **tenant houses** for its married employees and their families. Four original mid-nineteenth-century houses remain; they are of whitewashed stone with shingle roofs and wooden trim. The two-story stone **boarding-house** was used by single men.

The most imposing house at Hopewell Furnace is the mansion, also known as the **Big House.** Its northwest wing was built around 1771, and large additions were made in 1802 and 1820. The big house was home to the owner and his family, along with their servants and some workers. The basement dining room was the dining area for the single men of the community. Business was conducted in the second-floor study, and traveling businessmen slept on the third floor. The Victorian furnishings in the rooms open for viewing were acquired from the Brooke family.

Outbuildings include the **springhouse,** which supplied drinking water and stored perishables, the **bake oven,** and the **smokehouse.**

From late June through Labor Day, molding and metal casting demonstrations are given in the cast house. Living history programs may also be presented by the blacksmith, housewife, maid, and company clerk. Annual special events include a sheep shearing demonstration in May, craft demonstrations on Establishment Day (the first Sunday in August), Apple Harvest Day the last Saturday of September, and Iron Plantation Christmas on the second Sunday in December. Charcoal-making demonstrations, which last ten days, begin on Establishment Day and Apple Harvest Day.

SIDE TRIPS

French Creek State Park, the recreational portion of the Hopewell property purchased by the federal government, adjoins the historic site on three sides. The heavily wooded 7,339-acre park preserves this area's outstanding natural beauty. It has three lakes, a swimming pool, fishing, boating, hiking trails, picnicking, hunting in season, horseback riding, and environmental education programs, as well as several camping areas. French Creek State Park, Rt. 345, Elverson 19520, (215) 582-1514.

Visit **Valley Forge,** a National Historical Park. The 3,300-acre park commemorates the winter of 1777–1778, when George Washington's bedraggled Continental army camped here while British troops occupied Philadelphia. The park includes a **Visitors' Center,** the colonial-style **stone house** that was Washington's headquarters, **soldiers' huts, fortifica-**

tions, and **parade grounds.** Located north of PA Turnpike Interchange 24. Superintendent, Valley Forge 19481, (215) 783-7700. Admission charged.

See Ephrata Cloister, page 113, and Hagley Museum and Library, page 77.

EPHRATA CLOISTER

Restoration of mid-eighteenth-century German religious community; NR, NHL, HABS

Address: 632 W. Main St., Ephrata, PA 17522
Telephone: (717) 733-6600; (717) 733-4811
Location: In southeastern Pennsylvania, in Lancaster County, 5 miles south of PA Turnpike exit 21, 12 miles northeast of Lancaster
Open: Monday to Saturday, 9:00 A.M. to 5:00 P.M.; Sunday, 12:00 noon to 5:00 P.M.; closed Thanksgiving, Christmas, New Year's Day, Easter, Columbus Day, Veteran's Day, Martin Luther King Day, and President's Day
Admission: Adults, $5.00; groups and senior citizens, $4.00; children 6 to 17, $3.00
Shops: Museum Store
Facilities: Restored eighteenth-century buildings; Visitor Center with orientation slide show; guided tours; craft demonstrations; special events; picnic area

WHERE TO STAY

Inns/Bed & Breakfasts: Hackman's Country Inn, 140 Hackman Rd., Ephrata 17522, (717) 733–3498; Doneckers Inn, 318-324 N. State St., Ephrata 17522, (717) 733-8696, FAX: (215) 733-4248; 1777 House, 301 W. Main St., Ephrata 17522, (717) 783-8696; Smithton Country Inn, 900 W. Main St., Ephrata 17522, (717) 733-6094; Historic Strasburg Inn, PA 896, Strasburg 17579, (717) 687-7691, (800) 872-0201, FAX: (717) 687-6098
Motels/Hotels: Bird-In-Hand Family Inn, Box B, 2740 Old Philadelphia Pike, Bird-In-Hand 17505, (717) 768-8271, (800) 537-2535; Holiday Inn, Box 129, Denver 17517, (215) 267-7541, FAX: (215) 267-0515; Best Western Eden, 222 Eden Rd., Lancaster 17601, (717) 569-6444, FAX: (717) 569-4208
Camping: Starlite Camping Resort, 1500 Furnace Hill Rd., Stevens 17578, (717) 733-9655; Cocalico Creek Campground, 1055 Forest Rd., Denver 17517, (215) 267-2014; Dutch Cousin Campsite, 446 Hill Rd., Denver 17517, (215) 267-6911; Lancaster Reading KOA, 3 Denver Rd., Denver 17517, (215) 267-2112

Overview

Why are the strangest things the most interesting? I don't know, but I do know that the folks who lived at Ephrata Cloister lived a very unusual lifestyle, even by early-eighteenth-century standards. And Ephrata Cloister, site of one of the most notable communal societies in colonial America, is a most fascinating museum village set in Lancaster County, Pennsylvania's rolling green hills.

The Ephratans were a mystical Pietist religious group that originated in Germany. Led by Conrad Beissel, the founder of Ephrata Cloister, men and women lived communally in what they described as holy poverty. Inhabitants of the Cloister were celibate, and dressed in long, white, hooded robes. They lived in multistory, wooden, European-style medieval structures built in the first half of the eighteenth century, and slept in austere cells. Their daily lives revolved around prayer, meditation, music, work, and fasting.

The religious group, which eventually disintegrated, left a rich cultural heritage. In addition to some of the rarest architecture in America, their legacy includes their own and others' religious books and hymnals printed in German and English on their own presses. They also produced a body of original religious music, and many beautifully hand-illuminated manuscripts decorated with *Frakturschiften*, the medieval style of ornate lettering. Today, a visit to Ephrata, with its carefully restored buildings in a pastoral setting, presents an idyllic picture. A little imagination is required to recall the ascetic self-denial and discipline Ephratans practiced in their effort to achieve personal union with God.

History

Conrad Beissel, a German mystic and founder of the religious community at Ephrata, had been influenced in Germany by the preaching of the Pietists and the mystical books of Jacob Boehme. After being exiled from Germany for his unorthodox religious views, Beissel came to Pennsylvania in 1720, where he initially lived as a hermit.

A revelation caused Beissel to establish a cloistered community at Ephrata. His followers, inspired by his leadership and preaching, separated from the Dunkard Church, with which he had previously been affiliated, and followed him to the banks of Cocalico Creek. This religious communal society, founded in 1732, was based on the medieval concept of service to God through self-denial, meditation, and a life of extreme simplicity. It has been called one of the most thorough experiments in applied mysticism.

Ephrata Cloister, Ephrata, Pennsylvania
Dressed in a long white hooded robe similar to the garb worn in the eighteenth century by the brethren at Ephrata Cloister, an interpreter stands in the doorway of the restored 1750 Craft House at Ephrata Cloister, Ephrata, PA.
Photo by Patricia A. Gutek

Along with his converts, who were called brethren and sisters, Beissel fasted, grew a long beard, and preached celibacy to the prolific Pennsylvania Dutch population. Wives and husbands deserted their spouses to join him. People came from Europe to join the settlement of Seventh-Day German Baptists at Ephrata.

The community was composed of three orders: monastic brotherhood, monastic sisterhood, and married householders. The householders were craftsmen who lived nearby, worshiped at Ephrata, and supported the community's economy.

The cloistered orders spent their time in labor, meditation, and worship. They slept on narrow wooden planks eighteen inches wide, with only wooden blocks for pillows. They conducted midnight services that never lasted less than two hours and sometimes continued until dawn. Some people were said to fast for seven days at a time and to sleep only three or four hours out of twenty-four. The Ephratan diet consisted of bread, roots, greens, milk, butter, and cheese; usually there was only one meal a day. The solitary (the cloistered orders) wore white hooded habits; and for a time, the householders wore a similar habit of gray.

Between 1735 and 1749, the society constructed its log and stone buildings as its people remembered them in their Rhenish homeland. These structures were distinguished by many-storied gable ends; multiple rows of dormers on steep, graceful roofs; small, widely separated casement windows; and narrow central chimneys. They are rare examples of European-style medieval architecture in America. Their utter plainness spoke of spiritual, as opposed to material, beauty. Narrow hallways were to remind residents of the straight and narrow path, and doorways were low to inspire humility.

The community's economic life was not highly organized in the early years. Enterprise was concerned solely with supplying the barest material necessities. The members grew their own vegetables and grains. They manufactured wool and linen cloth for their clothes. Contributions to the community were on a voluntary basis and could consist of land, labor, money, or produce. Beissel managed the funds, keeping the settlement in holy poverty.

However, he believed in trying to alleviate the poverty he saw outside of his community. In 1732, even before the community was formally established, Beissel had a granary and bakehouse built, partly for the use of his followers but always available to the needy free of charge. He also started a free school for neighborhood children. The community offered clothing and housing to those in need.

In September 1777, 500 wounded soldiers from the Battle of Brandywine were brought to Ephrata. The community turned their buildings on Mount Zion, a hill rising above Cocalico Creek, into a camp hospital in which they cared for the sick. These buildings were later burned to arrest the spread of typhus fever, which killed both soldiers and Ephratans. A monument in the Mount Zion Cemetery marks the graves of many soldiers who died at Ephrata.

By 1740, the two celibate orders had grown to about seventy members each and the brethren, under the priorship of Israel Eckerling, wanted to establish the society on a better economic basis. They began by laying out extensive orchards (over 1,000 fruit trees) and even a small vineyard. In an effort to produce items for sale, brethren worked at weaving, shoemaking, and tailoring; and the sisters worked at spinning, sewing, quilting, embroidering, preparing household remedies, and making wax candles and paper lanterns. Ephrata industries, which were under the supervision of the four Eckerling brothers, included a gristmill, sawmill, paper mill, bakery, flaxseed oil mill, tannery, and printing press.

After meeting with much economic success, the cloistered members began holding secret worship services. During this time, Beissel lived apart from the community at the edge of the cloister property. In 1745, he reasserted his leadership, indicating his disapproval of the business enterprise. He enjoined the community to turn away from the worldly preoccupations and return to the monastic and meditative life. Most of the community members agreed with Beissel, except for the Eckerlings and some of their followers who were banished from the community. Beissel then disbanded the entire industrial establishment. Unfilled orders and contracts were canceled, and the horses, wagons, and oxen were sold. The orchard and vineyard were uprooted. The mills and craft operations were used only to supply the community's own needs.

Endeavors not banned by Beissel were writing music and printing books. The legacy left by the Ephratans includes hymns written by Beissel and his followers; *Frakturschriften*, the hand illumination of manuscripts, and a sizable quantity of hymnals, religious tracts, and theosophical dissertations published by the cloister press. From 1745 to the 1790s, the brethren printed books in both German and English, which the sisters embellished with their calligraphic art. These publications are considered among the rarest and most precious of early American documents. Ephrata's press also printed $25 million of Continental currency.

The most ambitious work of the cloister press was the translation and publication in 1748 of the 1,200-page *Martyr's Mirror*, a history of persecuted Christians. Printed for the Mennonites, it was the largest book produced in colonial America. It took fifteen printers three years to complete 1,300 copies.

Beissel died in 1768 and Peter Miller, whom Beissel had chosen as his successor shortly before he died, became the Ephratans' leader. The community was declining; old members were dying, and there were no new ones to replace them. Ephrata's communal celibate orders became extinct about 1800; the householders continued to use the cloister buildings until 1934.

The remaining buildings have been restored and are administered by the Pennsylvania Historical and Museum Commission.

TOUR

Guides explain the history and customs of this unique community as they take you through the saron, saal, and cabin. The rest of the tour is self-guided.

Purchase your admission tickets at the **Reception Center,** and begin your tour there with the slide show and museum displays of printing and *Frakturschriften,* including a copy of *Martyr's Mirror.* There is also a wooden communion service, thought to be a gift from George Washington for the cloister's care of soldiers wounded in the Battle of Brandywine.

The 1743 *Sisters' House,* also called the **saron,** is an outstanding example of medieval German architecture. A three-story building, it was originally occupied by married householders. In 1745, it was remodeled to accommodate the celibate sisterhood. Each floor is designed with a central kitchen joined on either side by a common workroom and sleeping cells. The cells are small, provided only with wooden plank beds and wooden block pillows. Meals were eaten in the refectory, which is furnished with simple tables and benches. A room in which the sisters practiced the art of *Frakturschriften* contains a display of that work. The interior is very plain, with white walls, wooden plank floors, narrow halls, and low doorways.

Sisters led an austere life, dividing their time between work and prayer: private prayer, from 5:00 to 6:00 A.M., work from 6:00 to 9:00 A.M., prayer from 9:00 to 10:00 A.M., work from 10:00 A.M. until noon, a church service from noon to 1:00 P.M., work from 1:00 to 5:00 P.M., private prayer from 5:00 to 6:00 P.M., a vegetarian meal at 6:00 P.M., singing or *Frakturschriften* school from 7:00 to 9:00 P.M., sleep from 9:00 P.M. to midnight, service from 12:00 midnight to 2:00 A.M., and sleep from 2:00 to 5:00 A.M..

The **Meetinghouse,** or **saal,** which adjoins the saron, was built in 1741. Church services were held on the lower floor of this two-story building; singing and writing schools were upstairs. There are four original benches and some original candlesticks inside. Framed *Frakturschriften* hang on the walls.

In Ephrata, the Sabbath was on the seventh day, Saturday. The service was an informal meeting consisting of singing and extemporaneous discourses. Many of the hymns were written by Beissel himself. He also prescribed a unique method of choral singing; visitors commented that its falsetto intonation created an otherworldly effect. No other instruments were used. The service also included communion, and sometimes foot washing.

The meetinghouse refectory was used for love feasts. Normally vegetarians, the Ephratans would eat lamb stew and bread at a feast. Any member could initiate a love feast at any time by inviting other members to this meal. Everyone ate out of the same bowl.

The small community **Bakehouse** is probably the oldest building at Ephrata; it was erected prior to the founding of the cloister. Bread baked here was distributed free to the needy. The building is now the site of a candle-making demonstration.

Adjoining the old bakehouse is the **Beissel Cabin,** a small clapboard-sheathed log house built in 1748. This hermit's cabin is sparsely furnished with benches and tables made at Ephrata and is heated by a 1756 five-plate stove. Beissel was a hermit for part of his life, and even after founding the cloister, he spent a great deal of time alone.

The 1735 **Almonry** (a place where alms were given out) is a large three-story stone building where male travelers or the homeless could find free shelter. Women in need of shelter would spend the night in the Sisters' House. This tradition of hospitality was common in European convents. The squirrel-tail ovens, located to the side and rear of the almonry's large fireplace, were used for baking bread.

A mid-eighteenth-century two-story frame cabin has been furnished as a typical **Householders Cabin**; however, most of the householders would have lived away from the cloister. The cabin has been restored to look as it would have around 1800; the furnishings are simple but not as stark as those in the saron.

The **Craft House,** built around 1750, is architecturally interesting because it is one of the few remaining colonial, half-timbered structures. The construction consists of a pegged timber framework chinked with stone. The interior walls are mud-plastered, and the outside is clapboarded. The ceiling beams, which extend to the outside of the building, are particularly unusual.

The **Printshop** contains a press built in Philadelphia and brought to Ephrata in 1804. It is the oldest American-made press still in operation.

The **Solitary House** is a mid-eighteenth-century cabin. It shows the domestic life of a celibate member of the cloister society who chose to live as a hermit.

The **Graveyard** is surrounded by a rebuilt stone wall. Many of the graves are above ground. Conrad Beissel and Peter Miller are buried here. Here is a translation of the German inscription on Beissel's gravestone:

> Here rests offspring of the love of God, Friedsam (Beissel was known as Father Friedsam Gottrecht at the Cloister), A Solitary. But later

became leader, guardian and teacher of Solitary and of the congregation in Christ in and about Ephrata. Born at Eberback in the Palatine. Called Conrad Beissel. Fell asleep July 6th Anno 1768. Aged according to his spiritual age, 52 years, but according to his natural 77 years and 4 months.

After visiting the cemetery, walk over to the **Academy.** This building dates from 1837, new by Ephrata standards. A private academy was operated by the church until the time of the Civil War, when it was leased to the township and used as an elementary school until 1926. The two-story building with a belfry displays schoolroom furniture of the 1840s. There is a Christmas candlelight tour in December.

SIDE TRIPS

Ephrata is located in Lancaster County, Pennsylvania, home of many Amish farmers, who do indeed drive horse-drawn buggies on the roads. These plainly dressed people adhere to a simple way of life that forbids such modern inventions as electricity and cars. They do not encourage, nor do they benefit from, busloads of people driving past their farms. Taking pictures of the Amish is especially offensive because graven images are forbidden by their religion. Out of respect for the Amish, we will not recommend any of the organized tours. Only designated tourist sites are included here.

The city of **Lancaster** was founded in 1718 and served as the country's capital for a single day, September 27, 1777. On that day, the Continental Congress was fleeing the British in Philadelphia and held a meeting in Lancaster. Ninety-minute narrated walking tours of the historic downtown area are available at 15 West King Street, Lancaster, (717) 392-1776.

Wheatland was the residence of President James Buchanan. The 1828 Federal mansion has been restored to the period of Buchanan's occupancy, 1848 to 1868. 1120 Marietta Ave., Lancaster. Located 1 1/2 miles west of Lancaster on Route 23, (717) 392-8721. Open daily, April to November, 10:00 A.M. to 4:15 P.M. Admission charged.

The **Strasburg Steam Railroad** offers a forty-five minute, nine-mile round trip to Paradise, Pennsylvania, in late-nineteenth-century coaches pulled by antique locomotives. Daily, May to October; weekends March, April, October, and November. P.O. Box 96A, Route 741, Strasburg 17579, (717) 687-7522. Admission charged.

See also Hopewell Furnace, page 105, and Hagley Museum and Library, page 77.

LANDIS VALLEY MUSEUM

A museum village of Pennsylvania German rural life from the colonial era through the nineteenth century

Address: 2451 Kissel Hill Road, Lancaster, PA 17601
Telephone: (717) 569-0401
Location: In southeastern Pennsylvania, in Lancaster County, 2½ miles northeast of Lancaster, on Rt. 272/Oregon Pike
Open: Tuesday to Saturday, 9:00 A.M. to 5:00 P.M.; Sunday, 12:00 noon to 5:00 P.M.; closed Mondays and holidays except Memorial Day, July 4, and Labor Day; primary season is from May through October; one-hour guided tour of five buildings from November through April
Admission: Adults, $7.00; seniors, $6.00; children 6 to 17, $5.00, from May through October; adults, $6.00; seniors, $5.00; children 6 to 17, $4.00, from November through April
Restaurants: Landis Valley House Hotel
Shops: Weathervane Shop
Facilities: Visitor Center with exhibit gallery; picnic areas; mostly handicapped accessible; special events; living history and craft demonstrations; heirloom seed project

WHERE TO STAY

Inns/Bed & Breakfasts: Cameron Estate, RD 1, Box 305, Donegal Springs Rd., Mount Joy 17552, (717) 653-1773, FAX: (717) 653-9432; General Sutter, 14 E. Main St., Lititz 17543, (717) 626-2115; Buona Notte B&B, 2020 Marietta Ave., Lancaster 17603, (717) 295-2597; Meadowview Guest House, 2169 New Holland Pike, Lancaster 17601, (717) 299-4017
Motels/Hotels: Hilton Garden Inn, 101 Granite Run, Lancaster 17601, (717) 560-0880, FAX: (717) 560-5400; Best Western Eden, 222 Eden Rd., Lancaster 17601, (717) 569-6444, FAX: (717) 569-4208; Holiday Inn North, 1492 Lititz Pike, Lancaster 17601, (717) 393-0771, FAX: (717) 299-6238
Camping: Indian Rock Campground, 436 Indian Rock Dam Rd., York 17403, (717) 741-1764; White Oak Campground, 372 White Oak Rd., Quarryville 17566, (717) 687-6207; Old Mill Stream Camping Manor, 2249 Rt. 30 E., Lancaster 17602, (717) 299-2314; Beacon Camping Lodge, West Newport Rd., Intercourse 17534, (717) 768-

8755; Lancaster/Reading KOA, 3 Denver Rd., Denver 17517, (215) 267-2112

OVERVIEW

Landis Valley Museum is an outdoor museum of Pennsylvania German rural life from the mid-eighteenth century to 1900. Of the more than two dozen buildings at the museum, some historical buildings are original to Landis Valley, while others have been moved from sites in Lancaster County. Reconstructions of structures typically found in the area make up the remainder of the buildings.

The founders of the Landis Valley Museum were two men who collected a huge number of Pennsylvania German artifacts. The Landis brothers, George and Henry, were interested in the material culture of their German ancestors—their tools, textiles, implements, and vehicles. When industrialism ended the era of small farmers and craftsmen, the Landis brothers felt a need to preserve for future generations the material aspects of a preindustrial lifestyle. They spent a great deal of time and money acquiring anything owned or made by the immigrants from Germany and their descendants who populated this region of Pennsylvania.

Rural lifestyles in Pennsylvania during the Colonial, Federal, and Victorian periods are depicted within a sixteen-acre area. A mixture of old and new buildings houses more than 80,000 objects collected by the Landis brothers.

HISTORY

Pennsylvania, one of the original English colonies, was founded by William Penn. He was granted a charter from King Charles II in 1681 based on a proposal for a "Holy Experiment" in the New World. Anyone who believed in God, regardless of their religious affiliation, would be welcome. Penn himself was a Quaker who advocated peace, justice, equality, and Christian simplicity. Penn wanted Pennsylvania's political principles to include ordered liberty, freedom of conscience, and broad participation in government.

During the seventeenth century, freedom to practice the religion of your choice was a powerful attraction to those Europeans who had suffered greatly when they veered from the official state religion. What is now present-day Germany had been especially divided by religious conflicts when a religious reform movement met massive resistance from the established church and state. Consequently, many German-speaking people responded to the opportunity to migrate to William Penn's colony.

Landis Valley Museum, Lancaster, Pennsylvania
The reconstructed stone and wood bank barn with an overhanging forebay typifies
those built throughout southeastern Pennsylvania from the late 1700s to the 1900s.
Cattle and horses were stabled on the lower level while a threshing floor and a hay
mow were above. At Landis Valley Museum, Lancaster, PA.

Photo by Patricia A. Gutek

Inexpensive land was another attraction for people looking for new
economic opportunities and a secure and prosperous future. Europe had
been engaged in devastating, bloody wars for decades. Freedom from war
and oppression was still another reason for folks to migrate from German-
speaking areas including the Palatine, Switzerland, Austria, and Czecho-
slovakia. Pennsylvania German or Pennsylvania Dutch were terms applied
to the German-speaking Europeans who immigrated to Pennsylvania from
1683 until 1820. The word "Dutch" is an English word which refers to the
Germanic language and those who spoke it rather than the country of
Germany. Germans settled in the fertile Lancaster area about 1711. Lancaster County was established in 1729.

German settlers applied their Old World agricultural methods to the

Pennsylvania soil. The good climate, abundant streams and springs, excellent soil, and plentiful forests combined with farming expertise led to success. Pennsylvania became the leading agricultural colony by the 1760s. Adults and children all contributed to meet the family's needs for food, shelter, and clothing. In addition to agricultural skills, many Pennsylvania settlers were expert blacksmiths, carpenters, wheelwrights, glassmakers, gunsmiths, wagon builders, potters, or weavers. Almost all of the necessities of life were produced in a community. Work was labor-intensive, products were custom-made, and tools were hand-made. With industrialism came agricultural machinery and factory-produced products which negatively impacted small family farms and individual craftspeople.

The collections of the Landis Valley Museum were started by brothers, George and Henry Landis, whose ancestors settled in the area named Landis Valley in the 1730s. Henry was born in 1865 and George was born two years later in Lancaster County. The brothers retired in 1924 to the family homestead and continued collecting in earnest. They wanted to establish a museum focused on the cultural skills and interests of the Pennsylvania Germans who in 1790 comprised forty percent of the population of southeastern Pennsylvania. They collected local agricultural and craftsmen's tools, hardware, quilts, coverlets, clothes, musical instruments, china, glass, firearms, and fraktur documents. In 1925, they opened their "Barn Museum" to the public.

In 1941, the Carl Schurz Foundation, administrator of the Oberlaender Trust, lent financial support, and the Landis Valley Museum was formally incorporated. Exhibit buildings were erected. In 1953, the Landis Valley Museum was deeded to the Commonwealth of Pennsylvania. The village is a recreation; no actual town existed at this location. The museum is on the old Landis homestead and some of its original structures remain. The Pennsylvania Historical and Museum Commission has expanded the museum by acquiring additional land and historical houses.

TOUR

Begin your tour at the **Visitor Center** in which a gallery displays changing exhibits on aspects of Pennsylvania cultural history. Not all museum buildings are open every day during the May through October season. A one-hour guided tour of only five buildings is given during the November through April season.

The **Print Shop and Leatherworking Shop** are in a dwelling built around 1800. The small white building is constructed of square hewn logs covered with weatherboards. The early-nineteenth-century print shop has a wooden framed 1825 press from Warren County, cases of type, and wood-block and metalplate engraving equipment. In the Leatherworking Shop, the harnessmaker made and repaired harnesses, saddles, leather fire buckets, hide-covered trunks and boxes, saddlebags, valises, and whips. Those products as well as leathermaking tools are displayed in the shop.

Reconstructed buildings at the **Log Farm** represent a typical German farmstead of the late 1700s. The one-story house with a central chimney was constructed of logs hewn on at least two sides. People from the wooded Alpine and South German areas traditionally built with logs. The two-room cabin has a kitchen and living room/bedroom with rope beds. Farm outbuildings include a log barn, a hay barracks, a stone springhouse built over a spring and used for storing perishable food, a pig sty, and a bake oven and smokehouse. A kitchen garden has been planted with historical vegetables, flowers, and herbs. Landis Valley Museum has an heirloom seed project in which traditional strains of historic, non-hybrid vegetables, herbs, and flowers are acquired and grown. The museum sells these seeds through a catalog. Geese, chickens, sheep, horses, pigs, and cows can be seen in the farm area.

The restored **Brick Homestead** was the home of Jacob and Elizabeth Landis, a Mennonite family who purchased the land in 1820. The large two-and-one-half-story house they built is in the vernacular style with Federal touches. The two front doors, one leading into the formal parlor and the other into the informal sitting room, are a Pennsylvania German feature. About 1840, Jacob Jr. married. Soon afterward, a one-story brick house was built nearby for the senior Landises. The solid houses and substantial furnishings indicate the prosperity of the Landis family.

Behind the main house is a reconstructed stone and wood bank barn with an overhanging forebay. These two-level barns, built throughout the southeastern part of the state from the late 1700s to the 1900s, stabled cattle and horses on the lower level while a threshing floor and a hay mow were above.

The **Blacksmith Shop,** moved from the Gettysburg area, was constructed around 1870. The forge and most of the tools date from the 1880 to 1900 period. In the **Transportation Building** are horse-drawn vehicles from the eighteenth to the early twentieth century including a number of sleighs and Conestoga wagons.

Victorian furnishings decorate the restored **Landis Valley House Hotel,** built around 1856 by the same Jacob Landis, Jr., who lived at the Brick Farmstead. Two rooms in the hotel are now used as dining rooms for serving lunch to hungry museum visitors.

The **Maple Grove School,** built in 1890 near Leola in Lancaster County and used until the 1960s, is a very large one-room school. It has six rows of desks and a pot-bellied stove.

A reconstruction of a late 1800s **Country Store** is filled with items from the mid-1800s through about 1915. Most of the inventory was factory-made and included crockery, tinware, medicines, farm tools, candy, and yard goods. The **Firehouse,** also a reconstruction, holds equipment used in Lancaster County during the latter 1800s.

The **Tin Shop** is in a reconstructed tollhouse. Tin objects and tools used in tinmaking are displayed. Another craft shop is the **Pottery Shop** which is lined with shelves filled with redware and stoneware.

The **Landis House,** which belonged to the brothers who founded the museum, was built in the late 1880s by their parents. The interior of the two-story frame house is decorated in the Victorian style with wallpaper, carpets, machine-made furniture, and kerosene lamps. There is an iron cook stove in the kitchen and the house is heated by coal stoves. Landis family heirlooms include the kitchen sideboard and one-door cupboard which were wedding gifts to Henry and Emma. The family kept their horses and vehicles in the stable behind the house.

The **Yellow Barn** was built in 1939 by George and Henry Landis using rafters and trusses from the original barn associated with the Brick Farmstead. It was used as an exhibit building for their collections. Now it shelters an exhibit on traditional Pennsylvania agricultural practices and tools. Farm tools which range from simple handmade items to complex tools manufactured in factories are exhibited in the **Farm Implement Shed.**

The **Erisman House** is a late-eighteenth-century, square-hewn log house covered with weatherboards on the front and board and batten siding on the back and sides. Moved from the city of Lancaster, it is furnished as the home of a seamstress. Her work room is filled with sewing equipment and fabric.

A reconstructed **Tavern** reflects an early-1800s country tavern. Taverns were most numerous during the turnpike road era, from 1790 to 1830. The tap room in the tavern is based on an 1813 painting by John Krimmel. The **Gun Exhibit** has many examples of the Pennsylvania rifle, a gun developed by German and Swiss craftsmen in southern Lancaster County in the mid-1700s. Another immense Conestoga wagon which originated in Lancaster County is displayed in the **Conestoga Wagon Shed.**

Special events include Charter Day in early March, Herb Faire in early May, Sheep Shearing in May, a Fair in early June, Harvest Days in

October, Pumpkin Patch in October, Days of the Belsnickel in early December, and Christmas at Landis Valley. Craft and living history classes for adults and children are given on Saturdays during July and August. Adult workshops and seminars on early Pennsylvania arts, crafts, and folklore are taught in late June.

SIDE TRIPS

Visit the **Cornwall Iron Furnace,** an iron plantation built by Peter Grubb in 1739. It operated from 1742 until 1883. A National Historic Landmark and a National Historic Mechanical Engineering Landmark, it has survived fully intact. In the 1850s, the furnace was enlarged and stone buildings replaced earlier wooden ones. These Gothic Revival style buildings in their rural setting make you feel like you have been transported to the English countryside. The nearby Miners Village, housing built around 1865 for employees, is still occupied and contributes to the British flavor. Tours of the Furnace are given daily except Mondays. Rexmont Rd. at Boyd St., P.O. Box 251, Cornwall 17016, (717) 272-9711. Admission charged.

Harpers Ferry NHP

WEST VIRGINIA

Colonial Williamsburg

Shaker Village of Pleasant Hill

VIRGINIA

KENTUCKY

Historic Rugby

Old Salem

TENNESSEE

NORTH CAROLINA

ARKANSAS

Old Washington HSP

SOUTH CAROLINA

MISSISSIPPI

ALABAMA

GEORGIA

LOUISIANA

Westville

Vermilionville

The LSU Rural Life Museum

FLORIDA

Spanish Quarter & Castillo de San Marcos NM

SOUTH AND SOUTHEAST

ARKANSAS
Old Washington Historic State Park, Washington

FLORIDA
Spanish Quarter and Castillo de San Marcos National Monument, St. Augustine

GEORGIA
Westville, Lumpkin

KENTUCKY
Shaker Village of Pleasant Hill, Harrodsburg

LOUISIANA
The LSU Rural Life Museum, Baton Rouge
Vermilionville, Lafayette

NORTH CAROLINA
Old Salem, Winston-Salem

TENNESSEE
Historic Rugby, Rugby

VIRGINIA
Colonial Williamsburg, Williamsburg

WEST VIRGINIA
Harpers Ferry National Historical Park, Harpers Ferry

OLD WASHINGTON HISTORIC STATE PARK

Restoration of southwestern Arkansas town during territorial and early statehood periods, 1824–1874; NR

Address: P.O. Box 98, Washington, AR 71862

Telephone: (501) 983-2684; (501) 983-2733

Location: In southwest Arkansas, about 30 miles northeast of the Texas border; on AR 4, nine miles northwest of Hope, at I-30, Exit 30

Open: Daily, 8:00 A.M. to 5:00 P.M.; closed Thanksgiving, Christmas, and New Year's Day

Admission: Day Passes for all Old Washington sites during guided tours: adults, $9.00, children 6 to 12, $4.50; Pioneers, Planters, Printers tour or Living in Town tour: adults, $4.50, children 6 to 12, $2.50; Museum Experience self-guided tour: adults, $3.00, children 6 to 12, $1.50

Restaurants: Williams' Tavern

Shops: Old Washington Merchantile

Facilities: Visitor Center; Southwest Arkansas Regional Archives; guided tours; special events

WHERE TO STAY

Inns/Bed & Breakfasts: Old Washington Jail B&B, P.O. Box 179, Washington, AR 71862, (501) 983-2461

Motels/Hotels: Best Western Inn of Hope, I-30 and AR 4, Hope 71801, (501) 777-9222, FAX: (501) 777-9077; Holiday Inn, I-30 & AR 4, Hope 71801, (501) 777-8601, FAX: (501) 777-3142

Camping: Bois d'Arc Lake and Reservoir, Hope 71801, (501) 777-3153; Crater of Diamonds State Park, Rt. 1, Box 364, Murfreesboro 71958, (501) 285-3113; Millwood State Park, Rt. 1, Box 37AB, Ashdown 71822, (501) 898-2800; White Oak Lake State Park, Star Route, Bluff City 71722, (501) 685-2748, (501) 685-2132

OVERVIEW

During the Civil War, Washington became the Confederate state capital of Arkansas from 1863 until 1865 while Federal troops occupied Little Rock. Earlier, the Cherokees passed through the town on their exodus to Oklahoma. Washington also served as a rendezvous point for volunteers in the Mexican-American War. Due to a series of destructive fires and being bypassed by the railroad, the town declined.

Old Washington Historic State Park preserves a number of restored nineteenth-century buildings in the small, living town of Washington. The restored buildings are interspersed with privately owned and occupied residences. Washington retains a mid-nineteenth-century air with quiet streets, huge magnolia trees, spacious lawns, and lovely gardens. Hundreds of daffodils bloom in the spring. The peacefulness of the historic town contributes to the sense of being in a time warp.

Washington is nine miles northwest of Hope, the birthplace of President Bill Clinton.

HISTORY

Old Washington was once a part of the Louisiana Purchase, that great piece of North America claimed by France and eventually sold to the United States in 1803. When the Louisiana Purchase was opened to settlement, homesteaders streamed into the Arkansas Territory. Many traveled on the Southwest Trail which ran from the Mississippi River across a corner of present-day Missouri, then went southwest across Arkansas for almost three hundred miles to the Red River. The town of Washington is located along the Southwest Trail near the Red River.

Because so many settlers traveled on the Southwest Trail, the Rev. William Stevenson, a Methodist preacher, decided to hold Methodist revival camp meetings on it. He chose a spot in the southwest corner of the Arkansas Territory which he dubbed The Ebenezer Campground. In 1819, he built a huge log shed on the side of the hill by the Black Bois d'Arc Creek. The town of Washington developed around Stevenson's campground.

One of the first businesses in Washington was a tavern opened by Elijah Stuart. In 1824, the commissioners of Hempstead County decided to locate the county's permanent seat of justice at the head of the Black Bois d'Arc Creek. The Court of Common Pleas for Hempstead County was held in Elijah Stuart's tavern until 1825, when the hewn log Hempstead Courthouse was built. That same year, the Hempstead County commissioners plotted lots in the town they called Washington.

In the early nineteenth century, white settlers were encroaching on the lands occupied by American Indian tribes. The conflict was especially intense in the southeastern states. President Andrew Jackson was determined to end the conflict by forcefully relocating the eastern American

Indian tribes across the Mississippi River, thus affirming the rights of white settlers to occupy American Indian lands. Some tribes agreed to removal, but many, especially the Cherokee, refused. The Removal Bill of 1830 provided for the American Indians forcible removal. Some of the forced marches of tribes passed through Washington on the Southwest Trail. More than 3,000 Choctaws from Mississippi on their way to Oklahoma walked through Washington from 1831 to 1833. Some Washington businessmen obtained government contracts to sell food to these Choctaw and Chickasaw Indians.

Arkansas attracted a growing number of settlers. By 1836, its population had increased sufficiently for it to be admitted as a state.

Because of Washington's proximity to the Texas border, it became a favorite point of entry to Texas, then a part of Mexico. Sam Houston, who wanted to free Texas from Mexican rule, met with Stephen Austin and Jim Bowie at the Washington tavern to plan the Texas Revolt of 1835–1836. Davy Crockett and his men spent several days in Washington in November 1835 before joining Houston's army in Texas.

Washington was a convenient rendezvous point for volunteers in the Mexican-American War which began in 1846. The first volunteers arrived in late June and more soldiers kept coming all during the summer and fall, camping in and around Washington.

A story told in Washington is that a town blacksmith, James Black, made the first Bowie knife. It is claimed that in 1831 Jim Bowie asked Black to make a knife he had designed. Bowie had whittled an outline of the knife out of a cigar box cover. Black made two knives, one according to Bowie's design and one of his own design. Bowie bought Black's design, and Bowie's name became associated with the famous knife. This is just one of several stories of the origin of the Bowie knife.

Washington's most important historic claim is linked to the Civil War when Arkansas joined the Confederate states that seceded from the Union. After General Frederick Steele's Union forces captured Little Rock in September 1863, many of its residents fled to the southwestern part of the state still held by the Confederates. The attics and basements of every house in Washington were used to house women and children. Washington became the Confederate state capital of Arkansas from 1863 until 1865 while Federal troops occupied Little Rock, the state capital. Arkansas Governor Harris Flanagan moved to Washington, as did the state government. Setting up headquarters in the Hempstead Courthouse, the general assembly and the supreme court continued to function.

Washington became the center of state Confederate activities, and its newspaper, *The Washington Telegraph,* was the only rebel newspaper still being published in the state. Some companies of the Confederate army also moved southwest, and the fields near Washington were used for military encampments. The crowded little town also served as Confederate Army headquarters for Arkansas.

After the Civil War ended, townspeople began rebuilding their community. Washington was dealt a severe blow when the Cairo and Fulton Railroad came to southwest Arkansas in 1874, bypassing Washington by eight miles to run through the new town of Hope. When fire swept through Washington in 1874, burning many businesses, many business people decided to relocate to Hope. When another fire burned twenty-four businesses in 1883, the same phenomenon occurred. Washington's population fell.

Restoration efforts by the Foundation for the Restoration of Pioneer Washington began in Washington in 1958. In 1973, the Arkansas State Parks and Tourism Department joined the restoration project and Old Washington Historic State Park was formed. The Southwest Arkansas Regional Archives, dedicated to collecting and preserving documents and photographs of southwest Arkansas, began in 1978. In 1980, the Ethnic Minority Memorabilia Association was incorporated to preserve and interpret African American history in the area.

Tour

The **Hempstead County Courthouse,** built in 1874, is the historic state park's **Visitor Center.** It served as the county courthouse until 1939 when Hope became the county seat. Then it was used as a school from 1940 to 1975. The red brick, two-story Victorian building has 1874 in black iron numbers over its door. The 1874 courtroom has been restored.

Old Washington offers a variety of guided tours organized around themes. One is called Pioneers, Planters, Printers, and Merchants Bring Life to Old Washington. It interprets Washington's history from 1824 to 1840. Living in Town: The Washington Community—1840–1875 is a tour which focuses on Washington as a political, social, economic, and professional center of southwest Arkansas. The Old Washington Museum Experience is a self-guided tour of the commercial sites of frontier Washington.

The **Tavern Inn** is a reconstruction of the original tavern built by Joshua Morrison in the 1830s. The two-story, white frame building has wide verandas on both the first and second floors. The first-floor taproom is a large, bright room with a wooden bar, a fireplace, tables and chairs for card playing, an 1850 reed organ, and a piano. The inn's large detached kitchen has cathedral ceilings and a huge brick fireplace. It is furnished with a large table, a pie safe, a loom, spinning wheel, and oversized baskets of cotton.

The **Blacksmith Shop** is a log reconstruction of the shop where James Black is said to have made the first Bowie knife. It is a working blacksmith shop with demonstrations by a guide who also retells the Bowie legend.

The most important historic site in Washington is the white frame **Courthouse** which was built in 1836 and was used as the Confederate state capital from 1863 to 1865. On the first floor are original yellow pine floors, ceilings, panelled walls, and hand-hewn columns. Fireplaces stand at opposite ends of the room. The walls are adorned with portraits of Robert E. Lee, Stonewall Jackson, Bradley Johnson, and General P.G.T. Beauregard.

The **B. W. Edwards Weapons Museum,** housed in a 1925 bank building, displays the guns collected by Edwards. Among the hundreds of foreign and American weapons are rifles, pistols, revolvers, swords, Remingtons, flintlocks, and Bowie knives. A collection of printing equipment is exhibited in the **Printing Museum,** a 1920 building which had been Washington's Post Office.

The **Sanders House,** a Greek Revival structure, was built in 1845 by Simon T. Sanders. One of Sanders' daughters, Sarah Virginia, married Augustus H. Garland, who became the governor of Arkansas, U.S. senator, and attorney general under President Cleveland. The house has fifteen-foot ceilings and original cypress floors. Some bedrooms and the dining room can only be accessed from the outside porch.

The **Purdom House,** built around 1850, was the home of Dr. James A. L. Purdom who practiced medicine until 1866. The restored building holds medical exhibits.

The **Royston Log House,** which was built around 1835, was moved from the Royston Plantation. It is a two-room house built of logs that have been covered by planks. A double-sided fireplace serves both the kitchen and bedroom.

The **Block House,** a Federal-style structure, was built by the Abraham Block family in 1832. The **Royston House** is a Greek Revival house built in 1845 for Grandison D. Royston. A magnolia tree planted in 1839 by Grandison Royston is the largest in Arkansas.

The 1883 **Goodlett Cotton Gin** is one of the few surviving steam-powered gins in the United States. It was built by David M. Goodlett and was used by the Goodlett family until 1966.

The **Williams Tavern Restaurant,** which serves as the park restaurant, was built by John W. Williams in 1832 at Marlbrook, seven miles northeast, and moved to Washington. The entry has a cage bar while the dining rooms have wooden plank floors, beamed ceilings, and fireplaces.

SIDE TRIPS

Although neither house is open to the public, the **birthplace** and **childhood home of President Bill Clinton** in Hope can be viewed from the exterior. Clinton's grandparents' home, in which his mother lived at the time of his birth, is at 117 S. Hervey Street, Hope. His mother's marriage to Mr. Clinton occasioned the family's move to Clinton's childhood home at 321 E. 13th Street, Hope.

SPANISH QUARTER & CASTILLO DE SAN MARCOS NATIONAL MONUMENT

Restoration and reconstruction of an eighteenth-century Spanish colonial settlement; NR, NHL, HABS

Restoration of a seventeenth-century Spanish fort; NR, HABS

Address: Spanish Quarter: Historic St. Augustine Preservation Board, P.O. Box 1987, St. Augustine, FL 32085; Castillo de San Marcos NM: 1 Castillo Dr., St. Augustine, FL 32084

Telephone: Spanish Quarter: (904) 825-6830; Castillo de San Marcos NM: (904) 829-6506

Location: St. Augustine is on Florida's northeast Atlantic coast, 36 miles south of Jacksonville; both sites are in downtown St. Augustine

Open: Spanish Quarter: daily, 9:00 A.M. to 5:00 P.M.; Castillo de San Marcos NM: daily, 8:45 A.M. to 4:45 P.M.; closed Christmas Day

Admission: Spanish Quarter: adults, $5.00; children 6 to 18, $2.50; families, $10.00; Castillo de San Marcos NM: adults, $2.00; seniors and children 16 and under, free

Restaurants: Many in St. Augustine's historic district

Shops: Spanish Quarter: Museum Store; Castillo de San Marcos NM: Bookstore

Facilities: Spanish Quarter: orientation center; craft demonstrations; Castillo de San Marcos NM: ranger talks; cannon firing demonstrations; tours

WHERE TO STAY

Inns/Bed & Breakfasts: Kenwood, 38 Marine St., St. Augustine 32084, (904) 824-2116; St. Francis, 279 St. George St., St. Augustine

32084, (904) 824-6068; Westcott House, 146 Avenida Menendez, St. Augustine 32084, (904) 824-4301

Motels/Hotels: Monterey, 16 Avenida Menendez, St. Augustine 32084, (904) 824-4482; Quality Inn Alhambra, 2700 Ponce de Leon Blvd., St. Augustine 32084, (904) 824-2883; Ramada Inn-Historic Area, 116 San Marco Ave., St. Augustine 32084, (904) 824-4352, FAX: (904) 824-2745; Ponce De Leon Resort, 4000 N. US 1, St. Augustine 32085, (904) 824-2821, (800) 228-2821, FAX: (904) 829-6108

Camping: Anastasia State Park, Anastasia Island, St. Augustine 32084, (904) 829-2668; Faver-Dykes State Park, US 1, St. Augustine 32084, (904) 794-0997; Ocean Grove Camp Resort, 4225 Hwy. Ala South, St. Augustine 32084, (904) 471-3414, (800) 342-4007; North Beach Campresort, 4125 Coastal Hwy., North Beach, St. Augustine 32095, (904) 824-1806

OVERVIEW

In the sixteenth century, European nations such as Spain, France, and England extended their empires to North America. In what is now the United States, England and Spain established colonies on the Atlantic coast. Spain claimed territory in the Southwest and Florida. St. Augustine, a city founded in 1565 by Don Pedro Menéndez de Avilés, is part of that Spanish colonial heritage.

The colonial village served as a garrison town charged with protecting Spanish fleets sailing along the Florida coast en route to Spain. After repeated attacks by pirates in the seventeenth century, a huge star-shaped Spanish fort, Castillo de San Marcos, was built. In the early 1700s, St. Augustine became a walled city, one of only three in the United States. Today, the walls are gone but the fort remains on St. Augustine's harbor.

The Spanish Quarter is a restored and reconstructed Spanish colonial village of the 1700s located within St. Augustine's historic area. Since the town burned many times, the oldest extant buildings are from the eighteenth century. A tourist town, St. Augustine's narrow streets are lined with privately owned eighteenth-century Spanish colonial architecture used as homes, bed and breakfasts, shops, and restaurants. They are small buildings with pastel stucco walls, windows with shutters or wooden grills, intricately carved doors, second-story balconies hanging over the street, and walled courtyards.

HISTORY

St. Augustine is the oldest permanent European settlement in North America and the nation's oldest continuously occupied city. On Septem-

**Spanish Quarter and Castillo de San Marcos National
Monument, St. Augustine, Florida**
Tourists line the walls of the restored seventeenth-century Spanish fort to get a
good view of the parade of soldiers in replica eighteenth-century Spanish uniforms.
At Castillo de San Marcos National Monument, St. Augustine, FL.
Photo by Patricia A. Gutek

ber 8, 1565, fifty-two years after Florida's discovery by Ponce de Leon,
Don Pedro Menéndez de Avilés arrived in the Spanish territory with 700
colonists. He named the colony St. Augustine because Florida had first
been sighted on St. Augustine's Day, August 28.

The expedition, ordered by King Philip II of Spain, was intended to
settle the territory and drive out the French, who had been encroaching on
the Spanish claim and threatening Spanish treasure fleets along Florida's
shorelines.

Although Menéndez was highly successful on both counts, St. Augustine's status as a permanent Spanish colony and military base was constantly challenged. In 1586, Sir Francis Drake pillaged and burned the
town; and in 1668, Captain John Davis, a pirate, plundered the homes and

killed many people. In 1670, the English settled Charleston in the Carolinas, and England and Spain agreed to respect each other's possessions.

Castillo de San Marcos, St. Augustine's star-shaped stone fortress, was begun in 1672 and took more than twenty years to complete. It was made of native shell stone, called *coquina*, and a cementlike mortar made from shell lime. The white plastered walls were thirty feet high and up to thirteen feet thick.

Carolinians attacked St. Augustine in 1702 after destroying Spain's northern missions but could not penetrate the fort, though they tried for fifty days. The British Carolinians burned the entire city except for the fort and then withdrew. The settlement was rebuilt with stone. To protect the town from future destruction, earthworks and palisades, buttressed at strategic points with redoubts, were built from the Castillo, making St. Augustine a walled city.

Another attack on St. Augustine was attempted in 1740 by British General James Oglethorpe of Georgia, but again, the castillo withstood the assault.

Toward the end of the French and Indian wars, Spain formed an alliance with France against the British. After the British captured Havana, Spain agreed to cede Florida in return for the Havana port. England held St. Augustine for twenty years (1763 to 1783). During the American Revolution, the Florida outpost remained loyal to England.

A treaty signed by England, France, and Spain in 1783 returned Florida to Spain. St. Augustine remained a Spanish possession until July 10, 1821, when Spain ceded Florida to the United States.

In 1836, Seminole Indians attempted to regain control of Florida, and the *castillo* was used by the Americans as a military prison. After the Seminole War ended in 1842, Florida became the twenty-seventh state in the Union.

During the Civil War, Florida seceded from the Union; and in 1861, Confederate troops took possession of the *castillo*, a federal fort. In March 1862, a Union blockade squadron demanded the surrender of St. Augustine. The small Confederate garrison withdrew, and the city was occupied by Union forces for the duration of the war.

After the war, Northern visitors began going to St. Augustine because of its mild winter climate. Henry Flagler, a cofounder of Standard Oil Company, built three luxurious hotels in the Spanish Renaissance style. But although the tourists Flagler attracted brought vitality and income to St. Augustine, older buildings were sacrificed to new construction. Fires in 1887 and 1914 also destroyed many historic buildings.

Castillo de San Marcos was renamed Fort Marion by the United States. It was decommissioned as an active military installation in 1900. In 1924, the fort was declared a National Monument and it was transferred to the National Park Service in 1933.

In 1959, the St. Augustine Historical Restoration and Preservation Commission was established by the Florida legislature. The group, renamed the Historic St. Augustine Preservation Board, has concentrated on preserving and restoring the city's historic section.

TOUR

Begin your tour of the Spanish Quarter at the **Triay House** which serves as the orientation center. A reconstruction, the two-room Spanish Colonial home contains historical exhibits on the discovery of the Spanish colonies. Another exhibit focuses on Spanish Catholicism and includes a display of religious medals and statues or **santos.**

The **Lorenzo Gomez House** is a reconstructed timber-frame house on its original foundation as determined archaeologically. It is typical of those built in the first Spanish period (1565 to 1763). A modest one-room dwelling, it represents a house occupied in the 1760s by a Spanish infantryman on a small salary. Gomez also operated a trading center in his home in an attempt to supplement his income. He sold or bartered goods like pottery, ropes, and kegs of rum obtained from supply ships.

The **Martin Martinez Gallegos House** is a reconstruction of a two-room tabby house with a walled garden. (Tabby is a type of concrete made from oyster shells and lime.) Among the simple furnishings in the white plastered rooms is a small altar with a candle and a *santos*.

Eighteenth-century blacksmithing skills are practiced in the **Blacksmith Shop,** also a tabby structure. Spinning and weaving are demonstrated in the **Bernardo Gonzales House,** constructed of coquina. Costumed docents weave on a 1798 double harness loom. Gonzales served in the Spanish cavalry.

A house that was filled with children during the eighteenth century belonged to **Geronimo de Hita Y Salazar,** a soldier with a large family. Now his house is visited by school children who are given a chance to try chores the Salazar children performed hundreds of years ago.

Two rooms of the **Antonio de Mesa and Juan Sanchez House** were constructed at the end of the first Spanish period (1565–1763). During the second Spanish period (1783–1821), Juan Sanchez expanded the house and added a second story. The house is furnished as it would have looked during the American Territorial Period (1821–1845).

A duplex built during the British Period (1763–1783) was lived in by Jose Peso de Burgo and his family from Corsica and the Francisco Pellicer family from Minorca. A reconstruction, the building now houses the Museum Store.

Outside the Spanish Quarter but also a project of the Historic St. Augustine Preservation Board is the **Government House Museum.** Located across from the Plaza, a building on this spot served as the Spanish Governor's office as early as 1598. The present structure was reconstructed in 1936 based on a 1764 painting of Government House. Portions of walls built in 1713 have been retained. The museum explores St. Augustine's history from early native settlements through the European period to the Flagler era. Exhibits focus on St. Augustine's archaeological findings, early building techniques, religious influences, and the bounty from shipwrecks off the Florida coast. 48 King Street, (904) 825-5033. Daily, 10:00 A.M. to 4:00 P.M. Admission.

The **Spanish Military Hospital,** 8 Avilés Street, is a reconstruction of the original hospital and pharmacy, Nuestra Señora de Guadalupe, built during the second Spanish period (1783 to 1821). The building is authentically furnished and equipped with an apothecary shop, a morgue, a doctor's office, an isolation ward, an officers' ward, and an enlisted men's ward. On the second floor, there is a museum of Florida medical history.

Castillo de San Marcos National Monument was begun in 1672 and finished in 1695, replacing a succession of earlier wooden forts. The star-shaped coquina fort is the oldest masonry fortification in the continental United States. Castillo de San Marcos, later known as Fort Marion, was built by American Indians, slaves, and Spanish soldiers. Based on a medieval plan, the fort has thirty-foot-high walls, a council chamber, officers' quarters, storerooms, dungeons, and watchtowers and is surrounded by a moat. It was never captured by an enemy.

The Officers' Quarters contains exhibits on Spanish sea routes, and the building of the Castillo.

Exhibits focus on the military history of the Spanish era, construction of the Castillo, and American Indians held at the Castillo during the 1870s and 1880s. Live cannon firing demonstrations, preceded by a parade of soldiers in eighteenth-century Spanish uniforms, attract the attention of many tourists.

Side Trips

The **Gonzalez-Alvarez House** at 14 St. Francis Street is often referred to as the **Oldest House.** Although its exact date is not known, it is believed to have been built between 1703 and 1727, making it the oldest Spanish residence in the country. It was originally a one-story building with coquina walls and tabby floors. It became the home of Major Joseph Peavett during the British colonial period (1763 to 1783), and Peavett added a wood frame second story, fireplace, and glass windowpanes. Open daily. Admission charged.

Another oldest, the **Old Wooden Schoolhouse,** 14 St. George Street, is believed to be the oldest school building in the United States. Records indicate it was built at the end of the first Spanish period, which lasted until 1763. Open daily. Admission charged.

The Greek Orthodox Church in America has restored **Casa de Avero,** a house dating from the first Spanish period, at 41 St. George Street. Now known as **St. Photios Shrine,** it commemorates the first colony of Greeks to arrive in the New World in 1768; Greek Orthodox religious services are conducted here. Open daily,

The **Alcazar Hotel** is one of three Spanish Renaissance–style hotels built by oil magnate Henry Flagler in 1888. It is now occupied by the **Lightner Museum,** which contains the personal collection of O. C. Lightner, founder and publisher of *Hobbies Magazine*. 75 King St. Open daily. Admission charged. The **Ponce de León Hotel** has become **Flagler College,** and **Zorayda Castle,** built to resemble the Alhambra, now houses oriental art treasures. 83 King St. Open daily. Admission charged.

Cross and Sword, an outdoor musical drama about the founding of St. Augustine, is presented in the **St. Augustine Amphitheater.** The play, which was written by Paul Green, is presented nightly except Sunday at 8:30 P.M. from mid-June to late August. On State Road 3-A1A, (904) 471-1965. Admission charged.

WESTVILLE

Recreation of a mid-nineteenth-century Georgian antebellum farming community

Address: S. Mulberry Street, Lumpkin, GA 31815

Telephone: (912) 838-6310

Location: In southwestern Georgia, 35 miles south of Columbus, at the intersection of US 27 and GA 27

Open: Tuesday to Saturday, 10 A.M. to 5:00 P.M.; Sundays, 1:00 P.M. to 5:00 P.M.; closed Mondays, Thanksgiving, Christmas, and New Year's Day, and early January

Admission: Adults, $6.00; senior citizens, $5.00; students, $3.00; children under five, free

Restaurants: Snacks available in village kitchens; restaurants in town of Lumpkin

Shops: Handicrafts and reproduction items in Randle-Morton Store

Facilities: Picnic area; mule-drawn wagon rides; special events include an old-fashioned Independence Day celebration; the Fair of 1850 and Yuletide Season in mid to late December; site is partially handicapped accessible

WHERE TO STAY

Inns/Bed & Breakfasts: The Plains B&B, P.O. Box 217, Plains 31780, (912) 824-7252; Jenny May and Sapp's B&B, 229 Broad St., Buena Vista 31803, (912) 649-7307; The Cottage Inn, P.O. Box 488, Hwy. 49N, Americus 31709, (912) 924-6680; Merriwood Country Inn, Rt. 6, Box 60, Americus 31709, (912) 924-4992

Motels/Hotels: Windsor Hotel, 104 Windsor Ave., Americus 31709, (912) 924-1555; Columbus Hilton, 800 Front Ave., Columbus 31901, (706) 324-1800; Courtyard by Marriott, 3501 Courtyard Way, Columbus 31904, (706) 323-2323; Holiday Inn South, 3170 Victory Dr., Columbus 31903, (912) 689-6181; Days Inn, 3452 Macon Rd. (I-85 & Macon Rd. Exit 4), Columbus 31907, (706) 561-4400

Camping: Stewart County Campground, Trotmon Road, Lumpkin 31815, (912) 838-6769; Florence Marina State Park, GA 39C at Lake Walter F. George, Omaha 31821, (912) 838-4244

Westville, Lumpkin, Georgia
The 1843 McDonald House was the home of Scotsman Edward McDonald. In 1859, a second floor was added to what had been a modest two-room house, and its was remodeled into a Greek Revival mansion. At Westville, Lumpkin, GA.
Photo by Patricia A. Gutek

OVERVIEW

Westville, a recreated museum village, depicts daily life in preindustrial Georgia during the 1850s. More than thirty buildings have been relocated, then restored, to form a typical mid-nineteenth-century west Georgia town. Westville never existed in Georgia's historical past, but is a recreated town which functions as an outdoor museum. Preservation of the crafts of 1850 is one of the primary goals of this museum village. Visitors witness the lifestyle of a Southern town 150 years ago as docents practice appropriate crafts and perform appropriate chores. Westville has one of the largest displays of mid-nineteenth-century Georgia-made decorative art. Vegetable and flower gardens throughout the village bloom with plants popular in the nineteenth century.

HISTORY

West Georgia was originally inhabited by Native American cultures including the Mississippian from 800 to 1400 A.D. They left two large Indian Mound Systems: Rood and Singer-Moye. Next came the Muskogean or Creek culture from 1400 to 1836. Pioneers were anxious to settle the land, and the Treaties of Indian Springs opened West Georgia for nonnative settlement in 1827. The last native culture, the Lower Creeks, sold their land to the state and moved west. West Georgia land was distributed by a lottery open to legal residents of the United States held in May 1827. Each lot was 202½ acres. Lumpkin is in Stewart County, one of the west Georgia counties settled at this time. By 1850, Stewart County's population was more than 16,000 persons, almost half of whom were African American slaves.

Westville is named for Colonel John Word West, a historian who served as acting president of North Georgia College. The village developed from the 1966 purchase of his private collection of historic buildings and artifacts. After a fifty-acre site in Lumpkin was donated for the museum, the process of moving buildings to Westville began in 1968. The museum village opened to the public on April 2, 1970. It is a project of Westville Historic Handicrafts, Inc., a not-for-profit, educational corporation.

TOUR

Westville is a fifteen-block town encompassing fifty-eight acres with more than thirty restored buildings. One of the first buildings you'll see after passing through the village gates is **Stewart County Academy** (1832) with its collection of period textbooks. Academies were generally private educational institutions for students in their teens. Unlike the New England states, Southern states did not establish common or public schools until after the Civil War.

The **Grimes-Feagin House** (1842), from Stewart County, is a one-story, Greek Revival cottage. It was built by John Grimes for his son-in-law, Henry Feagin. Doll making and quilting are demonstrated by village craftspeople here.

The **McDonald House** (1843 and 1859) was the home of Scotsman Edward McDonald, a man of wealth and social status. Originally, it was a modest two-room house to which two front parlors and a second floor were added. Now, the impressive Greek Revival mansion has a two-story portico with six columns. It is furnished with mid-nineteenth-century Empire-style pieces, including an ornate square piano, elaborate bedroom wardrobes, a hand-carved rosewood bed, and an oversized dining room table.

The Empire style (which takes its name from the Second French Empire) is more elaborate than the earlier Federal style and was popular with wealthy Americans.

Chattahoochee County Courthouse, a two-story frame building, was the seat of county government. Built in 1854, it was used until 1975, and much of its furnishings and woodwork are original. President Jimmy Carter's great-grandfather and grandfather served as county officials in this building. Southern political life centered on the county, in contrast with the town government prevalent in New England. Today, the courthouse is the home of Westville's educational programs.

The **Bryan House** (1831) was built in Stewart County by Loverd Bryan, a wealthy cotton gin operator. The two-story frame house is in the plantation plain style with Federal influences. "Plantation plain" is a Southern term for "I-frame." This style was popular in the South from 1750 to 1950. Inside, a craftsperson spins cotton yarn and weaves fabric on a loom. Across from the Bryan House is an 1850 cotton press and a gin house. The **Bagley Gin House** was built in the 1840s. This cotton gin, which is mule-driven, has an adjacent cotton screw press for baling cotton after it has been ginned. The cotton gin, invented by Eli Whitney in 1793, was essential to the Southern economy. Before its invention, little cotton was produced in the United States because the process of separating the fiber from the seeds by hand was too time-consuming. The mechanical efficiency of the gin helped to make cotton "king" in the American South. Westville's gin is one of the few remaining in the United States.

The **Doctor's Office** (1845) was built by Dr. William Lewis Paullin of Fort Gaines. It displays medical and dental instruments. Physicians in small towns and rural areas were general practitioners and often among the few college graduates in a community.

Many early settlers in Stewart County were farmers and the **Patterson-Marrett Farmhouse and Farm** represent their lifestyle. The rambling two-story log house has a dog-trot which is an open breezeway between two separate wings under one roof. It was built in South Carolina in 1850. The farmhouse kitchen was built separately from the main house to minimize the threat of fire. Displayed in the large open fireplace are iron frying pans, ovens, pots, and other utensils; there is also a brick oven in the chimney that was used for baking. Near the farmhouse are the mule barn, whiskey still, sugarcane mill, and syrup kettle. The fields are planted with sugarcane, and there are vegetable, herb, and flower gardens as well as fruit trees growing near the house.

The **Yellow Creek Camp Meeting Tabernacle,** built in 1840 in Hall

County, is a large, open structure with a roof supported by twelve-inch-square, hand-hewn beams. It contains a pulpit and benches. The camp meeting, peculiar to the South and the frontier, was a social event as well as a religious revival that attracted widely scattered families. Lasting anywhere from three to ten days, camp meetings were characterized by highly emotional reactions to the preaching of the minister.

The **Singer House,** built in Lumpkin in 1838, was once the home and shoemaking shop of Johann Singer. Perhaps because his family of eleven children outgrew their quarters, the cobbler built a separate shop next to his home in 1839. The two-story building has the shop on the first floor and sleeping accommodations for Singer's apprentices upstairs. Singer family furnishings include a cradle and a small spinning wheel brought from Germany.

The **Moye Whitehouse** (1840) is an excellently proportioned cottage of Greek Revival influence. It was moved from its original location on a 3,000-acre plantation near Cuthbert. The **West House** (1850) was the residence of Colonel John Word West's grandparents.

One of the major purposes of Westville is to keep alive and to demonstrate the crafts of early preindustrial America. Among the shops where crafts are demonstrated are the blacksmith shop, the cabinetmaker's shop (1836), and the shoemaker's shop (1838). The pottery shop, pug mill, and kiln are an example of a jug factory, where churns, jars, pitchers, and other items were made. Craft items are sold at the Randle-Morton Store.

Special events at Westville include a spring festival, a May Day celebration, an old-fashioned Independence Day celebration; the Fair of 1850, held in the fall and patterned after cultural fairs of the pre–Civil War era; and Yuletide Season in December, featuring traditional German, English, and Scotch-Irish holiday festivities.

SIDE TRIPS

In the town of Lumpkin, visit the **Bedingfield Inn** located on the town square. Built in 1836, it is a restored stagecoach inn. Open 1:00 P.M. to 5:00 P.M., Wednesday to Sunday. Admission charged.

Providence Canyon State Conservation Park is a natural area of 1,108 acres of chasms, crevices, and canyons. Referred to locally as the "little Grand Canyon," the park is especially known for its spring wildflowers. There are hiking trails, an interpretive center, and picnic areas. Open daily, 7:00 A.M. to 9:00 P.M., April 15 to September 15, 7:00 A.M. to 6:00 P.M., rest of year. Box 158, Route 1, Lumpkin, GA 31815, (912) 838-6202; 7 miles west of Lumpkin on Hwy. 39C

Andersonville National Historic Site is a 475-acre park consisting of the national cemetery and prison site. Camp Sumter, its official name, was the largest Confederate military prison established during the Civil War. As many as 32,000 Union soldiers lived on a 26½-acre site at one time. During its fourteen months of operation, more than 45,000 Union soldiers were confined at Andersonville; 13,000 of them died there. Andersonville is open 8:00 A.M. to 5:00 P.M. daily. Free. Located 10 miles northeast of Americus on GA 49, its address is: Rt. 1, Box 85, Andersonville, GA 31711. (912) 924-0343.

SHAKER VILLAGE OF PLEASANT HILL

Restoration of a nineteenth-century Shaker community; NR, NHL

Address: 3500 Lexington Road, Harrodsburg, KY 40330

Telephone: (606) 734-5411

Location: In central Kentucky, 25 miles southwest of Lexington and 7 miles northeast of Harrodsburg; on U.S. 68

Open: 9:30 A.M. to 5:00 P.M. daily from mid-March through November; some exhibition buildings closed December through mid-March

Admission: Village: adults, $8.50; students 12 to 17, $4.00; children 6 to 11, $2.00; family (2 adults & unlimited children), $20.00; Riverboat: adults, $5.50, students 12 to 17, $3.50; children 6 to 11, $2.00; Combination Village/Boat: adults, $11.50; students 12 to 17, $6.00; children 6 to 11, $3.00; family, $27.50

Restaurants: Trustees' Office Restaurant (reservations essential); Summer Kitchen in West Family Dwelling

Shops: Post Office craft shop; Carpenters' Shop craft shop

Facilities: Paddlewheel riverboat rides; craft demonstrations; conference facilities; music and dance programs; winter weekends; special events; overnight accommodations in historic buildings

WHERE TO STAY

Inns: Shaker Inn at Pleasant Hill (80 rooms in 15 original Shaker buildings), 3500 Lexington Road, Harrodsburg 40330, (606) 734-5411 (reservations essential)

Motels/Hotels: Best Western, 1680 Danville Road, Harrodsburg 40330, (606) 734-9431

Camping: Chimney Rock Campground, Harrodsburg 40330, (606) 748-5252; My Old Kentucky Home State Park, Bardstown 40004 (502) 348-3502; Pioneer Playhouse Campground, Danville 40422 (606) 236-2747

OVERVIEW

One of two Shaker communities in the South, both of them in Kentucky, Shaker Village of Pleasant Hill recreates aspects of the lifestyle of

Shaker Village of Pleasant Hill, Harrodsburg, Kentucky
Two doorways, one for men and one for women, contribute to the symmetry which
characterizes Shaker architecture. The 1821 West Family Dwelling has been
adapted for use as overnight lodging for visitors to Shaker Village of Pleasant Hill,
Harrodsburg, KY.

Photo by Patricia A. Gutek

the American communal religious group who lived there for more than a
century. Celebrated today for their simple, functionally designed, yet exquisite furniture and their serenely restored historic sites, the Shakers
numbered 17,000 Americans who practiced a religion based on Christian
beliefs, celibacy, exuberant worship services, sexual equality of religious
leadership, pacifism, and a communal economy in the years between the
American Revolution and the Civil War.

Though there are no longer Shaker brothers and sisters at Pleasant
Hill, the Shaker spirit permeates the site today. Picturesquely situated in
Kentucky bluegrass country, the museum village is surrounded by 2,700
acres of rolling fields edged in stacked flagstone fences. An evening mist
often envelopes the site contributing to its aura of separation from the

modern world. First-time visitors to Pleasant Hill are struck by a sense of harmony in everything they see, from the orderliness of the setting to the pleasing proportions of buildings, to the elegant simplicity of the furniture, to the plain utilitarianism of the tools. White picket fences, stone walkways, lanterns hung on posts, and guides in Shaker costumes add to the sense of rural serenity.

Shaker Village at Pleasant Hill is one of our favorite restorations. The buildings are original and architecturally impressive. The group of people who lived here is fascinating. The Shaker furniture is authentic, and the collection large and varied. The site is of medium size and do-able without courting exhaustion, the guides knowledgeable, and the craft stores well stocked with good reproductions. Lodging and dining rooms retain an attractive and authentic atmosphere. It is one of those rare self-contained villages where you can eat and sleep as well as see the sights. Once you spot the hand-stacked fieldstone fences lining the highway and pull into the parking lot, you will not need your car again until you leave.

We encourage you to immerse yourself in the atmospheric surroundings, soak up history, enjoy the lovely bluegrass countryside, walk the lantern-lit paths at night, and feast in the charming dining rooms. We have recommended this interesting and relaxing destination to everyone from historians to honeymooners—it's ironic these celibate people created such a romantic environment. They have all enjoyed their sojourn at Pleasant Hill and remarked on its restorative value.

There are 80 rooms for guests in fifteen original Shaker buildings. Even though these buildings are restored to nineteenth-century standards, the guest rooms are heated, air-conditioned, and electrified and have their own bathrooms. They are charmingly furnished with reproduction Shaker rockers, beds, desks, and handwoven rugs. The Shaker pegs that are seen in all the exhibit buildings line the walls for hanging clothes.

The dining rooms are in the Trustees' House. Meals are moderately priced, and the Shaker and Kentucky recipes showcase American cuisine at its finest: fresh foods properly prepared and beautifully served. No alcohol is sold.

HISTORY

On January 1, 1805, three Shaker missionaries (see the Appendix for a brief history of the Shakers) from New Lebanon, New York, traveled 1,200 miles to central Kentucky. They had heard about the Great Kentucky Revival, in which a wave of camp meetings had reawakened religious sentiments among thousands of people. After making some converts, the Shaker group gathered on Shawnee Run, a few miles from Harrodsburg.

Two years later, in 1807, a permanent settlement was established on the elevation that came to be called Pleasant Hill. In January 1809, two elders and two eldresses were sent from Union Village in Ohio to form the first ministry. In 1809, the first building in the village, the first Centre Family Dwelling, now known as the Farm Deacon's Shop, was built. Of the 270 buildings erected over the ensuing century, 30 remain today.

The Shakers were active craftspeople. They produced brooms, cooper's wares, weaving implements, shoes, woolen goods, pressed cheese, medicinal products, seeds, and herbs. By 1816, they had begun to make trading trips to New Orleans to sell their surplus goods.

Pleasant Hill's membership had increased to nearly 500 by 1820. During the course of the century, 1,500 Shakers lived in this prosperous community. Their landholdings reached approximately 4,000 acres, and they grew wheat, rye, oats, flax, Indian corn, broomcorn, and potatoes. There were also extensive fruit orchards.

The society was divided into five communal families, each numbering from 50 to 100 members and governed by two elders and two eldresses. Each family was a semiautonomous unit, with its own dwelling, shops, barns, fields, and orchards.

During the late 1850s, Pleasant Hill, like the other Shaker communities, began to experience the effects of the Industrial Revolution. Mass-produced items turned out on factory assembly lines were cheaper than the Shaker-made handicrafts. As their markets declined, so did Pleasant Hill's prosperity.

Along with a declining economy, the Kentucky Shakers faced the sectional issues generated by the Civil War. Although a border state with many Southern sympathizers, Kentucky remained loyal to the Union. The Shakers were pacifists and refused to fight. Elder Frederick Evans of Mount Lebanon persuaded President Abraham Lincoln to exempt Shakers on religious grounds. The Pleasant Hill Shakers, like their brothers and sisters elsewhere, generously fed, housed, and nursed both the Confederate and the Union troops that marched through their village. This impartiality angered their neighbors, who were also intolerant of the Shaker practice of buying and freeing slaves and accepting them into full membership in the society. The Shakers' stores of food, cattle, horses, wagons, and flatboats were often confiscated by the military.

In 1898, the Trustees' Office and hundreds of acres were sold. By 1900, three of the families had disbanded, and their vacant buildings were rented out. On September 12, 1910, the last of the property was sold and the society, four brothers and eight sisters, was dissolved. Between 1910 and 1960, the property was redivided and resold. The buildings, used for various purposes (including a bus station), were neglected, and two were destroyed by fire.

In 1961, a group of people led by Earl D. Wallace of Lexington decided to restore Pleasant Hill. They formed a nonprofit educational corporation known as Shakertown at Pleasant Hill, Inc. James L. Cogar, a former curator of Colonial Williamsburg, became Pleasant Hill's first president, and the village opened to the public in the spring of 1968.

Cogar is responsible for restoring the thirty original buildings according to the principle of adaptive use. The three functional uses are exhibitions that tell the story of the life and customs of the Shaker society; education by means of seminars, symposia, and conferences; and hospitality, dining, and overnight accommodations. Pleasant Hill is the only museum village in which all overnight accommodations for guests are in restored buildings.

TOUR

Begin your self-guided tour at the **Centre Family Dwelling.** The Centre, or First, Family was the highest rank according to the spirituality of the members and was given the place of honor nearest the meetinghouse. The T-shaped second Centre Family Dwelling was started in 1824 and completed in 1834. Master architect and carpenter Micajah Burnett laid out the plan of the village and designed the buildings, including this one.

The symmetry of the double doorways and two inside stairways to separate the men's quarters from the women's, along with the utter simplicity of the wide halls, white walls, high ceilings, arched doorways, wood trim, and plain wooden floors, contributes to the beauty of this outstanding building.

Burnett's design was based on early New England Shaker building style with elements of Federal classicism. The roof has square gabled ends and three massive chimneys. There are forty rooms in this four-story Kentucky limestone building, the largest erected at Pleasant Hill; it housed 100 Shakers. It is now the major exhibition building.

All rooms contain authentic Shaker furniture from the early nineteenth century, much of it made at Pleasant Hill. There is a kitchen complete with cooking utensils, a dining room, a meeting room, an infirmary, and simply furnished sleeping rooms.

The **Meetinghouse** was the spiritual center of the community. (Shaker religious services are described in the Appendix.) The one at Pleasant Hill was built in 1820 and has the double doorways typical of Shaker architecture. The white frame building rests on a heavy limestone foundation. Roof and ceilings are supported by a series of interlocking cantilever-type trusses and overhead studdings and rafters; this construction made it possible to have a meeting room large enough to accommodate all the worshipers.

The **Farm Deacon's Shop,** built in 1809, was the first permanent structure in the village. Originally the dwelling house for the Centre Family, it was used as a tavern after 1817 and, finally, as an office for the farm deacons. The two-foot-thick walls of this two-and-a-half-story structure are built of white limestone quarried from cliffs along the nearby Kentucky River. The ash floors are original. Artifacts relating to the Shakers' herb industry are displayed on the first floor; the second floor is used for guest lodgings.

In 1833, Micajah Burnett devised a water system that provided every house and barn in the village with running water. The yellow frame **water house** contains the machinery and tanks for the first public waterworks in Kentucky.

Next to the water house is the small **Brethren's Bath House,** built in 1860. Each family was a self-sufficient unit with its own large dwelling for eating and sleeping; a craft shop for women; separate bathhouses for men, women, boys, and girls; a washhouse; and various other outbuildings.

On the first floor of the **East Family Brethren's Shop** (1845), a broom maker works in his fully equipped shop. Across the hall, a carpenter uses traditional tools. The **East Family Sisters' Shop** (1855) houses spinning and weaving demonstrations on the first floor. The second floor of each shop now accommodates overnight guests.

The **Trustees' Office,** built in 1839 by Micajah Burnett, is one of the finest examples of Shaker architecture extant. It was used by the Shakers to conduct business with the outside world and to house and feed guests. Trustees were the people appointed to transact that business. The building is of flemish-bond brick and has a single front door. As you enter it, you'll be struck by the impressive twin spiral staircases.

Today, the first floor is used as a restaurant and a registration office for overnight guests. Upstairs, there are lodging rooms. The trundle beds for children are a delight.

Coopering demonstrations are conducted in the **Cooper's Shop** which was remodeled in 1847. The **East Family Wash House** has its original cauldrons, and parts of their washing apparatus. The 1848 **Post Office** and the 1815 **Carpenters' Shop** are craft shops which sell many Shaker reproductions and Kentucky crafts. A Research Library is in the 1859 **Preserve Shop** where Shaker sisters prepared jars of sweetmeats. The 1875 **Scale House** and the 1840 **Drying House** are undergoing restoration.

Pleasant Hill has two gardens: the **Vegetable Garden** by the Trustees' Office and the **Medic Garden** by the Centre Family Dwelling. You will also want to stroll over to the peaceful Shaker graveyard.

Special events at Shaker Village include demonstrations of beehive-oven baking, silk culturing, candle dipping, vegetal dyeing, basketry, cider making, and hearth cooking. There are also programs on Shaker songs.

You can take a one-hour ride on a paddlewheel riverboat, the *Dixie Belle*, from May through October. The rides on the Kentucky River leave from **Shaker Landing,** east of the village entrance.

THE LSU RURAL LIFE MUSEUM

Recreation of a nineteenth-century Louisiana working plantation

Address: Museum entrance: Essen Lane at I-10, Burden Research Planta-
tion, Baton Rouge, LA 70808;
mailing address: 6200 Burden Lane, Baton Rouge, LA 70808
Telephone: (504) 765-2437; FAX: (504) 765-2639
Location: Baton Rouge is in southeast Louisiana, eighty miles northwest
of New Orleans; entrance is at the intersection of I-10 and Essen
Lane
Open: Monday to Friday, 8:30 A.M. to 4:00 P.M.; open weekends on sea-
sonal basis; closed on some university holidays
Admission: Adults, $3.00; children 5 to 11, $2.00
Facilities: Group tours

WHERE TO STAY

Inns/Bed & Breakfasts: Nottoway Plantation, P.O. Box 160, White Castle 70808, (504) 545-2730, FAX: (504) 545-8632; Pointe Coupee,
401 Richey St., New Roads 70760, (504) 638-8254, (800) 832-7412
Motels/Hotels: Hampton Inn, 4646 Constitution Ave., Baton Rouge
70808, (504) 926-9990, FAX: (504) 923-3007; Crown Sterling
Suites, 4914 Constitution Ave., Baton Rouge 70808, (504) 924-
6566, FAX: (504) 387-1111, ext. 7647; Residence Inn by Marriott,
5522 Corporate Blvd., Baton Rouge 70808, (504) 927-5630, FAX:
(504) 926-2317; Sheraton Baton Rouge, 4728 Constitution St.,
Baton Rouge 70898, (504) 925-2244, FAX: (504) 927-6925; Wilson
Inn, 3045 Valley Creek, Baton Rouge 70808, (504) 923-3377
Camping: Baton Rouge KOA Campground, 7628 Vincent Rd., Denham
Springs 70726, (504) 664-7281; Knight's RV Park, 14740 Florida
Blvd., Baton Rouge 70819, (504) 275-0679

OVERVIEW

Louisiana State University's Rural Life Museum focuses on the culture, lifestyle, work skills, and architecture of nineteenth-century Louisiana plantation workers. Southern plantations have been glamorized and

romanticized in the movies, and much attention has been paid to the lifestyle of their owners who occupied the big house. However, the majority of plantation workers, both black and white, were hard-working farm laborers whose lifestyle was anything but glamorous.

Nineteenth-century rural homes and workshops have been relocated to Louisiana State University's Burden Research Plantation. These historic buildings typify those found on a southern Louisiana working plantation of that era. Artifacts in the buildings date from the preindustrial age. Louisiana State University has done a fine job of selection, presentation, and historical interpretation at this museum complex.

HISTORY

During the eighteenth and nineteenth centuries, indigo, tobacco, sugarcane, and cotton were cultivated on plantations in Louisiana's Mississippi Valley. Large numbers of people worked the fields, harvested the crops, and plied the crafts necessary to the plantation's economic success.

A folk museum to preserve aspects of the material culture from Louisiana's preindustrial era was conceived about 1970 by Steele Burden, Ione Burden, and Cecil G. Taylor, all of whom were connected to Louisiana State University. The museum would focus on Louisiana's rural heritage in that era when Louisiana settlers depended on land and water for their livelihood.

The Rural Life Museum is located on the Burden Research Plantation, a 430-acre agricultural research experiment station owned by Louisiana State University. Formerly the Windrush Plantation, the land was donated to Louisiana State University by the Burden Foundation.

TOUR

The Rural Life Museum is divided into three areas. The **Barn** holds collections of Louisiana artifacts related to cotton, bathroom fixtures, washing implements, textiles, vehicles, blacksmithing tools, woodworking tools, entertainment, lumbering, wildlife, hunting and trapping, the Civil War, American Indian artifacts, steam-operated machines, and Louisiana history. Exhibits cover Louisiana residents from the earliest American Indian civilizations to preindustrial times.

The **Working Plantation** consists of homes and shops related to farming and the laborers who made up the farming community. One essential building was the **Commissary** or General Store which was built between 1830 and 1835 as a storeroom on the Welham Plantation in St. James Parish. Converted into a general store in 1880, its position on the

The LSU Rural Life Museum, Baton Rouge, Louisiana
A small frame slave cabin from the first half of the nineteenth century displays a
rare example of folk art. Farm tools hang on the front of the cabin. At the LSU
Rural Life Museum, Baton Route, LA.

Photo by Patricia A. Gutek

banks of the Mississippi facilitated supplies being loaded directly from river steamboats.

Also from the Welham Plantation is the **Overseer's House** which dates to about 1835. An early 1800s construction method, *briquette entre poteaux,* or brick between posts, can be seen on the exposed front wall of the house.

A second *briquette entre poteaux* structure is the **Kitchen,** built around 1855 on Bagatelle Plantation in Union. Kitchens were often built separately because of the heat and the danger of fire. The Kitchen has a brick floor and a large fireplace in which cooking was done.

The **Sick House,** from Welham Plantation, was a slave cabin built in the 1830s. Plantation communities usually did not have a doctor, so the sick were often nursed by the wife of the overseer or plantation owner. One room of the house was used as a treatment room while the other served as the infirmary. The seriously ill were kept in the infirmary which has three rope beds with poles for mosquito netting.

The 1835 **Schoolhouse** served only the children of the white overseers and neighboring farmers. Plantation owners' children were privately tutored and African American slave children were not formally educated.

The **Blacksmith's Shop** was reconstructed using the 1835 frame of a blacksmith's shop from Welham Plantation. Inside are blacksmith tools and a fully operational forge.

Several simple frame **Slave Cabins** furnished with almost nothing but a bed indicate the rudimentary lifestyle of the plantation's African American slave laborers. Entire families lived in these little houses. After the Civil War, they were occupied by tenant farmers and sharecroppers.

The 1880 **Cane Grinder** and the reproduction **Sugarhouse** were needed for sugar manufacturing. Implements indicate that the open kettle method of making sugar which came from the West Indies was used. Corn was ground on a reproduction animal-powered **Grist Mill.**

The **Folk Architecture** exhibit features structures built by and for the people who occupied them using tradition and custom as their guidelines. Most of Louisiana's structures before the twentieth century would fall into that category.

A **Country Church** built in 1870 in Convent, Louisiana, served the College Grove Baptist congregation. An extremely simple version of the Gothic Revival style, its pews and altar are original. Windows are plain glass which have been painted red and white to resemble stained glass. Now used as a religious museum, it holds religious articles from a number of faiths. Across the road from the church is a simulated **Cemetery** with grave markers from various parts of Louisiana.

The **Pioneer's Cabin** was built in 1810 in Sunny Hill, Washington Parish, of heart pine logs that were planed smooth and pegged together. Its one room has a fireplace and is furnished with a bed, pie safe, and desk. There is a loft upstairs and a corncrib outside.

A reproduction, **Acadian House** is based on houses using *bousillage* construction techniques built in southern Louisiana by Acadian settlers. The outside stairway to the second floor sleeping area is typical of Acadian style homes. The gabled roof covers the house as well as the detached kitchen which is separated by an open porch. Furnishings include a prayer stand which attests to the strong religious fervor of the Acadians.

Two other forms of folk architecture are the **Dogtrot House** and the **Shotgun House.** The Dogtrot House, built in 1870 in the Kisatchie Forest west of Alexandria, consists of two self-contained rooms or cabins under one roof with an open space between them. Wooden frame chimneys packed with red clay and pine straw stand at each end of the house.

The Shotgun House takes its name from the arrangement of its rooms which are one behind another. From the Bayou Goula area, this house was typical of those built for share croppers after Reconstruction.

Adjacent to the museum are the **Windrush Gardens,** designed by Steele Burden, which may be toured. There is an All-American Rose Testing Garden, an annuals garden, an herb garden, nature trails, and wooded areas.

SIDE TRIPS

Plantations in the Baton Rouge area which may be toured include **Magnolia Mound Plantation,** 2161 Nicholson Dr., Baton Rouge 70802, (504) 343-4955; **Nottoway Plantation,** LA 1, White Castle 70788, (504) 545-2730; **Houmas House,** River Road, Burnside 70725, (504) 473-7841 or (504) 522-2262; and **Tezcuco,** River Rd., Darrow 70725, (504) 562-3929. Admission charged.

An historic ship, a steamboat, and the Old State Capitol are among the attractions at **Riverfront Park** in Baton Rouge's downtown area on the banks of the Mississippi River. The U.S.S. *Kidd,* a World War II destroyer, may be toured Tuesday to Sunday. Admission charged. (504) 342-1942. Take a cruise on the Mississippi aboard the *Samuel Clemens* steamboat. Daily, April to August; Wednesday to Sunday, rest of year. Admission charged. (504) 381-9606. The 1849 Old State Capitol whose architectural excesses nearly sent Mark Twain into apoplexy will be open for touring after a recent restoration and installation of exhibits has been completed.

VERMILIONVILLE

Recreation of Cajun and Creole culture in southern
Louisiana bayou village, 1765–1890

Address: 1600 Surrey Street, Lafayette, LA 70501
Telephone: (318) 233-4077, (800) 99-BAYOU
Location: Lafayette is in south central Louisiana; Vermilionville is four
miles south of the I-10 and I-49 intersection
Open: Daily, 9:00 A.M. to 5:00 P.M.; closed Christmas and New Year's Day
Admission: Adults, $8.00; seniors, $6.50; children 6 to 18, $5.00
Restaurants: La Cuisine de Maman; Le Quartier Creole (Food Quarters);
Bakery
Shops: La Boutique in the Visitor Center
Facilities: Visitor Center; cooking school; handicapped accessible; craft
demonstrations; band and dance performances; special events; the-
ater productions

WHERE TO STAY

Motels/Hotels: Quality Inn, 1605 N. University, Lafayette 70501, (318)
232-6131, FAX: (318) 232-6285; Hotel Acadiana, 1801 W. Pinhook
Rd., Lafayette 70508, (318) 233-8120, (800) 826-8386; Ramada
Inn-Airport, 2501 SE Evangeline Thrwy, Lafayette 70508, (318)
234-8521, FAX: (318) 232-5764; Hilton & Towers, 1521 W. Pinhook Rd., Lafayette 70505, (318) 235-6111, FAX: (318) 261-0311
Camping: Lake Fausse Pointe State Park, St. Martinville 70582, (318)
229-4764; Acadiana Parks Campground, Lafayette, (318) 234-3838;
KOA Lafayette, Rt. 2, Box 261, Scott 70583, (318) 235-2739; Harry
Smith Lodge & RV Park, P.O. Box 448, Broussard 70518, (318) 837-
6286

OVERVIEW

Southern Louisiana bayou culture is the focus of Vermilionville,
which is a living history museum of Cajun and Creole folklife on the banks
of Bayou Vermilion. In addition to a recreated village of historic structures
furnished with authentic artifacts, Vermilionville features Cajun and Creole music, crafts, and food.

Louisiana was a seventeenth-century French colony in North
America. The two French groups who settled on the rivers and bayous of
Southern Louisiana developed a distinctive culture based on their French

Vermilionville, Lafayette, Louisiana
The style of the recreated La Chapelle des Attakapas is modeled on a 1773
Catholic church at St. Martinville which served Louisiana's Acadians. Next to the
church is Le Presbytere, the priest's house, which is an 1840 structure called
Maison La Grange. Its outside staircase to the sleeping loft is characteristic of
Acadian architecture. At Vermilionville, Lafayette, LA.
Photo by Patricia A. Gutek

heritage and their adaptation to frontier life along the remote, subtropical
waterways. Even today, in this age of homogenized American culture, contemporary Cajun culture is unique. Yet the French ancestors of these Loui-
sianans have been in North America for more than 300 years, the
Acadians having lived in maritime Canada for 100 years before coming to
Louisiana, and the Creole group descendants of original French colonists
in Louisiana.

HISTORY
Southern Louisiana's Creole and Acadian/Cajun populations have
their roots in France though their ancestors have been in North America

for more than 300 years. Decades of civil and religious warfare, famine, and epidemics drove French peasants from France's Centre-Ouest provinces of Poitou, Aunis, Angoumois, and Saintonge to immigrate to Maritime Canada, now the provinces of Nova Scotia and New Brunswick. Between 1632 and 1654, French colonists sailed to a proprietary colony operated by the Company of New France which Samuel Champlain had founded for France in 1604. It was named La Cadie which was a Micmac word for land of plenty. Later the colony came to be called l'Acadie or Acadia. Thus, its settlers were Acadians.

In eastern Canada, the Acadians developed a distinctive society based on their geographic isolation and frontier mentality, common French origins and language, social solidarity, and strong extended kinship system. As a result of ongoing strife between France and England, Acadia became a British colony. When the Acadians were ordered to take an oath of allegiance to the British crown, the fiercely independent French-speaking Acadians refused. Consequently, in 1755, the Acadians were expelled by the British from Acadia, now renamed Nova Scotia, where they had lived for 100 years.

Called the Grand Derangement, the expelled Acadians were dispersed to the English middle colonies, France, and the French Antilles. Families were broken up. No compensation was made for the farms, houses, and other possessions left behind. Many deportees died enroute, and the destitute survivors found only hardship and misery. In an effort to reunite their families and reestablish their lifestyle, the Acadians looked to Louisiana, a sparsely settled French colony then under Spanish rule. Eventually, many found their way to southern Louisiana arriving between 1765 and 1785. The Spanish government welcomed the industrious, anti-British settlers and supplied them with modest amounts of land, tools, and food.

The French explorer, Robert Cavelier de La Salle, had claimed all the North American land drained by the Mississippi for France in 1682. A small number of French colonists migrated to Louisiana in the early eighteenth century. Their descendants, those born in Louisiana, were called Creoles, a term that meant homegrown, not imported, and adapted to the environment.

Class differences separated the two French groups in Louisiana. The Acadians were peasant farmers while the French Creoles had developed large farms and plantations on which they used captured Africans as slave workers. African slaves who were born in Louisiana were called Creole slaves.

Louisiana was sold to the United States in 1803. Several states were carved out of the Louisiana Purchase. When the state of Louisiana was defined, it lumped together the southern, French-occupied parishes with the northern, English-speaking parishes although the two parts of the state had little in common culturally.

In southern Louisiana, Acadians settled near the waterways, the rivers, and bayous, including the Mississippi River. Strip villages developed along the riverbanks. Other Cajun settlements were in Louisiana's swamps and marshes or on its prairies. Many Cajuns operated small farms, fished, and hunted. Travel was by waterway rather than road. The Acadians intermarried with their Louisiana neighbors who included Native American Houmas, Chitmachas and Attakapas, German Alsatians, Spanish, Anglo-Americans, Irish, and Scots. Louisiana Acadians came to be called Cajuns, a corruption of the term Acadian.

Because of the remoteness of the bayou area, residents had little contact with the larger American culture. The Acadians maintained a separate culture even during the Civil War. Their high desertion rate indicated their lack of commitment to the South's causes. They continued to speak French which was the language used in their schools. Their values were family, the Catholic religion, hard work, and the joy of life evident in frequent celebrations with their distinctive food and music.

The Cajun subculture managed to stay intact until about 1900 when several factors speeded up its Americanization. Discovery of oil in 1901 brought in outsiders and created salaried jobs and a cash economy. The Education Act of 1916 made English mandatory in the schools. Roads, railroads, communications, and commercial and tourist facilities have all impacted the area and its people. The Cajun culture still exists today in southern Louisiana, but with adaptations to modern times.

In 1984, the Lafayette Parish Bayou Vermilion District was created to establish a living history museum depicting the lifestyles and cultures of the Cajuns, Creoles, and others who settled the Attakapas District of south central Louisiana between 1765 and 1890. Vermilionville, a non-profit museum, opened in 1990 on a 22-acre site in Lafayette's Beaver Park. Vermilionville was an earlier name of the city which was renamed Lafayette one hundred years ago.

TOUR

Vermilionville is organized into three sections: the festive area, the folklife area, and the living history area.

The **Festive Area** contains replicas of buildings typically found on a Creole plantation. The **Visitor Center** or *Bienvenue Chez Nous Autres* is modeled after a Creole plantation house. An orientation film is shown here. A plantation overseer's house is occupied by the restaurant, La Cuisine de Maman, while The Food Quarters or Le Quartier Creole is in plantation slave quarters. The **Performance Center,** based on the design of a cotton gin, is used for dance demonstrations, daily band performances, plays, and lectures. There is also a Bakery and a Cooking School featuring authentic Cajun and Creole recipes.

The **Folklife Area** contains a recreated village of restored historic buildings from southern Louisiana, along with some recreated structures. Costumed craftspeople demonstrate weaving, quilting, broom making, woodworking, basketry, musical instrument making, toy making, furniture making, candle making, soap making, decoy carving, and homebuilding and renovation. Many tour guides and craftspeople are bilingual Cajuns.

Most Cajun houses are small, frame structures built on stilts with steep pitched roofs, and front and back porches. The style of architecture that evolved in southern Louisiana was based on the environment. Raising a house on tree stumps or bricks prevented flooding. Steep roofs allowed the frequent rains to run off rapidly. Roofed porches provided cooler air, shade, and a place to socialize.

Beau Bassin, a two-room house that blends Creole and American Greek Revival styles, was built around 1840 in the Carencro area of Lafayette Parish. The builders were the children of Louis Arceneux, who was one of Henry Wadsworth Longfellow's models for Gabriel in his poem "Evangeline." Today, the home is used to demonstrate spinning, weaving, quilting, and dyeing.

Le Magasin, a replica of an early Acadian barn, is used for water-related crafts, including boat building, decoy carving, and net and trap making. ***L'Academie de Vermilionville*** is a replica of an 1890s schoolhouse. Children are often taught French songs or given a history lesson here. Woodworking is done in ***La Maison Mouton,*** a reconstruction of an 1810 four-room house. Behind the house is ***La Forge,*** a working blacksmith shop where many of the woodworker's tools were made.

La Maison Acadienne was built in 1860 as a two-family, or double-pen cabane, slave cabin near Carencro. Later, it was used as a school for the grandchildren of Jean Mounton, the founder of the city of Vermilionville. It is not completely restored, but is left as a work in progress to display construction techniques. ***La Maison Boucvalt,*** built in the late nineteenth century in Opelousas, is a four-room, white, frame house with a center chimney. Craftspeople fashion rosaries from seeds and ropes from horse hair. Fiddle making, chair caning, and basketry are demonstrated in the 1803 **La Maison Buller** from Ville Platte. An unusual feature is its stranger's room, a bedroom used by travelers, which did not connect to any other room in the house.

La Chapelle des Attakapas is a replica church based on the eighteenth-century Catholic churches at Pointe Coupee and St. Martinville. Inside the simple church are a white wooden altar, wooden pews, and black, wrought-iron chandeliers. The priest's house, called **Le Presbytere,** was known as Maison La Grange when it was built in Grand Coteau in 1840. The simply furnished house has a bed, a kneeler for praying, religious pictures, a desk, and a small fireplace.

Fausee Pointe, the living history area, is the Amand Broussard farmstead which includes a farmhouse, kitchen, barn, garden, and farm animals. The 1790 Broussard House belonged to the wealthy cattle rancher and his family of fourteen children. Construction methods used in this house include *colombage* and *bousillage*. There are four rooms downstairs and a dormitory upstairs. Mattresses are filled with moss.

Costumed docents perform everyday chores done by the Broussard family 200 years ago. They cook, tend gardens, feed animals, and speak as if they were living a century or two ago.

Special events at Vermilionville include Cajun and Creole weddings, baptisms, Mardi Gras festivities, Christmas, Bastille Day, Native American Rendezvous, and plays performed by the village's own theater group.

SIDE TRIPS

The **Acadian Cultural Center,** a feature of the Acadian Unit of Jean Lafitte National Historical Park and Preserve, includes museum exhibits, a bookstore, and a theater with a film on the Acadian people.

Also in the Acadian Unit is **Prairie Acadian Cultural Center** in Eunice and the **Wetlands Acadian Cultural Center** in Thibodaux.

Another museum village that sheds light on Cajun culture is **Acadian Village.** Restored Acadian historic structures have been moved from the local area. Admission charged. 200 W. Broussard Road, Lafayette 70506, (318) 981-2364.

OLD SALEM

Restoration of an eighteenth-century Moravian community;
NHL, NR

Address: Box F, Winston-Salem, NC 27108
Telephone: (919) 721-7300
Location: Winston-Salem is in northwest North Carolina; Old Salem is
near the intersection of I-40 and US 52
Open: Monday to Saturday, 9:30 A.M. to 4:30 P.M.; Sunday, 1:30 P.M. to
4:30 P.M.; closed Christmas Eve, Christmas, and Thanksgiving
Admission: Old Salem: adults, $10.00; children 6 to 14, $5.00; Old Salem
and Museum of Early Southern Decorative Arts: adults, $13.00; chil-
dren 6 to 14, $6.00
Restaurants: Old Salem Tavern; Mayberry's
Shops: T. Bagge Merchant; Salem Gift and Book Store; Winkler Bakery
Facilities: Visitor center with orientation film; special events; Museum of
Early Southern Decorative Arts

WHERE TO STAY

Inns/Bed & Breakfasts: The Augustus T. Zevely House B&B, 803 South
Main St., Old Salem, Winston-Salem 27101, (919) 721-7300;
Brookstown Inn, 200 Brookstown Ave., Winston-Salem 27101,
(919) 725-1120, (800) 845-4262, FAX: (919) 773-0147; Manor
House, Box 1040, Clemmons 27012, (919) 766-0591, FAX: (919)
766-8723
Motels/Hotels: Best Western Regency Inn, 128 N. Cherry St., Winston-
Salem 27101, (919) 723-8861, (919) 723-2997; The Mark, 460 N.
Cherry St., Winston-Salem 27101, (919) 725-1234, FAX: (919)
722-9182; Stouffer Winston Plaza, 425 N. Cherry St., Winston-
Salem 27101, (909) 725-3500, FAX: (919) 722-6475
Camping: Tanglewood Park, Clemmons 27012, (919) 766-0591; Hanging
Rock State Park, Walnut Cove 27016, (919) 593-8480; Pilot Moun-
tain State Park, Pinnacle 27041, (919) 325-2355

OVERVIEW

Dating from before the American Revolution is a North Carolina
planned town founded in 1766 by a pietistical religious group from Moravia, now in the Czech Republic, called Moravians. Sometimes called "The
Williamsburg of the South," Old Salem's nine museum buildings are

Old Salem, Winston-Salem, North Carolina
In the congregational town planned by the Moravians, the half-timbered Single Brothers' House was built in 1769 with a brick addition in 1786. The restored two-story building at the corner of Academy and Main Streets is now used for demonstrations of traditional crafts at Old Salem, Winston-Salem, NC.

Photo by Patricia A. Gutek

within a sixteen-block area of Moravian-built eighteenth- and nineteenth-century buildings. To ensure an authentic appearance in the historic area, more than a hundred nonconforming structures within the congregation town limits were demolished when restoration efforts began. Like at Williamsburg, many buildings in the historic area are privately owned, but their exteriors have been restored. Because of the large number of original historic structures, the European-style architecture, the historically interesting group that lived in Salem, the beautiful gardens, and the high-quality restoration work, Old Salem ranks very high on our list of fine museum villages.

Salem was a congregational community, strictly planned by Moravian church leaders. The site for Salem ("peace" in Hebrew) was chosen because of its good water supply, proper drainage, and southern exposure. The principal structures, which included houses for the single brothers, single sisters, a community store, and a tavern, were built around an open square.

Not an agricultural center, Salem was conceived as a trading center for artisans and craftsmen. The busy, industrial city of Winston-Salem has grown up around the colonial town of Salem so that it now is a historic eighteenth-century area in a modern twentieth-century city.

Even though admission is charged to enter museum buildings, you are free to stroll the brick paths through the restored area at any time, eat at the Salem Tavern, or shop in museum stores.

Salem is architecturally interesting because of the number of large eighteenth-century buildings that show strong European influence. Houses sit flush with the sidewalks and have half-timbered walls, tile roofs, central chimneys, and symmetrically placed windows.

History

The Moravians, who founded Salem in 1766, trace their faith to the Bohemian Protestant martyr, Jan Hus. Hus died at the stake in 1415 because of his unrelenting opposition to corruption in the Roman Catholic Church. A faithful band of his followers known as *Hussites* sought refuge in Moravia, a province in the present-day Czech Republic. In 1457, they formed a society known as *Unitas Fratrum* (Unity of Brethren), renounced the authority of Rome, and began to ordain their own ministers.

Despite persecution, the Unity flourished, spreading across Moravia, Bohemia, and into Poland until the Counter Reformation and Thirty Years War (1618 to 1648) destroyed all but a remnant of the group and forced its members into exile.

Pietism, the "religion of the heart," was kept alive by the distinguished educator and Moravian bishop of the *Unitas Fratrum*, John Amos Komensky, (1592–1670), also known by his Latin name, Comenius. The Moravians who eventually emigrated to the New World incorporated many of Comenius's educational ideas into their efforts to convert the American Indians to Christianity.

The brethren followed the rule that the spirit of love should be constantly maintained toward all the children of God, regardless of race or creed. In their daily lives, the brethren strove to preserve purity and simplicity. Like other Protestant denominations, the Moravians, as members of the Unity were commonly called, turned to America as a place where they could practice their beliefs free from persecution and whose American Indian tribes offered unlimited opportunities for missionary activity.

By 1740, the brethren had founded a successful colony at Bethlehem, Pennsylvania. Their reputation as industrious, law-abiding people attracted the attention of a British nobleman, Earl Granville, who approached the Moravian leaders with an offer of land. In 1753, a 98,985-acre tract was purchased in what is now Piedmont, North Carolina. The Carolina purchase was named *der Wachau* after the Austrian estate of Count Nicholas Ludwig von Zinzendorf, an important patron of the sect. The settlement came to be known as *Wachovia*.

Salem was planned as Wachovia's trade center, a town where economic development and architectural details would be regulated as strictly as people's lives. Construction began in 1766, and by the spring of 1772, most of the major buildings had been completed, and early settlers and the government of Wachovia proceeded to move in.

The Moravian beliefs combined pietistic behavior with a zeal for commerce. A person's work and the profit it yielded were considered essential to spiritual growth. Whether a candlemaker or tinsmith, a Moravian craftsman should develop his skills to the utmost in order to glorify the divine taskmaster.

The guild system was the way that the brethren accomplished their many objectives. A Salem youth began his apprenticeship, with elaborate ceremony, at about the age of fourteen and with rare exceptions remained in that status for a full seven years. The guild system yielded high-quality products that were sold for profit.

Because the Moravians did not separate church and state, the business of running the town and enforcing the rules of the congregation was vested in three main boards or committees. The duties of the *Aufseher Collegium* (board of overseers) were to superintend trade, enforce zoning laws and building codes, discipline wayward apprentices and masters, control community accounts, and allocate funds for capital-improvement projects. The board, which was made up mostly of laymen and was concerned primarily with secular matters, also turned a harsh eye on tradesmen accused of immoral conduct. Matters of a strictly spiritual nature were referred to the Elders Conference. Another important body was the Congregation Council, which dealt mainly with issues involving all members of the community.

The Moravian "choir" system arose out of the belief that a close association of persons of like age, sex, or marital status promoted spiritual growth. There were choirs for married people, children, single brothers, single sisters, older boys, older girls, widows, and widowers. Some of the choirs—single brothers, widows, single sisters—lived in their own choir houses. All choirs worshiped together on a regular basis.

The choir system was closely linked with a sense of shared life and property, but by the time of Salem's founding, the brethren were allowed greater latitude in their economic lives. They were free to live in their own homes, though the church's leasehold system retained a right to the land on which the houses stood, and could also choose their own building styles. In the early days, only confirmed Moravians were allowed to live in or own houses in Salem.

Moravians were allowed to use alcohol and tobacco in moderation, but dress codes were severe, particularly for women. Each sister wore an ankle-length dress and, at church services, a traditional *Haube* (head covering). However, the colors of their clothing were the gayest that could be wrung from their homemade dyes.

As the area surrounding Wachovia grew more populous, the highly regimented congregation system of Salem lost much of its appeal. Gradually, the old rules were either relaxed or abandoned; and by the middle of the nineteenth century, Salem had ceased to function as a congregation town. Today, only the church, an active Protestant denomination, remains as a Moravian entity.

Although the original Salem ceased to exist, many of its buildings remained standing. But the founding of a new town, Winston, on its northern borders in 1849, the growth of Winston's tobacco and textile industries, the merger of Winston and Salem in 1913, and the gradual spreading of the city until it all but engulfed the old Moravian town led to its deterioration and near extinction.

In the spring of 1950, a broad-based, nonprofit organization known as Old Salem, Inc., brought together Moravians and non-Moravians in an effort to preserve the historic town. More than fifty buildings have now been restored or reconstructed on their original sites, recreating another era in the heart of a bustling metropolis.

TOUR

After viewing the slide show on Moravian history at the **Reception Center,** begin your tour at the town square, which was originally farmland. Later, it was used for grazing sheep, but it eventually came to resemble a New England commons. The only major building on the square is the **Market-Fire House,** built in 1803. This reconstructed brick firehouse contains an exhibit of early fire-fighting equipment.

The northern, half-timbered portion of the **Single Brothers' House** dates from 1769; the southern, brick portion was added in 1786. Because the lime needed for mortar was scarce in Wachovia, oak timbering was used in 1769 to reinforce the house's brickwork. By 1786, when the addition was built, lime was more plentiful, and the community used brick in all its building projects.

Typically, a Salem boy entered the Moravian guild system at fourteen. He left his home, moved into the Single Brothers' House, and began a seven-year apprenticeship under one of the master craftsmen. After achieving journeyman status, he continued to live with the single brethren until he married. At that time, he moved into his own home and started his own business.

The Single Brothers' House is a long, two-story structure with a high basement and two attics. It was not only a residence but also contained the shops of the master craftsmen. The restored building contains craft shops stocked with appropriate tools, and craftspeople demonstrate and explain their work. These shops include a **tin shop, gun shop, dye shop, weaver's room, tailor's shop, potter's shop, cooper's shop,** and **joiner's shop.** The productivity of the brothers, along with the high quality of their products, was a major factor in the economic success of Salem.

The **Boys' School,** a brick building erected in 1794, also faces Salem's square. Built by master builder Johannes Gottlob Krause, it is noteworthy for the artistry that appears in the pattern of the brick masonry on the west gable, the coved cornices, and the belt course of brick on the east gable. Until 1896, the school was attended by boys aged six to fourteen; but in that year, it became the home of the Wachovia Historical Society. Collections of artifacts acquired by Moravian missionaries were displayed here until the 1950s, when Old Salem, Inc., restored the building and assumed management of the collection. Exhibits in the **Wachovia Mu-**

seum now relate directly to the history of Wachovia: Moravian pottery, church history, Moravian music, ironwork, lighting devices, and a restored classroom. Moravians placed great emphasis on education, and the boys' curriculum included geometry, Latin and English grammar, geography, history, penmanship, and German.

North of the square is the **Miksch Tobacco Shop.** This 1771 building was the first privately owned house in Salem. Matthew Miksch not only lived in but also operated a tobacco business from this house. The house was built of logs, but because the brethren disapproved of plain log houses on their main street, it (like others) was covered with clapboards. Originally, the house had two rooms, but Miksch added a third room at the back and a loft.

The **Winkler Bakery** was built in 1800 for a baker named Thomas Buttner. In 1808, Christian Winkler acquired the shop. Bread is still being baked in the wood-fired domed brick bake oven attached to the south side of the building. Eighteenth-century baking processes are used to produce European-style white bread, Swedish rye, whole wheat, and Moravian sugar cake and sugar cookies. All these products are sold at the bakery, and the aroma of fresh-baked bread permeates the restored area.

South of the square is the **John Vogler House,** which was built in 1819. This house has many Federal characteristics and thus represents a departure from Salem's Germanic architectural tradition. Vogler was an accomplished silversmith who also dabbled in clock making, gun-smithing, jewelry making, and silhouette making. Seventy percent of the furniture in the house belonged to the Vogler family. One room is used as a Vogler family museum, with their silver, guns, and artwork exhibited. Another room is used for Vogler's silversmithing shop, and many of his spoons, ladles, and snuffboxes are displayed.

The **Schultz Shoemaker Shop** was built in 1827. Samuel Schultz originally operated his business from his 1819 home but decided to construct a separate building adjacent to it. This home and shop are typical of those owned and operated by married craftsmen. The shop displays the tools and products of early-nineteenth-century shoemaking.

The **Vierling House** was built in 1802 and was the last and largest masterwork of Johannes Krause. Unique features of this brick Georgian house are the exposed-stone foundation and the herringbone gable patterns. Krause was commissioned to build the house by Dr. Samuel Benjamin Vierling, the most renowned of Salem's early physicians. It was in this house that Dr. Vierling practiced the professions of physician, surgeon, and apothecary. He is said to have performed mastectomies, skull trepans, and other major operations in his apothecary. The restored house contains both living quarters and medical offices.

The **Salem Tavern Museum** (1784) is a plain three-story brick building with a veranda. Taverns to accommodate travelers were a high priority of the congregation town, and this one had a fine reputation for its food and drink. Among the prominent Revolutionary War figures who stopped at Salem was George Washington, who spent two days at this tavern in 1791.

The first floor has a **Publick Room** where the ordinary (a standard meal at a fixed price) was served each day. Across the hall is a **Gentlemen's Room** for the more elite clientele. It is furnished with private tables and Windsor chairs instead of long tables and benches. Cooking was done in the twin fireplaces of the large kitchen. There are several sleeping rooms in addition to the innkeeper's bedroom, with its canopy bed.

Salem Tavern (1816), where today's visitors can stop for a meal, was originally a boardinghouse built as an adjunct to the main tavern building. The outside is restored to its 1816 appearance; the inside has been adapted for dining in a hospitable tavern atmosphere.

Gardens were part of the early congregational town plan. Each family maintained its own garden to supply vegetables for the table. A landscaping program has restored many gardens to various time periods: the **Treibel** and **Miksch Gardens,** 1759 to 1761; **Eberhardt Garden,** 1814; **Levering Garden,** 1820; **Leinbach Garden,** 1822; **Cape Fear Bank Garden,** 1847; and **Anna Catharina Garden,** 1772. There is also an arboretum of native trees near the Museum of Early Southern Decorative Arts.

Operated by Old Salem, Inc., the **Museum of Early Southern Decorative Arts** was founded by Frank L. Horton, Old Salem's first director of restoration, in 1965. Nineteen rooms representative of the early South have been removed from their original locations and reassembled in the museum. They are decorated with furniture, paintings, metal-work, pottery, and glasswork produced by Southern craftsmen. A large part of the collection was donated by Mr. Horton and his mother, Mrs. Theo Liipfert Taliaferro. The museum emphasizes the products of craftspeople used in the three principal cultural regions of the Old South: the Chesapeake, the Carolina low country, and the back settlements during the years between 1640 and 1820.

God's Acre, founded in 1779, is the graveyard for Salem's Moravian congregation. Long rows of identical gravestones attest to the sect's belief in equality. People were buried with their fellow choir members rather than with their families. A large square is provided for each choir: married women and widows, married men and widowers, single men and boys, and single women and girls. An Easter sunrise service has been held in God's Acre every year since 1772 and attracts thousands of visitors.

Salem Academy and College, a four-year liberal arts college for women, is an outgrowth of a girls' boarding school operated by the Moravians. The first building for the school was erected in 1805 and has been restored to its 1837 appearance and now serves as a dormitory. College buildings are not open to tourists.

The **Home Moravian Church** was built in 1800. Although it has undergone many interior renovations, its exterior looks much as it originally did. This church has been occupied continuously by the Moravian congregation since 1800.

Two shops are operated at Old Salem. One is in the southern half of the restored 1775 **T. Bagge Community Store** and the other, the Salem Gift and Book Store, is in an 1850 addition to the 1810 **Inspector's House.** The shops carry reproductions made by the village's working craftsmen, including pottery, candles, quilts, wooden toys, tinware, and needlework kits. There is also a fine selection of books, many of them about Moravians.

Many educational and special events are held at Old Salem throughout the year. There are classes or lectures on weaving, wool dyeing textiles, candle making, vegetable and flower gardening, nineteenth-century architecture, rug hooking, beehive-oven baking, and ice creams of the colonial period. Concerts are scheduled throughout the year.

Special events include a Spring Festival in April, a Civil War Encampment in June, a Torchlight Procession on the Fourth of July, and Salem Christmas in December.

SIDE TRIPS

Historic Bethabara ("house of passage" in Hebrew) is the site of the first Moravian settlement in North Carolina. Archaeological research has uncovered the foundation walls and cellars of many of the original buildings. The 1756 **palisade,** a fort that gave refuge to outlying settlers in times of trouble, has been reconstructed. The 1788 **Gemein Haus** (Congregation House), a fine example of Moravian architecture, the 1782 **potter's house,** and the 1803 **brewer's house** have all been restored as exhibit buildings. The **Visitors' Center** contains exhibits on the early settlers, including many artifacts found on the site. Nature trails lead to the Moravian graveyard called **God's Acre.** Located at 2147 Bethabara Road, Winston-Salem 27106. Open Monday to Friday, 9:30 A.M. to 4:30 P.M., and

Saturday and Sunday, 1:30 P.M. to 4:30 P.M., from Easter to Thanksgiving. For information, call (919) 924-8191. Admission is free.

A museum of American art now occupies the former estate of Richard J. Reynolds, founder of the R. J. Reynolds Tobacco Company. **Reynolda House,** Route 67 and Reynolda Road, Winston-Salem 27106, is open Tuesday to Saturday, 9:30 A.M. to 4:30 P.M., and Sunday, 1:30 P.M. to 4:30 P.M. For information, call (919) 725-5325. Admission charged.

Tanglewood Park is a 1,000-acre public resort in Winston-Salem. Its facilities include golf courses, tennis courts, a lodge, cottages, campsites, restaurants, swimming, and riding trails. It is open year-round and can be reached by exiting at Clemmons from I-40 West. P.O. Box 1040, Clemmons 27012, (919) 766-0591. Admission charged.

HISTORIC RUGBY

Restored nineteenth-century Victorian English village; NR

Address: P.O. Box 8, Hwy. 52, Rugby, TN 37733
Telephone: (615) 628-2441; (615) 628-2430
Location: In northeastern Tennessee, about one hundred twenty-five miles northeast of Nashville and about seventy miles northwest of Knoxville; 35 miles from both I-75 exit 141, and I-40 exit 300; on State Highway 52
Open: Monday to Saturday, 9:30 A.M. to 5:00 P.M.; Sunday, 12:00 noon to 5:00 P.M., February through December; tours by appointment only in January
Admission: Adults, $4.00; senior citizens, $3.50; students, $2.00
Restaurants: The Harrow Road Cafe
Shops: Rugby Craft Commissary; Board of Aid Bookshop
Facilities: Visitor Centre; guided tours; archive and research centre; craft workshops; special events

WHERE TO STAY

Inns/Bed & Breakfasts: Newbury House; 1880 Pioneer Cottage; and Percy Cottage, P.O. Box 8, Hwy. 52, Rugby 37733, (615) 628-2441, (615) 628-2430
Camping: Big South Fork National River & Recreation Area, P. O. Drawer 630, Oneida 37841, (615) 879-4890

OVERVIEW

Nestled among the lush vegetation of Tennessee's Cumberland Plateau is a restored village of English Victorian cottages, vestiges of a planned experimental community for younger sons of England's landed gentry. Founded by Thomas Hughes, the late-nineteenth-century town was designed as a haven for well-educated but discontented second-, third-, and fourth-born sons who could establish a new life, own land, and work at careers of their choice without the traditional constraints imposed by England's rigid social structure.

Rugby's location, as much as anything, makes this museum village outstanding. Travelers have no clue that Tennessee's Cumberland Plateau has a charming English Victorian village hidden in its backwoods. The village is adjacent to the southern portion of the 105,000-acre Big South Fork National River and Recreation Area. A winding road from the inter-

Historic Rugby, Rugby, Tennessee
The Thomas Hughes Free Public Library is housed in its original 1882 one-story
frame building with a cupola. Gold lettering on the arched frosted glass panels of
the front doors announces its opening on October 5, 1882. At Historic
Rugby, Rugby, TN.

Photo by Patricia A. Gutek

state passes through scenic but sparsely populated rural and mining hamlets so remote that they only received electricity in the 1950s.

More than twenty original or reconstructed buildings remain in the Victorian village, about half of which are privately owned. Buildings open for touring are Christ Church Episcopal, the Thomas Hughes Library, Kingstone Lisle, and the Schoolhouse Visitor Centre.

Rugby's wooded setting is isolated; make sure you have enough toothpaste, aspirin, and batteries for your camera. Seclusion is an asset for a historic site; the restaurant and inn make complete immersion in the past possible. Overnight accommodations are available in restored buildings, the Newbury House Inn and Pioneer Cottage and reconstructed Percy Cottage.

History

Thomas Hughes, a second son of a English upper-class family, deplored the idle, useless lifestyle assigned to many young Englishmen. Primogeniture, wherein upper-class first-born sons inherited their fathers' titles and estates, was the traditional inheritance pattern in England. Younger sons, who were not heirs, were educated at elite public schools, really prestigious private schools, like their older brothers, yet second sons would never own their own land. They were encouraged to earn their living by entering the professions of ministry, law, medicine, public service, or the military.

In fact, many younger sons did not enter the overcrowded professions and were left with a life of unemployment, and an inadequate allowance as their only source of income. Hughes condemned the aristocracy who would rather see their children starve like gentlemen than thrive in a trade or profession considered beneath them. "Yes; of the many sad sights in our England, there is none sadder than this, of first-rate human material going helplessly to waste . . ." (Hughes, *Rugby*, p. 6)

A prolific writer, Hughes' most famous book was *Tom Brown's School Days*, a fictional account of his education at Rugby, one of England's prestigious public schools. Hughes attended Rugby from 1833 to 1841 and was influenced by the ideas of Thomas Arnold who advocated reform of the public schools. English public schools, contrary to their name, were highly selective, prestigious boarding schools that prepared the scions of upper-class families to be English gentlemen who would be comfortable on the playing field as well as in the drawing room. Their curricula emphasized the classics, literature, and history but ignored science, the professions, and technical study. Public school education stressed the inappropriateness and social stigma attached to engaging in business, trades, or the manual arts.

Hughes studied law at Oxford, practiced law in London, and was a member of the House of Commons from 1865 to 1874. He was a social reformer who championed Christian socialism, supported the cooperative movement, the trade-union movement, and was involved in founding and running the Working Men's College in London. After visiting the more socially open United States in 1870, Thomas Hughes proposed founding a community there of English gentlemen farmers.

While in the United States, Hughes met Franklin W. Smith, a Boston capitalist who headed a company known as the Board of Aid to Land Ownership. The company had an option on 100,000 acres of East Tennessee land intended as a relocation site for unemployed Boston workers. Because of an upturn in the economy, the Tennessee property was no longer needed for that purpose, and the American group offered it to Hughes. After obtaining financial backing from Henry Kimber and John Boyle of London, Hughes became the official spokesman for the land company which retained the name Board of Aid to Land Ownership, Limited. The property was beautifully situated on a heavily wooded high plain between two deep river gorges.

Because the Board of Aid to Land Ownership, Limited was a commercial venture, the land was made available to all buyers, not just English second sons. Hughes believed that the settlement should be open to all who subscribed to his principles and ways, whether Englishmen or Americans. According to Hughes, participants would lead a peasant's life during working hours but find themselves in a cultivated society when their work was done. Hughes named the community Rugby after the school he had attended, and the town officially opened in October 1880. Three weeks later, Rugby's population was 120, and by the following January, it had grown to 200 English and Scottish people with a good percentage of Americans, some of whom were natives of the Tennessee mountains. Despite the emphasis on sons, the population was almost evenly divided between men and women.

By the summer of 1881, Rugby had a cafe, a boarding house, a three-story hotel, private homes, and a cooperative commissary. Because many of the British residents were well-educated members of a leisure class, recreational and cultural pursuits were important considerations. The community had tennis courts, bowling greens, bridle paths, and a gentlemen's swimming hole. Croquet, hunting, and musical events were popular. A number of clubs were formed including the Lawn Tennis Club, the Rugby

Social Club, Rugby Musical and Dramatic Club, the Philharmonic Society, the Masonic Lodge, the Ladies Church Working Society, and the Cornet Band. A weekly newspaper, the *Rugbeian*, began publication in 1880. The Rugby Schoolhouse was constructed in 1880, and in 1882, a public library was built. Religious services were held in the school as Christ Church was not built until 1887. Colonists dressed for afternoon tea at four o'clock. Since Hughes was a temperance advocate, liquor was prohibited in the village.

The population of Rugby fluctuated as residents faced arduous weather, a typhoid epidemic, leadership problems, and the burdens of manual labor. Although John Boyle, who had been sent by Hughes to survey the suitability of the Cumberland Plateau land, had raved about the pure and genial atmosphere and temperature which at once attracted him favorably towards the climate, the first winter in Rugby was harsh and very cold, the worst winter in that part of Tennessee in twenty-five years. When typhoid broke out in August 1881, twenty cases were reported and seven people died. The contamination was traced to one of the earliest buildings constructed in Rugby, a three-story hotel called the Tabard Inn. Though the inn was closed, frightened residents fled the community and the population plunged from 300 to 60 by December.

Despite this inauspicious beginning, Hughes was determined to make the colony succeed. Acknowledging prior mistakes in management, changes were made. The Tabard Inn was reconditioned and reopened. A school mistress was hired. Thomas Hughes was not himself a resident of Rugby although he visited the community for a few months annually. His brother Hastings did live in Rugby, and in 1881, Thomas' and Hastings' mother, Margaret Hughes, moved to Rugby where she lived until her death at ninety in 1887. Margaret Hughes' presence had a steadying effect on the morale of the shaky community.

Gradually, the population increased. By 1884, there were between 400 and 450 residents, and some sixty-five buildings in Rugby. Commercial activities included farming, a canning company, a sawmill, boarding houses, public stables, a drug store, blacksmith shops, and summer tourism with guests accommodated at the Tabard Inn. Unfortunately, the Tabard Inn was destroyed in a fire in October 1884. A new Tabard was opened in the summer of 1887, the year that Christ Church was built.

Rugby survived from 1880 to 1887 with various successes and setbacks, but from 1887 on, it gradually declined. Many factors contributed to the community's demise. Very few of the English pioneers brought any kind of manual skill, business ability, or agricultural knowledge to the community. The canning factory closed. An English public school for young gentlemen, the Arnold School, lasted only from 1885 to 1887. The newspaper, *the Rugbeian,* ceased publication. Thomas Hughes' last visit to Rugby was in 1887, the year his mother died, and Hastings Hughes moved to Massachusetts. Hughes died in 1896 having lost a great deal of money in the Rugby venture as did the other stockholders of the Board of Aid to Land Ownership. In the early 1900s, that company sold its remaining 25,000 acres to American investors. Most original colonists had already left Rugby.

Rugby, Tennessee, overlooked and neglected for the following half century, existed as a small farming community. As with many historic sites, progress in terms of urban sprawl and highway construction destroys, while neglect preserves. Rugby's remote location helped much of the Victorian village remain intact. In 1966, a 16-year-old boy, Brian Stagg, led a Rugby restoration movement. Tours of historic buildings began in 1967, and in 1972, the village was placed on the National Register of Historic Places. Historic Rugby, Inc., has restored several buildings and reconstructed several others. A master plan for the historic site includes restoration and rebuilding of even more buildings.

Tour

Tours begin at the **Schoolhouse Visitor Centre,** a two-story frame structure built in 1907 and used as a school until 1951. It replaced a three-story schoolhouse built in 1880 that was destroyed by fire in 1906. Exhibits in the Schoolhouse focus on Thomas Hughes, Rugby, cottage Victorian architecture, and the Cumberland Mountains, and include photographs and documents. Guided tours leave from the Schoolhouse.

Rugby's piece de resistance is the **Thomas Hughes Free Public Library** housed in its original 1882 one-story frame building with a cupola. The collection of 7,000 rare books includes 2,000 volumes brought from England and 5,000 donated books. Gold lettering on the arched frosted glass panels on the front doors announces the Hughes Public Library was opened October 5, 1882. One of the finest collections of Victorian literature in the United States, no volume published after 1899 is on the shelves, and the oldest book was printed in 1687. The books are in remarkably good condition. The building has no electricity and is unheated. Floor to ceiling bookshelves line the walls in addition to free-standing bookcases, wooden tables, and chairs.

Christ Church Episcopal was built in 1887 and still holds Sunday services today. The Carpenter Gothic church, designed by Cornelius Onderdonk, has board and batten siding with maroon and gray trim. Its interior is paneled with native yellow pine, which was not painted or stained but has darkened naturally. The stained-glass window above the altar was dedicated to Margaret Hughes and Mary Blacklock. Other windows, which are original, are clear although they had previously been covered with rice paper to give the illusion of stained glass. The original oil lamps were electrified in the 1950s. The rosewood, harmonium reed organ was made in London in 1849 and is still in use.

Kingstone Lisle is the house that was built in 1884 for Thomas Hughes who made annual visits to Rugby. The wooden walls, ceilings, and floors of the interior are yellow pine. Furnishings were either made in Rugby or brought from England by Rugby colonists. The parlor has a Weber piano and a silver plate for calling cards. Windows have long puddling drapes. In the bedroom is Thomas Hughes' green felt-covered writing desk as well as his trunk.

The reconstructed **Harrow Road Cafe** is a flourishing restaurant. Another reconstruction, the **Rugby Craft Commissary** is a craft store. This cooperative commissary supplied all the needs of the town's residents. Today it is a craft shop featuring Appalachian crafts such as quilts, baskets, and dulcimers. The **Board of Aid land office** is a bookshop.

Overnight accommodations are available in the simple one-story frame **Pioneer Cottage.** Built in 1880, it served as a temporary haven for early colonists until their houses were built. Thomas Hughes stayed at Pioneer Cottage during his first visit to Rugby. Another bed and breakfast, the **Newbury House,** 1880, was Rugby's first boarding house. The two-story, mansard-roofed inn has been restored, and its five bedrooms are furnished in the Victorian period. A third lodging facility is **Percy Cottage.** This Victorian cottage was reconstructed on its original foundation. The original Percy Cottage was built in 1884 for Sir Henry Kimber.

Many of the privately owned houses in Rugby have also been restored and can be seen from the outside. Once a year they are open for touring during the Rugby Pilgrimage held the first weekend in October. Another annual event is the Spring Music and Crafts Festival held in mid-May. The festival features craftspeople selling and demonstrating their crafts, as well as British and Appalachian music and dancing. Crafts are also available at the Thanksgiving Marketplace held Thanksgiving weekend. The Christmas at Rugby celebration, held in early December, features candlelight tours and a Victorian dinner.

Workshops are taught in a variety of crafts such as cane seating, hand-spinning, tatting, and basketry.

Colonists are buried in the **Laurel Dale Cemetery** on Donnington Road. From there, an 1880s trail leads to the **Gentlemen's Swimming Hole** a half mile away. This trail continues for one mile to the Meeting of the Waters, where Clear Fork River and White Oak Creek intersect.

SIDE TRIPS

Big South Fork National River and Recreation Area, just north of Historic Rugby, is a 105,000-acre park managed by the National Park Service. It is situated in a rugged gorge area of the Cumberland Plateau in southwestern Kentucky and northeastern Tennessee. Activities include hiking, camping, hunting, horseback riding, canoeing, kayaking, whitewater rafting, and fishing. For information, write Superintendent, P.O. Drawer 630, Oneida, Tennessee 37841.

COLONIAL WILLIAMSBURG

Restoration of the eighteenth-century capital of the English colony of Virginia; NR, NHL, HABS

Address: P.O. Box 1776, Williamsburg, VA 23187-1776
Telephone: (804) 229-1000; (800) HISTORY
Location: In southeast Virginia, midway between Richmond and Norfolk on I-64
Open: Daily, 9:00 A.M. to 5:00 P.M.
Admission: Patriot's Pass (admission to all major exhibits in Colonial Williamsburg for one year): adults, $29.00, children 6 to 12, $17.50; Royal Governor's Pass (admission to all major exhibits in the Historic Area plus Governor's Palace, the Abby Aldrich Rockefeller Folk Art Center, and the DeWitt Wallace Decorative Arts Gallery during current visit): adults, $26.50, children 6 to 12, $16.00; Basic Admission Ticket (admission to exhibits in the Historic Area, valid only for that day): adults, $24.00; children 6 to 12, $14.50; separate admission tickets available for Governor's Palace, Carter's Grove, Wallace Gallery, and Folk Art Center
Restaurants: Christiana Campbell's Tavern, King's Arms Tavern, Shields Tavern, Chowning's Tavern, Regency Dining Room, Bay Room, Cascades Restaurant, Wallace Gallery Cafe, Golden Horseshoe Clubhouse Grills, Woodlands Grill
Shops: Tarpley's Store; Raleigh Tavern Bake Shop; Hunter's Store; Prentis Store; Mary Dickinson Store; John Greenhow Store; Post Office; Golden Ball; McKenzie Apothecary; Craft House; Visitor Center Bookstore; Merchants Square; Everything Williamsburg; Sign of the Rooster at the Folk Art Center; Wallace Gallery Gift Shop
Facilities: Visitor Center with orientation film; craft demonstrations; Central Library; golf courses; bus transportation; special events; educational forums; handicapped accessible; DeWitt Wallace Decorative Arts Gallery; Winthrop Rockefeller Archaeology Museum; Abby Aldrich Rockefeller Folk Art Center; Carter's Grove; Basset Hall

WHERE TO STAY

Inns/Bed & Breakfasts: Colonial Houses & Taverns, Williamsburg, (800) HISTORY
Motels/Hotels: Williamsburg Inn, Williamsburg, (800) HISTORY; Williamsburg Lodge, Williamsburg, (800) HISTORY; Williamsburg

Colonial Williamsburg, Williamsburg, Virginia
Young fife and drum corps members outfitted in replicas of eighteenth-century
British soldiers' garb wend their weary way back after reveille.
At Colonial Williamsburg, Williamsburg, VA.

Photo by Patricia A. Gutek

Woodlands, Williamsburg, (800) HISTORY; Governor's Inn, Williamsburg, (800) HISTORY; Providence Hall, Williamsburg, (800) HISTORY; Fort Magruder Inn, 6945 Pochanontas Trail, Williamsburg 23187, (804) 220-2250, (800) 582-1010

Camping: Jamestown Beach Campsites, P.O. Box CB, Williamsburg 23187, (804) 229-7609, (804) 229-3300; Williamsburg KOA, 5210 Lightfoot Rd., Williamsburg 23188, (800) 635-2717, (804) 565-2907; Gloucester Point Campgrounds, Rt. 4, Box 199, Hayes 23072, (800) 332-4316, (804) 642-4316; Colonial Campgrounds, 4712 Lightfoot Rd., Williamsburg 23188, (800) 336-2734, (804) 565-2734

OVERVIEW

Williamsburg is the one museum village that virtually everyone has heard of, and it is usually their favorite. In an atmosphere that combines history and romance, it has everything: a huge restored area that takes several days to see; original eighteenth-century buildings on their original sites; an important historical connection to the American Revolution; 225 period rooms decorated with original American antiques; well-informed costumed guides; expert craft demonstrations; a park-like, well-landscaped site; exceptional museum collections of folk art and decorative art; restaurants in romantic colonial taverns; shops loaded with books, reproduction furniture, and craft items, as well as all the facilities found at resorts including fine hotels, tennis courts, and golf courses.

Without doubt, Williamsburg is the crown jewel of America's restored museum villages. Indeed, many of the other restored villages and communities that are described in this book owe their inspiration and design to Colonial Williamsburg. The quality and breadth of its restoration and its programs attract about a million visitors each year which means you need to plan in advance for accommodations during the busiest seasons at Colonial Williamsburg.

Today, the Historic Area of Williamsburg covers 173 acres of the original 220-acre town, based on the 1781 street plan. It is a mile long, with the Wren Building of the College of William and Mary at the western boundary and the Capitol at the eastern end; the average width is one-half mile. Within or adjacent to this area are eighty-eight restored houses, shops, taverns, public buildings, and dependencies. In addition to the Governor's Palace and the Capitol, more than fifty structures have been rebuilt on their original sites. Ninety acres of gardens have been planted in eighteenth-century style, and the Colonial Williamsburg area is surrounded by 3,000 acres of greenbelt.

HISTORY

Already well known for the College of William and Mary, which is named in honor of the British sovereigns, Williamsburg has many claims to significance in American history. In 1699, it became Virginia's second capital, replacing Jamestown, the first permanent English settlement in the New World, where colonists had faced continual famine, fire, and American Indian raids since its founding in 1607.

Williamsburg was both an outpost of the powerful British Empire in the New World and an ideological training ground for those who would help to lead America to independence. The magnificently restored Royal Governor's Palace (1720) was the official residence of the king's representative in Virginia, a royal colony. While the Governor's Palace affirmed the majesty and dominion of the Crown, the House of Burgesses, composed of elected representatives of Virginia's counties, broadcast the fledgling efforts of Americans to govern themselves.

Williamsburg eventually became a center of revolutionary activity. Here George Washington, Patrick Henry, George Wythe, Thomas Jefferson, and other Founding Fathers began the struggle that would lead to the birth of a new nation.

At Williamsburg on May 15, 1776, the Virginia Convention passed a resolution urging the Continental Congress to declare the colonies free and independent of Great Britain and to create a national confederation. Acting on that resolution, Richard Henry Lee proposed in Philadelphia that Congress declare the colonies "absolved from all allegiance to the British Crown." Congress adopted Lee's resolution on July 2 and approved the Declaration of Independence on July 4.

On June 12, 1776, the Virginia Convention at Williamsburg adopted George Mason's Virginia Declaration of Rights, which later became the basis for the first ten amendments of the Constitution of the United States.

In 1781, Williamsburg surrendered its role as Virginia's capital when the offices of the new commonwealth were moved to Richmond to be more convenient to the state's growing population and be better protected from enemy attacks.

Williamsburg is also significant in the history of restoration in the United States. Colonial Williamsburg is one of the finest historical restorations not just in the United States but in the world.

Colonial Williamsburg is the name identifying all the activities of the

Colonial Williamsburg Foundation, a nonprofit educational organization. Among its activities are the restoration and interpretation of the historic sections of Williamsburg, the development of an extensive educational and cultural program based on Williamsburg's historical significance, the management of visitor accommodations and services, and the operation and maintenance of the DeWitt Wallace Decorative Arts Gallery, the Winthrop Rockefeller Archaeology Museum, the Abby Aldrich Rockefeller Folk Art Center, Carter's Grove Plantation, and Bassett Hall, the home of Mr. and Mrs. John D. Rockefeller, Jr.

The concept of restoring Williamsburg originated with the Reverend Dr. W.A.R. Goodwin, rector of the Bruton Parish Church. In 1926, Goodwin discussed the idea with John D. Rockefeller, Jr., who agreed to provide financial support. It was decided to restore the extant buildings to their appearance during the colonial era. Important buildings such as the Governor's Palace and the Capitol, which no longer existed, were painstakingly researched and recreated.

TOUR

Because Colonial Williamsburg is large and complex, you should begin your tour at the official **Colonial Williamsburg Visitor Center.** This is a scene of often hurried activity, but you will nevertheless find the time used here to orient yourself well spent. Here you will find complete details on what to see and do, ticket sales, an orientation film, and cultural and historical exhibits. Information is available on accommodations, dining, special activities and programs, and travel attractions throughout tidewater Virginia. A guide for handicapped visitors is also available. Historic Area buses provide transportation for ticket holders.

Because of the size of the Williamsburg restoration, the site description follows the major streets and comments only on the buildings open to the public. Buildings front on the three major streets of the city: Duke of Gloucester, Francis, and Nicholson streets. But on each street you will also see a number of privately owned restored buildings.

The **Capitol,** one of the major landmarks, is a careful recreation of the first building that served as Virginia's capitol from 1704 until it was destroyed by fire in 1747. A second Capitol was completed in 1753, which incorporated the surviving walls of the first Capitol but was a different architectural style. In 1781, Virginia's government moved to Richmond.

Under the supervision of Henry Cary, a leading colonial architect, the foundations of the Capitol were laid in 1701, and construction was completed in 1705. The architecture is a simplified version of the Renaissance style. Note the round and arched windows and cupola. Since the Capitol was built during Queen Anne's reign, her coat of arms is emblazoned on its tower.

The building's H-shaped design reflects the composition of the colonial government, which was headed by a royal governor appointed by the British crown. One wing housed the elected House of Burgesses on the first floor and their committee rooms on the second. Among the distinguished Americans who served as burgesses were George Washington, Patrick Henry, Richard Henry Lee, and Thomas Jefferson. The Capitol's other wing housed the General Court Room and the Council Chamber. The Council consisted of the governor and his appointees. A costumed interpreter notes that burgesses met in a rather austere setting that contrasts with the more elegant Council Chamber.

Be sure to see the portraits of Edmund Pendleton, John Robinson, and Patrick Henry in the Conference Room and the large painting of George Washington by the famous American artist Charles Willson Peale that hangs in the hallway.

The **Pasteur & Galt Apothecary Shop,** built in 1760, was the shop of physicians Dr. William Pasteur and his partner, Dr. John Galt. The shop is marked with the mortar-and-pestle sign of the apothecary and the snake-entwined staff of the physician. It contains exhibits of the ointments, herbs, medicines, and elixirs of the colonial period. The room at the rear contains the doctors' apparatus and surgical instruments. Behind the shop is an herb garden.

The **Raleigh Tavern,** a reconstruction on the north side of Duke of Gloucester Street, was named for Sir Walter Raleigh, who encouraged English settlement in North America and popularized the use of tobacco in Europe. Colonial taverns were places of public receptions, meetings, and dining. Among the prominent persons who dined or met at the Raleigh were George Washington, Peyton Randolph, John Marshall, Thomas Jefferson, and the Marquis de Lafayette.

At the **Raleigh Tavern Bakery,** bread and cakes made according to colonial recipes are sold.

The **Golden Ball** is a reconstruction of a jeweler's shop that stood on the site from 1727 to 1907. The shop was first owned by James Craig. Displays in the shop feature eighteenth-century jewelry and silver. Both eighteenth-century reproductions and contemporary jewelry can be purchased, including silver, pewter, and replicas of pieces in the Williamsburg collection. As in most of the craft buildings, a costumed artisan is at work.

Wetherburn's Tavern is located on property purchased by Henry

Wetherburn in 1738. The restored white frame building, used continuously for the past 200 years, has been variously a tavern, store, girls' school, guesthouse, and inn. The detailed inventory of Wetherburn's estate was used as a guide in furnishing it. Added information came from archaeological excavations of the site, which uncovered 192,000 artifacts such as glass, pottery, porcelain, and bottles. In addition to the Wetherburn family, twelve slaves lived and worked at the tavern. A kitchen, dairy, and garden are behind the tavern.

The **Printing Office** was owned in the eighteenth century by William Parks, publisher of the *Virginia Gazette,* which first appeared in 1736. Site excavations unearthed pieces of type, bookbinder's ornaments, and other artifacts related to printing. The site is the location of the **Printing Office, Post Office,** and **Bookbindery,** which are craft shops. Of particular interest are the demonstrations of the printing press and bookbinding.

The **Market Square Tavern,** at the intersection of Queen and Duke of Gloucester streets, is operated as a hostelry of the Williamsburg Inn. Among the tavern's famous guests were Thomas Jefferson and Patrick Henry. The tavern has an attractive garden planted with the trees, flowers, and herbs that were popular in the eighteenth century.

Chowning's Tavern, which was opened in 1766 by Josiah Chowning, is a reconstruction operated as an eighteenth-century tavern, or *ordinary.* It serves luncheons and dinners featuring such popular period fare as brunswick stew, Welsh rabbit, oysters, clams, and draft ale. Behind the tavern is a delightful garden shaded by an arbor of scuppernong grape vines.

The **Magazine,** a substantial red brick, octagonal building, is a well-known landmark. Erected in 1715 by Governor Alexander Spotswood, it was used as an arsenal for the weapons, powder, and ammunition needed to defend the colony. It now houses a display of weapons of the French and Indian wars, including flintlock muskets, the standard arms of British and colonial troops.

The **Courthouse,** built in 1770, was used by Williamsburg and James City County until 1932. The restored red brick T-shaped building features arched windows, a white octagonal cupola, and overhanging pediments. As the chief government agency in colonial Virginia, the county court had wide judicial and executive powers. Inside, costumed interpreters take the roles of judges, clerks, lawyers, and citizens as they reenact eighteenth-century legal proceedings.

The **James Geddy House and Foundry,** a two-story L-shaped structure, was built in 1760. From 1760 to 1777, it was home to James Geddy, one of Williamsburg's leading silversmiths. Today, it is used for craft displays and demonstrations and includes a collection of watches and watchmaker's tools. In the foundry behind the house, skilled craftsmen cast objects of bronze, brass, pewter, and silver.

The **Bruton Parish Church,** at the corner of Duke of Gloucester Street and Palace Green, has been used as a place of worship since 1715. During the colonial era, the Church of England, or Anglican church, was established as the official religion. Today, the Bruton Parish Church functions as an Episcopal church, the contemporary American descendant of the Anglican church. Arched doors and windows reflect the architectural style of Anglican churches of the eighteenth century. The west gallery was reserved for students from William and Mary. The churchyard contains tombstones marking the graves of members of the congregation who died during the colonial period.

Merchants Square, located between the restored area of Colonial Williamsburg and the campus of the College of William and Mary, is an attractive shopping and commercial area that complements the architectural style of the colonial city. More than thirty distinctive specialty shops offer antiques, books, gifts, clothing, souvenirs, and food.

The **College of William and Mary,** located at the western end of Duke of Gloucester Street, is one of America's oldest institutions of higher learning. Among its famous graduates were Thomas Jefferson and John Marshall. Through the efforts of the Reverend James Blair, Episcopal commissary for Virginia, a royal charter issued in 1693 authorized the establishment of the college. The first building was completed in 1700.

When it was first established, the College of William and Mary had the mission of seeing "that the Church of Virginia may be furnished with a seminary of ministers of the Gospel." However, the original religious objective was tempered. In 1779, the original classical curriculum and the three original departments of grammar, philosophy, and theology were broadened to include more modern subjects such as mathematics, science, law, and history; and the college began to prepare educated gentlemen to be lawyers, physicians, and politicians.

The **Wren Building** was named for Christopher Wren, the noted English architect whose style influenced its design. The building has been restored to its 1716 appearance.

The **Chapel** was built in 1732. Several prominent Virginians, including John and Peyton Randolph, are entombed in its crypt.

The **President's House,** built in 1733, continues to be the official residence of the college's presidents. The **Brafferton Indian School,** built in 1723, was used as a boarding school for young Indian boys during the colonial era.

Bassett Hall, an eighteenth-century house that was the Williamsburg home of Mr. and Mrs. John D. Rockefeller, Jr., looks as it did when the Rockefellers restored and furnished the house in the mid-twentieth century.

The **DeWitt Wallace Decorative Arts Gallery,** on Nassau Street, displays high-quality art objects, furniture, silver, ceramics, textiles, and paintings from the Williamsburg collection. The modern, 62,000-square-foot museum is entered through the lobby of the reconstructed **Public Hospital** of 1773, the last major public building of eighteenth-century Williamsburg to have been reconstructed. The hospital had burned in 1885. Heartrending exhibits focus on the evolution of beliefs about and treatment of mentally ill people. Both an eighteenth-century, prison-like cell and a nineteenth-century, patient's apartment can be viewed.

The **Public Gaol,** a restored exhibition building, is located on the north side of Nicholson Street. It was built under the supervision of Henry Cary and completed in 1704. Debtors' cells were added in 1711, and the keeper's quarters were added in 1722. It was used by the colony until 1780 and served as the city jail of Williamsburg until 1910. In 1933, it became part of Colonial Williamsburg.

Anthony Hay's Cabinetmaking Shop was purchased by Anthony Hay in 1756; the shop's addition was built around 1770. The reconstructed building houses an operating craft shop. The cabinetmakers use the cherry, walnut, and mahogany woods so popular in the eighteenth century to produce handmade furniture. Also, in the shop, musical instruments of the period such as harpsichords and guitars are handcrafted.

The **Peyton Randolph House** is the imposing home of the distinguished statesman who served both colonial Virginia and the early American Republic. From 1766 to 1775, Randolph was speaker of Virginia's House of Burgesses. He was elected president of the Continental Congress in 1774. The western section of the house was built by Sir John Randolph, Peyton Randolph's father, in 1715. In 1724, a one-and-a-half-story house next door was purchased; a middle two-story addition was then built to join the two houses.

Robertson's Windmill has been reconstructed. The mill's lower chamber contained machinery to screen and sack flour and meal; the upper chamber held the shaft and millstones that ground the grain. The mill was wind-powered, by sails lashed to wooden frames.

The **Brush-Everard House,** a restored frame town house, was built in 1717 by John Brush, a Williamsburg gunsmith and armorer, as his residence and shop. The property was purchased by William Dering, an artist and dancing master, in 1742. It was then owned by Thomas Everard, a politician who was auditor of Virginia and mayor of Williamsburg. Everard enlarged the house by adding two wings that formed a U-shaped design.

The reconstructed **Governor's Palace,** which resembles a Georgian-style English country manor, is a splendid structure that recalls the power and majesty of the British Empire. Designed by Henry Cary and completed in 1720, it was the residence and official headquarters of seven royal governors of Virginia until the outbreak of the American Revolution in 1775. It then served as the official mansion of the Commonwealth of Virginia's first two governors, Patrick Henry and Thomas Jefferson.

The palace was destroyed by fire in 1781. Reconstruction of the building, begun in 1931, was based on archaeological excavations, which unearthed the foundations, and research that included the use of Thomas Jefferson's 1779 floor plan, records of the House of Burgesses, and a copper plate of the palace found in the Bodleian Library at Oxford University.

A visit to the Governor's Palace is a delightful experience, especially for children, who come face to face with American history. A guide accompanies visitors through the palace where they may encounter the governor's staff—the clerk of the council, the butler, and household servants. On one of our visits, a youngster eagerly accepted the assignment of presenting a petition to the governor's secretary. Of particular interest is the first-floor entry hall, with its collection of firearms and swords.

The formally designed palace garden features both native American and European trees and plants. As in many of the Williamsburg gardens, holly and boxwood are prominent. Behind the palace is a kitchen, and a stable with a working wheelwright.

The **George Wythe House** is a restored exhibition building that was once the home of George Wythe (1726–1806), a leading scholar and lawyer. A member of the House of Burgesses, Wythe served as the colony's attorney general and was a signer of the Declaration of Independence. In 1779, he was appointed as professor of law at the College of William and Mary. Among his famous students were Thomas Jefferson and John Marshall, a chief justice of the U.S. Supreme Court whose landmark decisions established many of the precedents for the country's legal system.

The handsome brick house has four rooms and a wide central passage on each floor. Two chimneys are between the paired rooms so that all eight rooms have fireplaces.

The **garden and yard area** is the location of an **orchard** and such reconstructed frame dependencies as the **kitchen, laundry, smokehouse, stable,** and **chicken house.**

The **Abby Aldrich Rockefeller Folk Art Center** is a museum and gallery housing the folk art collection given to Colonial Williamsburg in 1939 by Mrs. John D. Rockefeller, Jr. The museum, built in 1957, reopened in 1992 after adding a new building with 19,000 square feet that tripled the exhibition space. With 3,000 folk art objects dating from the colonial period to the present, it is the nation's leading folk art collection. Included are portraits, landscapes, fraktur drawings, still life paintings, shop signs, weather vanes, pottery, metalware, quilts and coverlets, carvings, furniture, and toys.

Christiana Campbell's Tavern, on Waller Street, is a reconstructed early-eighteenth-century building now operated as a restaurant. It specializes in seafood, steaks, and colonial fare.

SIDE TRIPS

Eight miles east is **Carter's Grove Plantation,** an 800-acre estate with a 200-year-old mansion house. Built in 1754 and restored to the 1930s, the Georgian-style brick mansion consists of five connected sections. Nearby, a slave quarter of the 1700s has been reconstructed on its original site. Half the population of eighteenth-century Williamsburg was African American. Also at Carter's Grove is the Winthrop Rockefeller Archaeology Museum, a new subterranean museum. It explains the discovery of Martin's Hundred, a 1619 plantation on the James River, whose principal settlement, Wolstenholme Towne, was lost in 1622. The seventeenth-century English town has been partially reconstructed.

An eight-mile scenic country road that winds through woodlands, meadows, marshes, and streams, leads from Carter's Grove to the Historic Area.

Jamestown National Historic Site, on Jamestown Island south of Williamsburg, was the location of the first permanent English settlement in North America, founded in 1607. It was Virginia's capital until 1699 and is part of the historic triangle of tidewater Virginia that also includes Williamsburg and Yorktown.

An orientation film is shown in the Visitor Center. Archaeological excavations have uncovered building foundations as well as countless artifacts and burial grounds. A 1647 brick church tower is the only structure remaining above ground. Craftsmen demonstrate glassblowing in the Glasshouse. Open daily. Admission charged.

Jamestown has a state-operated **Festival Park,** with replicas of the first fort, an Indian dwelling, and the ships used to transport the colonists across the Atlantic. For further information, contact the Superintendent, Colonial National Historical Park, Yorktown 23690.

Yorktown was the scene of the last major battle of the American War for Independence. On October 19, 1781, British General Charles Cornwallis surrendered to General George Washington, commander of the Continental army. Earlier, in 1691, Yorktown was established as one of Virginia's four official ports; its major export was tobacco.

Colonial National Historical Park, administered by the National Park Service, consists of 4,500 acres, including the battlefield area. **Yorktown Battlefield and Visitors' Center** is open daily. You can drive the 7-mile **Battlefield Tour,** which includes **Moore House,** where the surrender terms were negotiated, and the 9-mile **Allied Encampment Tour,** which features **Washington's Headquarters** and the **French Cemetery.** Admission is free.

HARPERS FERRY NATIONAL HISTORICAL PARK

Restoration of a mid-nineteenth-century village; site of John Brown's raid; NR

Address: P.O. Box 65, Harpers Ferry, WV 25425
Telephone: (304) 535-6298
Location: In eastern West Virginia, at the Maryland, West Virginia, Virginia borders; 65 miles northwest of Washington, D.C.; 20 miles southwest of Frederick, Maryland, via US 340
Open: Visitor Center: daily, 8:00 A.M. to 5:00 P.M.; closed Christmas Day; historic buildings open only during summer months
Admission: Vehicles, $5.00; if walk-ins: $3.00 per person
Shops: Bookstore in Information Center
Facilities: Visitor Center; Information Center; shuttle buses; audio-visual presentation; guided tours; picnic areas

WHERE TO STAY

Inns/Bed & Breakfasts: Hillbrook, Rt. 2, Box 152, Summit Point Rd., Charles Town 25414, (304) 725-4223; Bavarian Inn & Lodge, Rt. 1, Box 30, Shepherdstown 25443, (304) 876-2551, FAX: (304) 876-9355; Thomas Shepherd Inn, P.O. Box 1162, 300 W. German St., Shepherdstown 25443, (304) 876-3715

Motels/Hotels: Cliffside Inn, Box 786, Harpers Ferry 25425, (304) 535-6302, (800) 782-9437; Comfort Inn, P.O. Box 980, Union St. & WV 340, Harpers Ferry 25425, (304) 535-6391, FAX: (304) 535-6395; Sheraton Inn, 301 Foxcroft Ave, Martinsburg 25401, (304) 267-5500, FAX: (609) 868-2920; Days Inn, 209 Viking Way, Martinsburg 25401, (304) 263-1800

Camping: Harpers Ferry Camp Resort, Rt. 3, Box 1300, Harpers Ferry, 25425, (304) 535-6895, (800) 323-8899; Gambrills State Park, Frederick, MD, (301) 473-8360; Lazy A Camping, Rt. 2, Box 165, Hedgesville 25427, (304) 229-8185

OVERVIEW

A place of natural beauty as well as history, Thomas Jefferson described the scene at Harpers Ferry as being "worth a voyage across the

Atlantic." Harpers Ferry gained national prominence because of its connection to John Brown, an abolitionist who seized the U.S. Arsenal at
Harpers Ferry in 1859.

In 1859, Harpers Ferry was a thriving industrial center. Many factories, powered by water, lined the river banks. Because of lack of economic
opportunity and repeated flooding, the town did not grow and prosper,
thus retaining much of its mid-nineteenth-century appearance. Now restored by the National Park Service as a National Historical Park, the
buildings are typically three-story brick or stone structures grouped closely
together on the river banks and rising picturesquely up steep High Street.
The restoration is to 1859, the year of John Brown's Raid. Exhibits and
interpretive presentations are organized around the themes of Industry,
John Brown, Civil War, African American History, and Natural History.

HISTORY

Harpers Ferry's location has contributed to its role in history. The
town is situated at the confluence of the Shenandoah and Potomac rivers
on a point of land where Virginia, Maryland, and West Virginia meet in
the Blue Ridge Mountains. Early-nineteenth-century buildings climb the
hills from the banks of gray and green merging waters. Steep tree-covered
cliffs look down on the town. Here is how Thomas Jefferson described
Harpers Ferry in his *Notes on the State of Virginia*:

> The passage of the Patowmac through the Blue Ridge is per-
> haps one of the most stupendous scenes in Nature. You stand on a
> very high point of land. On your right comes up the Shenandoah,
> having ranged along the foot of the mountain a hundred miles to
> seek a vent. On your left approaches the Patowmac in quest of a
> passage also. In the moment of their junction they rush together
> against the mountain, rend it asunder and pass off to the sea. The
> first glance of this scene hurries our senses into the opinion that this
> earth has been created in time, that the mountains were formed first,
> that the rivers began to flow afterwards, that in this place particularly
> they have been so dammed up by the Blue Ridge of mountains as to
> have formed an ocean which filled the whole valley; that, continuing
> to rise, they have at last broken over at this spot and have torn the
> mountain down from its summit to its base. The piles of rock on
> each hand, but particularly on the Shenandoah, the evidence marks
> of their disruptions and avulsions from their beds by the most power-
> ful agents in nature, corroborate the impression. But the distant fin-

ishing which nature has given the picture is of a very different character. It is a true contrast to the former. It is as placid and delightful as that is wild and tremendous. For the mountain being cloven asunder, she presents to your eye, through the cleft, a small catch of smooth, blue horizon, at an infinite distance in that plain country, inviting you, as it were, from the riot and tumult roaring around to pass through the breach and participate in the calm below. Here the eye ultimately composes itself; and that way, too, the road happens actually to lead. You cross the Patowmac above the junction, pass along its side through the base of the mountain for three miles, the terrible precipice hanging in fragments over you, and within about 20 miles reach Fredericktown and the fine country around that. This scene is worth a voyage across the Atlantic.

Thomas Jefferson, *Notes on the State of Virginia*, 1785

It was not its beauty but its economic opportunity that lured Peter Stephens, the first white settler, to the area in 1733. Stephens, who was a trader, operated a ferry across the river. In 1747, a millwright and architect named Robert Harper purchased Stephens's ferry operation. In 1763, the Virginia General Assembly established the town of "Shenandoah Falls at Mr. Harper's Ferry" and gave Harper the exclusive right to maintain a ferry across the Potomac River. This ferry continued to operate until 1824, when the Wager family, Harper's descendants, built a double wooden span across the river, which they operated as a toll bridge until 1839.

George Washington decided Harpers Ferry would be a good location for a second national armory. In 1796, the government purchased 118 acres from the Wager family, and construction of the U.S. Armory and Arsenal began in 1799. Muskets, rifles, and pistols were manufactured in the twenty workshops and offices that made up the U.S. Musket Factory, which was located along the Potomac. A privately owned company, Hall's Rifle Works, produced breech-loading rifles for the government. Hall's business occupied nine buildings along the Shenandoah River.

Harpers Ferry gradually became an industrial transportation center linking the east-west Potomac routes with the north-south routes. In 1833, the Chesapeake and Ohio Canal reached Harpers Ferry.

It was the U.S. Armory that drew John Brown to Harpers Ferry. Brown, a 59-year-old abolitionist, decided to arm an uprising of slaves. At midnight on Sunday, October 16, 1859, John Brown, leading eighteen men who called themselves the "Provisional Army of the United States," captured the bridge watchman, and crossed the covered bridge into

Harpers Ferry. Without resistance, the raiders seized the Shenandoah bridge, Hall's Rifle Works, and the Federal Arsenal, barricaded the B & O bridge across the Potomac, cut telegraph wires, and took prisoners—all in the space of two hours.

John Brown intended to set up a free-African American stronghold in the mountains of Maryland and Virginia. A native of Connecticut, he had studied military strategy in Europe. He intended to create an army of liberated African Americans who would forcefully end slavery.

After his initial success at Harpers Ferry, Brown's plans began to deteriorate. Brown's raiders stopped the 1:20 A.M. Baltimore train but then allowed it to go through. News of the raid spread quickly. Militia companies from Virginia and Maryland were sent to Harpers Ferry where they captured or killed several raiders. U.S. marines commanded by Colonel Robert E. Lee and Lieutenant J. E. B. Stuart, both of whom were destined to win fame as generals of the Confederacy, recaptured the Federal Armory on Tuesday, October 18. Brown and his remaining raiders, along with their hostages, had barricaded themselves in the Armory's fire engine house, and were soon captured.

When it was all over, ten raiders had been killed, five were captured, and four escaped. Four townspeople, one marine, and a free African American named Heyward Shephard were dead. Shephard was the baggagemaster on duty at the train station the night of the raid. When he tried to investigate the unusual commotion outside, he was shot. Ironically, the first victim of John Brown's violent attempt to free slaves was a free African American.

Brown was tried and found guilty of murder, treason, and conspiring with slaves to cause insurrection. He was hanged at nearby Charles Town on December 2, 1859. Although Brown's unsuccessful raid did not free any slaves except those set free in the will of the murdered town's mayor, the widely publicized event dramatized the strong and divergent positions on the slavery issue that would lead to the Civil War.

On the day of his execution, Brown wrote, "I, John Brown, am now quite certain that the crimes of the guilty land will never be purged away but with blood. I had, as I now think, vainly flattered myself that without very much bloodshed it might be done." Less than a year and a half later, the Civil War began. Union armies marched off to face their Confederate adversaries singing the verse, "John Brown's body lies a moldering in the grave but his soul goes marching on."

Harpers Ferry's position was considered geographically strategic to both the Union and the Confederacy. Struggles to occupy the town and control the railroads were continuous and resulted in the town being passed back and forth between the two occupying forces several times.

When the Civil War began, Harpers Ferry was in Virginia; it was only later that West Virginia seceded from Virginia and became a state in 1863. On the day that Virginia seceded from the Union, April 17, 1861, the Armory became an immediate military target. When several companies of Virginia militia started marching toward the 100 Union troops guarding the Armory, Lieutenant Roger Jones decided to torch the Armory and Arsenal, burning some 15,000 arms by the time the Virginia militia entered the town. Confederate troops were able to confiscate and ship to Richmond the Armory's ordinance stock, machinery, and tools. When they withdrew in June, the Confederates burned the remaining Armory buildings.

Constant military occupation and loss of employment at the Arsenal left Harpers Ferry in ruins, physically and economically. Devastating floods in the late 1800s added to the demise of the once flourishing industrial town.

Harpers Ferry is now part of a national historical park operated by the National Park Service. The town has been restored to the way it was in 1859, when John Brown made his midnight raid.

TOUR

A new **Visitor Center** has been built outside the historic area. From there, you can board a shuttle bus into the lower town.

The **Stagecoach Inn** on Shenandoah Street is a two-and-a-half-story inn built in 1826 as a private residence but was operated as an inn by Major James Stephenson from 1830 to 1837. During the Civil War, the building was used by the federal government as a military warehouse and quarters for troops. It is now used as an information center and a bookstore.

Shenandoah Street had been part of the Charles Town & Smithfield Turnpike Co.'s toll road in the 1830s. The street has been restored to its 1833 macadamized finish, which consists of small broken stones compacted into a solid layer.

On Shenandoah Street are the **Provost Office** and a **Dry Goods Store** in an 1812 building that was used as quarters for the master armorer until 1858. The 1858 brick building next door was to be the new quarters for the master armorer. However, it was occupied by John E. P. Daingerfield, the paymaster's clerk at the time of the raid, and Daingerfield was taken hostage. The building is now a gun museum with exhibits on the history of gunmaking.

The **John Brown Museum** in another 1839 building focuses on the story of John Brown and his raiders. A movie on the raid is also shown here.

Across from the museums is **Arsenal Square,** where the foundations of two of the original buildings have been excavated. The buildings were burned in 1861, at the start of the Civil War.

John Brown's Fort is the ironic name given to the small, one-story 1848 Armory fire engine house and watchman's office. During the raid, Brown originally held hostages here. Later, he and his followers barricaded themselves there. When the marines' demand for surrender was turned down by Brown, they battered down the engine house door and took the raiders captive. The engine house was the only Armory building to survive the Civil War. In 1891, it was displayed at the Chicago World's Fair, where it met with little interest. It was returned to Harpers Ferry and placed at various locations until 1968, when the National Park Service moved it to its present location on Shenandoah Street, not far from its original location on Potomac Street.

Walk to the **Point,** where you can see the Shenandoah and the Potomac Rivers actually merge their green and gray waters. Then standing in West Virginia, you'll see Maryland on one side and Virginia beyond the ridge on the other.

Armory employees relaxed over a drink in the 1839 **Whitehall Tavern** on Potomac Street. In the **Confectionary** on High Street, built in 1845 and enlarged later, townspeople could buy Frederick A. Roeder's breads, cakes, and rolls.

The **Civil War Museum** focuses on the war's effect on Harpers Ferry. Constant troop movements, battles to occupy the strategic town, shellings from the bulwarks on nearby cliffs, occupation or burning of buildings, all combined to wreak havoc on the once prosperous town.

The **Black History Exhibit** focuses on the African American struggle to gain freedom.

Harper House, a stone house built on the side of a hill, is the oldest house in town. Robert Harper began building the house in 1775, but the Revolutionary War delayed completion until 1782. Unfortunately, Harper died that year without ever occupying it. The house was used as the town's tavern until 1803 and served such prominent guests as George Washington and Thomas Jefferson. It is restored as a tenant house of the 1850s with families living in crowded conditions on each level.

Stone steps, cut out of rock at the turn of the nineteenth century, lead to **St. Peter's Catholic Church,** which was built in the 1830s, and the ruins of **St. John's Episcopal Church,** which was built in 1852 and served as both a Confederate barracks and as a hospital during the Civil War.

Jefferson Rock is the shale rock where Thomas Jefferson is said to have stood in October 1783 while admiring the view he described in his *Notes on the State of Virginia.*

A footbridge leads to **Virginius Island,** a thirteen-acre island in the Shenandoah River that was a thriving industrial area in the 1800s. At the time of John Brown's raid, water supplied the power to a cotton factory, flour mill, saw mill, machine shop, iron foundry, and a blacksmith shop. Flooding was a continual problem and industry was especially hurt by the devastating flood of 1870. Now, only ruins remain in the heavily forested area.

At Harpers Ferry, the restoration and the town flow into each other. Most of the restored buildings are in the **Lower Town.** Buildings along High Street are historically and architecturally similar to restored buildings but are privately owned and used as businesses.

In the **Upper Town** near Filmore Street are a cluster of restored brick buildings built in the mid-1850s for armory officials, including the superintendent and the paymaster, and their clerks. Unused armory dwellings became campus buildings of Storer College, a normal school for the education of free African Americans. The college remained in operation until 1955. Now the buildings are used as a training center for National Park Service employees.

Harpers Ferry National Historical Park includes large tracts of land along the rivers. There are marked hiking trails in all areas, and we chose to hike in Maryland Heights because of the Civil War ruins and batteries along the trail. A magnificent view of Harpers Ferry and the converging rivers from Overlook Cliff, a sheer shale cliff, is well worth the climb.

Loudoun Heights, another part of the park, also figured in Civil War battles. The 2,000-mile Appalachian Trail, which extends from Maine to Georgia, runs through Loudoun Heights.

SIDE TRIPS

Antietam Battlefield, maintained by the National Park Service, is just across the state line in Sharpsburg, Maryland. It was the site of a major Civil War battle. On September 17, 1862, General Robert E. Lee invaded the North, pitting 41,000 Confederate troops against the 87,000 Union troops under General George B. McClellan. Intense fighting resulted in Union losses of 12,410 and Confederate losses of 10,700; it has been called the bloodiest day of the Civil War. Although the battle was not decisive, it was considered a strategic victory for the Union because the Confederate troops withdrew. British aid to the Confederates was withheld pending the outcome of this battle. The Visitors' Center is open daily, 8:30 A.M. to 6:00 P.M., June to August; to 5:00 P.M., rest of year. Antietam Battlefield is located north of Sharpsburg, on Route 65. For information, write to P.O. Box 158, Sharpsburg, MD 21782; (301) 432-5124. Admission charged.

Hikers and bikers can take the **C & O towpath** along the banks of the canal in the **Chesapeake and Ohio Canal National Historical Park.** The construction of the Chesapeake & Ohio Canal, which was supposed to provide an economical shipping route from Georgetown to Pittsburgh, was begun in 1828 and ended in the 1850s, when it had reached Cumberland, Maryland, a distance of 185 miles. The National Park Service maintains the towpath and walk-in campgrounds along the route. The campground at Sharpsburg, with thirty tent sites, is open all year. The address for all the campgrounds maintained by the park is P.O. Box 4, Sharpsburg, MD 21782. For information, telephone (301) 739-4200.

Historic
Fayette Townsite

WISCONSIN

MICHIGAN

Old World
Wisconsin

Henry Ford Museum
& Greenfield Village

Pendarvis

Amana
Colonies

NEBRASKA

IOWA

Hale Farm
and Village

Zoar Village SM

Stuhr Museum
of the Prairie Pioneer

Bishop
Hill

Harold Warp
Pioneer Village

INDIANA

OHIO

Nauvoo

ILLINOIS

Conner
Prairie

Lincoln's
New Salem

Historic
New Harmony

MIDWEST

ILLINOIS
Bishop Hill
Nauvoo
Lincoln's New Salem, Petersburg

INDIANA
Historic New Harmony, New Harmony
Conner Prairie, Noblesville

IOWA
Amana Colonies, Amana

MICHIGAN
Henry Ford Museum & Greenfield Village, Dearborn
Historic Fayette Townsite, Garden

NEBRASKA
Stuhr Museum of the Prairie Pioneer, Grand Island
Harold Warp Pioneer Village, Minden

OHIO
Hale Farm and Village, Bath
Zoar Village State Memorial, Zoar

WISCONSIN
Old World Wisconsin, Eagle
Pendarvis, Mineral Point

BISHOP HILL

**Restoration of an 1846–1861 Swedish religious commune;
State Historic Site; NR, NHL**

Address: Bishop Hill Heritage Association, P.O. Box 1853, Bishop Hill,
IL 61419; and/or Site Superintendent, P.O. Box D, Bishop Hill, IL
61419

Telephone: (309) 927-3899; (309) 927-3345

Location: In western Illinois, 157 miles west of Chicago; 17 miles east of
I-74; 20 miles south of I-80; 2 miles north of US 34

Open: Heritage Museum: daily, 10:00 A.M. to 4:00 P.M., April to December; Colony Church, Colony Hotel, and Bishop Hill Museum: daily,
9:00 A.M. to 5:00 P.M., closed Thanksgiving, Christmas, and New
Year's Day; hours may vary in winter

Admission: Heritage Museum: adults, $1.00; children, $.50; Colony
Church, Colony Hotel, Bishop Hill Museum: free

Restaurants: The Red Oak; PL Johnson's Dining Room

Shops: The Colony Woodshed; The Prairie Workshop; The Red Oak;
Bishop Hill Colony Store; Antik Affar; Village Smithy Gift Shop;
Hintze Pottery, Friends Weave, Prairie Paperworks and The Clothier
in Colony Blacksmith Shop

Facilities: Visitors Center with orientation film; special events

WHERE TO STAY

Inns/Bed & Breakfasts: Holden's Guest House, Bishop Hill 61419, (309)
927-3500

Motels/Hotels: Kewanee Motor Lodge, 400 S. Main St., Kewanee 61443,
(309) 853-4000; Jumer's Continental Inn, E. Main St. at I-74, Galesburg 61401, (309) 343-7151, (800) 285-8637, FAX: (309) 343-7151,
ext. 264; Ramada Inn, 29 Public Sq., Galesburg 61401, (309) 343-
9161, FAX: (309) 343-0157

Camping: Johnson Sauk Trail State Park, RR 3, Kewanee 61443, (309)
853-5589; The Timber, Rt. 2, Cambridge 61238, (309) 937-2314

OVERVIEW

Bishop Hill was a religious commune founded in 1846 by Swedish
immigrants under the leadership of Erik Jansson, a highly charismatic man
who attracted many followers. While in Sweden, Jansson condemned the
religious literature of the Lutheran Church, and he and his followers pub-

licly burned those books. This put them into direct conflict with both Sweden's religious and civil authorities; Jansson was arrested and imprisoned.

The freedom of worship guaranteed by the United States Constitution appealed to the persecuted Janssonists. Olof Olsson, sent to find suitable land in America, selected a site on the Illinois prairie. Adopting a communal lifestyle, the Janssonists sold their property and pooled their resources. Between 1846 and 1854, 1,500 followers of Jansson sailed from Sweden to the United States to participate in the religious commune in Bishop Hill, Illinois. From initial hardship they developed economic success through farming, orchards, a tannery, and mills. Many large buildings were constructed in Bishop Hill to accommodate the communal lifestyle. The religious colony lasted until 1861, when it was dissolved because of dissension among the members.

Bishop Hill is not an outdoor museum but a living town of approximately 140 people that has changed little since the 1850s. No appreciable expansion or construction has marred the mid-nineteenth-century atmosphere. Although some colony buildings are no longer standing, thirteen original buildings remain. Some are museums or shops; the others are privately owned and not open to the public. There are no reconstructions.

HISTORY

The story of Bishop Hill, founded in 1846 as a commune by 800 immigrants, began in Sweden with the charismatic religious leader Erik Jansson. In 1830, at age twenty-two, Jansson, who was a farmer, suffered a severe attack of rheumatism while tilling his fields. He prayed for and received healing and regarded his cure as a miraculous sign from God and became a lay preacher.

In the early 1840s, Jansson joined the Reader, or Lasare, movement established by Olof and Jonas Olsson. Readers were Fundamentalists who dissented from the formalism of Sweden's Lutheran church. Jansson became a leader of a pietistical group that conducted clandestine prayer meetings. His followers regarded him as a second Christ. They believed that the Bible was the only book that had religious authority. Janssonists attempted unsuccessfully to change the Lutheran church's position on religious books but eventually resorted to burning Lutheran literature, for which Jansson was arrested.

While being transported to prison in 1845, Jansson escaped, and he and his family began their journey to America. After a three-month ocean voyage, a trip across the Great Lakes, and a 150-mile trek on foot from

Bishop Hill, Illinois
The 1848 Colony Church, a three-story white frame gambrel-roofed building, was the first permanent building in the Swedish religious community. Colonists both lived and worshiped in the dual-purpose structure at Bishop Hill, IL.

Photo by Patricia A. Gutek

Chicago, Jansson and a group of 400 Swedish immigrants arrived at Bishop Hill, a community previously established, at Jansson's direction, by Olof Olsson. It was named after Biskopskulla, Sweden, where Jansson was born.

The Janssonists settled into dugout living quarters. These shelters, half cave and half timber, were built into the side of a ravine that ran through the town. Worship services were conducted in a tent. Ninety-six colonists died that first winter because of exposure and lack of food.

However, crops were planted in the spring, and a brick kiln was built in which adobe bricks were made for construction of a diversity of permanent buildings.

Approximately 1,500 immigrants left Sweden for Bishop Hill between 1846 and 1854. Many died en route or fell victim to epidemics. Others later became dissatisfied and moved to nearby towns. Approximately 1,100 Janssonists lived in Bishop Hill between 1846 and 1861, although the population never exceeded 800 at any one time. The Janssonists represented a cross section of the Swedish population: blacksmiths, tailors, shoemakers, weavers, tanners, carpenters, farmers, and servants.

Fifteen landowners in Sweden sold their large farms and contributed the money, as all the colonists did, to the communal fund to transport Janssonists to America. Although some left husbands and wives behind, great efforts were made to bring as many relatives as possible to America.

Erik Jansson supervised all activities in the colony. But in 1850, he was murdered by John Root, the husband of his cousin Charlotta. Root wanted to leave Bishop Hill with his wife and son, but their marriage contract stated that if he left, his wife would not have to go with him. Root made several attempts to force his wife and child to accompany him, but Jansson sent men to return Charlotta and her son to Bishop Hill. On May 13, 1850, when Jansson was in Cambridge, Illinois, attending to court cases involving the colony, Root shot him through a window of the courthouse.

After Jansson's murder, the religious leadership of the colony fell to Jonas Olsson. Seven governing trustees were selected, and in 1854, the colony was legally incorporated. Rapid economic growth followed. The colony's landholdings were 12,000 to 14,000 fertile, well-watered acres. Business prospered as the Janssonists sold such products as cloth, clothing, wagons, harnesses, saddles, shoes, furniture, and broomcorn to a growing frontier population. Between 1848 and 1861, Bishop Hill was a major center of commerce and the overnight stage stop between Rock Island and Peoria.

Eventually, dissension arose over religious and social issues; and despite economic prosperity, the colony was dissolved by mutual consent in 1861. Property was divided among the members, many of whom continued to live in the area. Most of today's residents of Bishop Hill and its vicinity are descendants of original colonists or later Swedish immigrants.

In 1947, Bishop Hill became an Illinois State Memorial and is now a National Historic Landmark and a State Historic Site. The Illinois Historic Preservation Agency owns and maintains the Colony Church, Colony Hotel, Village Park, and the Bishop Hill Museum. The Bishop Hill Heritage Association, a non-profit corporation interested in preservation, owns six of the original colony buildings and two post-colony buildings.

TOUR

The **Colony Church** (1848), Bishop Hill's first permanent building, was a dual-purpose structure. Community members both worshiped and lived there. The church is a three-story, white frame, gambrel-roofed building. Two sets of outside stairs lead to the second-floor sanctuary, which is beautifully but simply designed. Pale blue walls contrast with pews made of native black walnut and turned maple rungs. The pulpit panels were painted to resemble marble. A center divider separates the men's pews on the west side and the women's and children's pews on the east. The wood and wrought-iron chandeliers, whose design was inspired by the brass chandeliers found in Swedish cathedrals, are reproductions. The unheated sanctuary, which could seat 1,000 people, was used twice each weekday and three times on Sunday for services that lasted two hours or more.

On the first floor and in the basement were twenty dwelling rooms, ten on each floor. Each family had one room, which served primarily as a sleeping room; the cooking, laundry, and bathing were done in other buildings.

The colony church was restored to its 1848 appearance in the 1960s. The sleeping rooms now contain exhibits. **The Sweden They Left** depicts life in Sweden around 1850. Another room focuses on **The Immigration** and the route taken from Sweden to Illinois. Also displayed are items brought from Sweden by the colonists, including shoes, baskets, wooden and metal boxes, pots, Bibles, coins, and photographs of their homes in Sweden.

Another room displays tools used by the colonists and drums, uniforms, and weapons from Company D Fifty-seventh Illinois Infantry, the company Bishop Hill residents served in during the Civil War. Still another exhibit is devoted to the construction process used in building the colony church.

An extensive collection of paintings by Olaf Krans (1838–1916), exhibited in the **Bishop Hill Heritage Museum,** is one of the outstanding features of Bishop Hill. Krans emigrated from Sweden in 1850 at the age of twelve. This important American primitive painter's subjects were the founders, buildings, landscapes, and pioneer farming practices of Bishop Hill; the scenes were based on his childhood memories. He began the paintings in 1875 and presented the collection of nearly 100 paintings to the village in 1896 at its fiftieth-anniversary observance.

One distinctive though unsettling feature of Krans's portraits, most of which were based on turn-of-the-century photographs, are the subjects' pale blue eyes, which seem to follow the viewer as she or he moves through the room. The bearded, unsmiling men are usually dressed in black suits and white shirts, and the women wear dark dresses. The paintings are appreciated not only for their artistic beauty but also for their rendering of life in the colony during its relatively short existence.

The **Bjorklund Hotel** was built in 1852 as a two-story brick residence but was converted to a hotel when Bishop Hill became the overnight stop on the stage route between Peoria and Rock Island. A series of additions began in 1857. The first were a barroom on the first floor and the hotelkeeper's quarters on the second. Next, a kitchen and second-story quarters were added, making the building U-shaped. A third floor that included a ballroom and a large tower was the last addition.

The hotel was owned by the colony and managed by a noted clockmaker, Sven Bjorklund. In 1861, when the communal period of Bishop Hill ended, Bjorklund became the owner of the hotel, which he operated until his death. The Bjorklund family ran the hotel until the 1920s, when it was converted into a private residence.

The hotel's first floor and a bedroom on the second floor are open to the public. A clock made by Bjorklund still keeps time in the men's sitting room. Other furnishings include an original cherry table, beds, and a bureau. The kitchen has a bake oven with a forty-loaf capacity, a dry sink, a cupboard with white dishes, cooking utensils, and coffee bean roasters. Baskets, pottery, jars, and wooden boxes are on display in the pantry.

The **Steeple Building** was built in 1854 as a hotel but came to be used as a residence for colonists. This three-story Greek Revival brick structure is stuccoed on three sides. A classical portico dominates the facade, and there is a two-story octagonal wooden cupola. The clock, which was built by Sven Bjorklund, Lars Soderquist, and P. O. Blomberg, has four faces, each with one hand that marks the hours only.

The **Steeple Building** houses the **Bishop Hill Heritage Museum** which has exhibits on the immigration of Swedish people to America, lighting, textiles, clocks and watches, furniture, wood stoves, and brooms, as well as the Archives and Research Library for the Bishop Hill Heritage Association. It also serves as the visitors center and an orientation film is shown.

The **Colony Store** was the center of the colony's commerce with its neighbors. It sold shoes, clothes, cloth, liquor, medicine, lumber, wagons, and harnesses and provided millwork, grain grinding, and blacksmithing. Today, the store sells Swedish imports, Bishop Hill craft items, and books about the colony.

The **Blacksmith Shop** was built in 1857, at a time when trade and industry were becoming increasingly important. Blacksmiths made hardware for wagons, and a ramp at the back of the building led to the area where the wagons were assembled. The wagons were then lowered down the ramp and taken to the carpentry and paint shops.

The blacksmith shop is now a craft center with handmade items for sale, including handwoven shawls, blankets, and coverlets. Hand-thrown pottery and brooms are available in the 1882 Poppy Barn owned by the Heritage Association, while baskets and wooden objects are found in the Cobbler Shop. The carpenter and paint shop, built in 1852, is now a small grocery store and post office.

In the **Bishop Hill Cemetery,** a white marble monument marks Erik Jansson's grave. The ninety-six colonists who died during the first winter are buried in Red Oak Cemetery three miles west of town. The site of the dugouts is along the upper edge of the ravine that extends northwest at the north end of Park Street.

Special events at Bishop Hill include Spring Premier in April, Counted Cross-Stitch and Quilt Shows in May, Sundays in the Park Concerts in June, an Antique Show in July, Summer Market in August, Old Settlers Day in September, *Jordbruksdagarna* (Agricultural Days) in September, Art Show in September, *Julmarknad* (Christmas Market) in late November and early December, Lucia Nights (Festival of Lights) in mid-December, and *Julotta* (nondenominational candlelight service) on Christmas Day.

SIDE TRIPS

Carl Sandburg Birthplace, a State Historic Site, is the restored frame cottage where the Pulitzer Prize-winning poet and Lincoln biographer was born in 1878. The home is furnished with many Sandburg family items. Located behind the house is Remembrance Rock, where Sandburg's ashes were placed after his death in 1967. Open Tuesday to Sunday. Free. 313 E. Third, Galesburg, IL 61401, (309) 342-2361.

Nauvoo

Restoration of an 1830–1850 Mormon town; State Historic Site; NR, NHL, HABS

Address: Nauvoo Restoration Inc., P.O. Box 215, Nauvoo, IL 62354
Telephone: (217) 453-2237
Open: Daily, 9:00 A.M. to 5:00 P.M.
Admission: Free
Facilities: Visitors' Center with orientation film and Monument to Women sculpture garden; twenty restored buildings; temple site; *City of Joseph* Pageant; Christmas festival; musicals; free guided tours; carriage rides

Address: Joseph Smith Historic Center, P.O. Box 338, Nauvoo, IL 62354
Telephone: (217) 453-2246
Open: Monday to Saturday, 8:00 A.M. to 7:00 P.M., Sunday, 1:00 P.M. to 7:00 P.M., Memorial Day to Labor Day; Monday to Saturday, 9:00 A.M. to 5:00 P.M., Sunday, 1:00 P.M. to 5:00 P.M., rest of year
Admission: Free
Facilities: Visitor Center with orientation film, museum exhibits and gift and book shop; restored Smith Mansion House, Smith Homestead, Nauvoo House, Red Brick Store; Grave Site; guided tours
Location: In western Illinois on the Mississippi River, on Rt. 96, 185 miles north of St. Louis and 250 miles southwest of Chicago
Restaurants: In town of Nauvoo: Hotel Nauvoo Restaurant
Shops: Book and gift shop in Visitor Center of Joseph Smith Historic Center; Red Brick Store; antique and craft stores in town

Where to Stay

Inns/Bed & Breakfasts: Hotel Nauvoo, Box 398, Nauvoo 62354, (217) 453-2211; Mississippi Memories B&B, Box 291, Riverview Heights, Nauvoo 62354, (217) 453-2771; Ancient Pines B&B, Nauvoo 62354, (217) 453-2767; Ed-Harri-Mere B&B, (217) 453-2796; Ortman B&B, Nauvoo 62354, (217) 453-2249; Parley Lane B&B, (217) 453-2277
Motels/Hotels: Motel Nauvoo, Box 272, 150 N. Warsaw St., Nauvoo 62354, (217) 453-2219; Village Inn Motel, Box 191, 1350 Parley St., Nauvoo 62354, (217) 453-6634
Camping: Nauvoo State Park, P.O. Box 337, Nauvoo 62354, (217) 453-

2512; Breezewood Campground, (217) 453-6420; Camp Nauvoo, (217) 453-6404

OVERVIEW

As a historic restoration, Nauvoo is one of the nation's finest; it has been called the Williamsburg of the Midwest. Located on the east bank of the Mississippi River, Nauvoo's wooded bluffs offer a panoramic view to the traveler. Nauvoo's fame comes from its being a holy city, associated with Joseph Smith, founder of the Church of Jesus Christ of Latter-day Saints, known informally as the Mormons. The Latter-day Saints arrived in Nauvoo in 1839, plotted a city, built 2,500 log, frame, and brick houses, grew to a population of 20,000 and then abandoned the city after Smith's death in 1846. Split over the issue of succession, most Mormons followed Brigham Young west to the Utah territory while the smaller group eventually settled in Independence, Missouri.

Nauvoo Restoration, Inc., sponsored by the Church of Jesus Christ of Latter-day Saints, headquartered in Salt Lake City, and the Restoration Trail Foundation, sponsored by the Reorganized Church of Jesus Christ of Latter Day Saints of Independence, Missouri, have both participated in the restoration of the mid-nineteenth-century town with each having their own visitors center and historic properties. Only a small percentage of the original buildings from the 1840s still stand and are restored; large sections of land in the city are vacant.

Although Nauvoo's foremost historical significance is its relationship to Joseph Smith and the Church of Jesus Christ of Latter-day Saints, the town was also the scene of a later experiment in communal living by the Icarians, a group of French immigrants led by Etienne Cabet. In addition to being the scene of a significant restoration, today Nauvoo is an active small town with a population of about one thousand people.

HISTORY

An understanding of Nauvoo's importance in both American and religious history begins with its relationship to Joseph Smith, the founder and prophet of the Church of Jesus Christ of Latter-day Saints. Smith, a farmer's son, was born at Sharon, Vermont, on December 23, 1805. In 1819, the Smith family relocated to Manchester, near Palmyra, in New York. There Joseph experienced a series of divine communications that led eventually to the establishment of the church. It was in this area of New York that Smith, according to Mormon tradition, found the golden plates on the Hill Cumorah that he translated into the *Book of Mormon*. Smith

Nauvoo, Illinois

An interpreter sets type in the restored 1842 Print Shop from which the *Nauvoo Neighbor* and *Times and Seasons* were printed. From 1830 to 1850 Nauvoo was the home of the Church of Jesus Christ of Latter-day Saints founder, Joseph Smith, and his followers. At Nauvoo, IL.

Photo by Patricia A. Gutek

and his followers formally organized as the Church of Jesus Christ of Latter-day Saints on April 6, 1830, at Fayette, New York.

From 1831 until they purchased Nauvoo in 1839, the Saints, who faced hostility because of their doctrines, relocated several times. In their quest to establish the New Jerusalem, they first went to Kirtland, Ohio, in 1831. Six years later, in 1837, they migrated to Jackson County, Missouri, where they again faced opposition. In 1839, the Latter-day Saints came to the small Mississippi River town of Commerce, Illinois. They purchased land, drained the swamps, and called their new holy city Nauvoo (Hebrew for "the beautiful place").

In 1840, the Illinois legislature passed the Nauvoo charter, which gave the community virtual home rule. Smith, a skilled administrator as well as charismatic religious leader, organized an autonomous theocratic state within a state, with its own government, militia, school system, and university. Under his leadership, the Latter-day Saints created a prosperous community of 12,000 inhabitants, making Nauvoo Illinois's largest city at that time. Homes, shops, schools, a newspaper, and a temple were built as the religious group once again tried to establish their New Jerusalem. Nauvoo's growing political power and economic prosperity, as well as opposition to the Mormon practice of polygamy, ultimately provoked tension between the Mormons and the residents of the surrounding communities.

As tensions grew in western Illinois, Governor Thomas Ford ordered the Illinois militia to place Smith and his brother Hyrum in protective custody in the jail in nearby Carthage. On June 27, 1844, a mob stormed the jail and killed the brothers.

With the death of Smith, the majority of the Mormons, now led by Brigham Young, left Nauvoo to begin their arduous westward trek to Utah, where they founded Salt Lake City in 1847. An estimated 10,000 Latter-day Saints were part of this mass migration, one of the largest and most carefully planned in American history, into the territories west of the Mississippi.

When we visited Nauvoo, we met many people who had come to Nauvoo from Utah and Idaho to visit the city left by their ancestors. Many tour guides are Mormons, often retired couples who are spending some time in residence in Nauvoo as part of their service to the church.

The Reorganized Church of Jesus Christ of Latter Day Saints rejected Brigham Young's election as leader. The Reorganized church, which has its headquarters in Independence, Missouri, recognizes only direct descendants of Joseph Smith as presidents of the church. Thus, the first successor was Smith's son, Joseph Smith III. The Reorganized church maintains several sites at Nauvoo, distinct from those maintained by the larger church.

Although the physical remnants of the Icarians are few, their effort to found a communal society at Nauvoo is also a fascinating episode in American history. Led by the French political philosopher and utopian theorist Etienne Cabet, 260 persons from France and several other European countries came to Nauvoo in 1849 to establish a communal and egalitarian society. Their name, Icarians, came from the utopia that Cabet had described in his novel *Voyage to Icaria*. Although the Icarian experiment ended in 1860, descendants of the Icarians still live in Nauvoo.

Nauvoo's restoration began in the late 1950s with the efforts of Dr. James LeRoy Kimball, who restored the home of Heber C. Kimball, his great-grandfather. Dr. Kimball then got the Utah-based church involved in the project.

Most of the work has been done by Nauvoo Restoration, Inc., sponsored by the Church of Jesus Christ of Latter-day Saints, with headquarters in Salt Lake City, Utah. The state of Illinois purchased a 148-acre tract, now Nauvoo State Historic Site, to encourage further restoration.

TOUR

Nauvoo Restoration Inc. maintains a Visitors Center, the temple site, and twenty restored or reconstructed buildings. Costumed interpreters in every building narrate the history of the house and its occupants. Craft demonstrations are presented in many shops. You need two days to see all the restored buildings in Nauvoo which are spread over a fairly large area. You can walk, travel in your own car, or hop on the horse-drawn wagon.

The **Nauvoo Visitors' Center** is a large, red-brick building overlooking a sculpture garden. An audiovisual program and a scale model of Nauvoo in 1846 provide an excellent orientation to the historic site and its significance in Mormon and American history. Dedicated to women, the **Monument to Women sculpture garden** is a two-acre park featuring a heroic central sculpture of a woman and twelve life-size figures depicting women's roles in society. The Female Relief Society, associated with Emma Smith, Joseph's wife, was an important service organization in the church. The sculptures, the work of Florence Peterson Hansen and Dennis Smith, were done in the early 1970s.

The Nauvoo **Temple Site** (1841–1865), a well-landscaped four-acre park, contains the excavated ruins of the Nauvoo Temple. Excavated in 1962 by Southern Illinois University, the site illustrates the role of archaeology in restoration. Paintings of the temple, as well as a model, reveal a design of native gray limestone that incorporated classical, medieval, Renaissance, and nineteenth-century styles. Among its unique external features were large "moon stones" at the base and "sun stones" at the top of its thirty pilasters. One of the sun stones is located on the temple site. The temple was topped by a tower, belfry, observatory, and spire.

Construction began in April 1841, and the temple was dedicated on May 1, 1846. By that time, many Latter-day Saints had already departed. On October 9, 1848, a fire caused extensive damage to the temple. It was used by the Icarians from 1849 until 1850, when a tornado toppled the north wall. The building was later razed.

The **Seventies Hall** was reconstructed by Nauvoo Restoration, Inc., which, through archaeological excavation, uncovered the foundations of the original 1844 building. The hall was designed as an educational center for the *seventies*, laymen in the church who carry on missionary activities. The first floor was used for classes and lectures; the second, for offices, a museum, and library. The hall was sold in 1846 and used as a school from 1866 to 1895; it was demolished in 1915.

The two-story brick **Noble-Smith House** (1843), restored to its original condition by Nauvoo Restoration, Inc., was the home of Joseph Bates Noble until 1846 and then of Lucy Mack Smith, the mother of Joseph Smith.

The **Brigham Young Site and Residence** was the home of Brigham Young (1801–1877) from 1840 to 1845. Like many of the Mormons, Young was born in the East (Vermont) and, upon joining the church, followed Smith westward in the moves that eventually led to Nauvoo. Young had worked in the construction trade before his conversion and was a skilled builder and carpenter. Evidence of his craftsmanship can be seen in his house. After living in a log structure, Young completed the two-story brick house in 1843. During the summer of 1844, two wings, each one story high, were added. The east wing, which served as Young's office, was the place where many crucial decisions were made about the future of the church, especially the decision to move westward. Although the furniture and household items are not those of the Young family, they are authentic to Nauvoo's Mormon period. The outbuildings were reconstructed on their original foundations. The trees and plants are those of a typical 1840s garden.

The **Heber C. Kimball Home** is the restored 1845 residence of Heber Chase Kimball (1801–1868), a church leader, missionary to England, and chief advisor to Brigham Young. Kimball, a migrant from the East, had tastes that were sophisticated for frontier Illinois. His house, in the then-popular Federal style, was constructed of brick in the intricate flemish bond pattern.

The **Jonathan Browning Houses and Workshops** are the residence and factory of one of America's most innovative firearm manufacturers. Jonathan Browning learned his gun making and repairing skills as a youth in Kentucky, Tennessee, and Illinois. He developed multishot, repeating guns and rifles. His invention of revolving multiround cylinders for handguns and rifles made him well known throughout the American West. His son, John Moses Browning, secured patents for the famous Browning automatic rifle.

In 1843, Browning and his wife, Elizabeth, visited Nauvoo and after meeting Joseph Smith joined the Mormon church. They then sold their property in Quincy, moved with their nine children to Nauvoo, and purchased a lot on Main Street. There Browning built his log house and two-story brick house and workshops. The large two-story brick building has been restored to its original condition, while the log house is a reconstruction.

During the Mormon exodus, Browning was given the special assignment of locating at Kanesville, Iowa, to manufacture weapons for the Mormons who were migrating to Utah's Great Basin in large but separately organized wagon trains. Browning remained in Kanesville from 1847 to 1852. He and his family then joined the Mormon settlement at Ogden, Utah, where he lived until his death in 1879.

The **Wilford Woodruff House** (1843) was the first building in Nauvoo to be completely restored. Wilford Woodruff (1807–1898) was ordained by Joseph Smith as one of the church's Twelve Apostles. After serving as a missionary in England from 1839 to 1841, he returned to Nauvoo. There, in 1843, he built the Federal-style two-story brick house at the corner of Durphy and Hotchkiss Streets. In 1846, he and his family joined the Saints in Utah, where he had a distinguished career serving as the fourth president of the church, from 1887 to 1898.

The **Printing Office Complex** consists of three, red brick buildings erected in 1842 by James Ivins. John Taylor, a publisher and editor, purchased the complex in 1845. He used one store as a print shop from which Nauvoo's newspapers, *Nauvoo Neighbor* and *Times and Seasons*, were printed. The restored Print Shop has upper and lower type cases, as well as 1830 and 1860 printing presses.

John Taylor, who would serve as the third president of the LDS church, and his family lived in the restored two-story Federal-style house, now called the **Ivins-Smith-Taylor House.** As with most Nauvoo homes, furnishings in the Taylor Home are typical of the early to mid-nineteenth-century period rather than family possessions. However, there is a 150-

year-old rocking horse in the children's bedroom that belonged to John Taylor's young son. After the family left Nauvoo to head west, the boy cried continuously. Questioned by his parents, he finally admitted that he missed his rocking horse. His father returned on horseback to Nauvoo and under cover of darkness entered his abandoned home and rescued his son's rocking horse.

Flanking the house on the other side is the reconstructed **Post Office** which is a combination post office and general store. The store is stocked with groceries, dry goods, kitchen utensils, pottery, and agricultural tools as it was in the 1840s.

Stop in the reconstructed **Scovil Bakery** where you'll be given a gingerbread cookie to sample. Lucy and Lucius Scovil baked bread, cookies, cakes, and crackers in the ovens in the small, one-story red brick building. The outdoor oven behind the bakery was used in the summer.

The **Sarah Granger Kimball Home** is a one-and-one-half-story Greek Revival frame house built in 1840 during the pre-Mormon period. Sarah Kimball was instrumental in founding the Nauvoo Female Relief Society in 1842.

Lyon Drug and Variety Store dates to 1843 when the brick home and store were built. Jars of herbs line the drug store shelves as Windsor Lyon practiced herbal and botanical medicine. In addition to medications, the Lyon store stocked dry goods, groceries, crockery, glass, hardware, books, stationery, paints, baskets, wooden tubs, and military goods. Notice the herb garden outside.

Another attached house and business belonged to Sylvester Stoddard who operated a tinshop. The tinsmith, his wife Charity, and their family moved in 1844 into the two-story red-brick house, which has been reconstructed. In addition to producing a variety of tin utensils, Stoddard made stovepipe which he installed in many Nauvoo buildings.

The three-story, Federal-style **Cultural and Masonic Hall,** built in 1843, was used for masonic lodge meetings, musical and theatrical performances, and church business meetings. Now, the first floor is restored as a theater where musical dramas about Mormon history are performed. The second floor features a quilt exhibit, and the third floor is a gallery of Nauvoo paintings.

William Weeks was selected by Joseph Smith to be the temple architect of the Nauvoo Temple. He handled day-to-day construction problems, but the design of the temple was basically that of Joseph Smith. Weeks endured the perennial problem of builders whose clients change their minds during construction as Smith frequently had new visions about the temple design. Sketches and photographs of the temple are exhibited in the **Weeks Home.**

Other buildings that can be toured are **Clark Home and Store** which was a family home and general store, the **Riser Home and Shop** where George Riser made shoes and boots, the white frame **Coolidge Home** which furniture maker and cooper Coolidge built as a residence and shop in 1843, and the **Pendleton Log Home** built in 1843 where schoolteacher and herbal doctor Calvin Pendleton taught reading, writing, and arithmetic to Nauvoo children.

The **Webb Wagon and Blacksmith Shop** (1843) was operated by James Webb and his five eldest sons. The shop produced many of the wagons for the westward journey to Utah. The recreated building was erected on original foundations. The bellows, anvils, bench vice, and other tools are originals that were taken to Utah and then returned to Nauvoo to enhance the authenticity of the recreation.

The Reorganized Church of Jesus Christ of Latter Day Saints maintains the **Joseph Smith Historic Center,** a visitors center with an audiovisual orientation program, a book and gift shop, and museum exhibits. Included in the exhibits are the original headstones from the graves of Joseph, Emma, and Hyrum Smith. A new marker was placed at their grave site in 1991. Guided tours of the Smith homes and store leave regularly from the Visitors Center.

When Joseph Smith came to Nauvoo in 1839, he purchased a two-story log house which had been built in 1803. In addition to Joseph, Emma, and their children, visitors were accommodated and sick people were nursed by Emma at the **Homestead.** A one-story frame addition, a large keeping room, was added to the back of the Homestead in 1840. A two-story frame addition was later built on the west side. Smith family pieces include Emma's walking stick and a blanket chest with a false bottom used for storing important papers.

In 1843, the Smith family moved from the Homestead into the **Mansion House,** a two-story frame house with twenty-two rooms. To accommodate visitors, Smith added a hotel wing which was removed in 1890. The bodies of Joseph and Hyrum Smith lay in state in the Mansion parlor on June 28, 1844, and 20,000 people came to pay their respects. Fearing desecration of their bodies, that night Emma secretly buried Joseph and Hyrum in the dirt basement of the unfinished Nauvoo House. No one at the funeral realized that the closed coffins did not contain the Smith brothers' bodies. When construction of the Nauvoo House resumed a short time later, Emma moved the bodies under the Spring House near the

Homestead. In 1928, the skeletal remains of Joseph and Hyrum were found near the Spring House and moved to the **grave site** next to the Homestead.

Joseph Smith operated a general store in Nauvoo. Known as the **Red Brick Store,** the building also served as headquarters for the church. The second floor of the reconstructed building saw civil activity; in addition, Mayor Joseph Smith and his city council met there. Reproduction items similar to those available in the 1840s are sold in the Red Brick Store.

The National Icarian Heritage Society maintains the **Icarian Living History Museum** at 2205 East Parley Street, Nauvoo. It is in the restored 1846 Mix-Linge house which was lived in by Icarians, Emile and Annette Baxter, and is open from April through October, 2:00 P.M. to 5:00 P.M. When the Icarians came to Nauvoo in 1849, they purchased the temple block for $2,000. For a short time, they used the fire-gutted temple. The Icarians built many structures on the temple block, all of which have since disappeared.

The *City of Joseph,* a dramatic and musical pageant based on Joseph Smith's life at Nauvoo, is presented the last Friday and Saturday in July and the first Tuesday through Saturday in August. The Wedding of Wine and Cheese is an annual grape festival held on Labor Day weekend.

SIDE TRIPS

To complete the story of Joseph Smith and the Latter-day Saints in Nauvoo, travel twenty-three miles southeast to the **Carthage Jail.** A second-floor room in the restored limestone building which served as both jail and living quarters for the jailer and his family is the site where Joseph and Hyrum Smith were murdered on June 27, 1844. In addition to the restored jail, there is a visitors' center and memorial gardens. From Nauvoo, take IL 96 south to US 136 east. 307 Walnut Street, Carthage 62354, (217) 357-2989. Open daily; free.

Nauvoo State Park is a 148-acre park with a 13-acre lake, campsites, playground, and museum. Acquired by the state of Illinois in 1948, the park lies along Route 96 on the south edge of Nauvoo. Campsite permits must be obtained from the site manager. For information, call (217) 453-2512.

LINCOLN'S NEW SALEM

Reconstruction of the 1830s frontier village lived in by Abraham Lincoln; State Historic Site; NR

Address: RR 1, Box 244A, Petersburg, IL 62675
Telephone: (217) 632-4000
Location: In central Illinois, 200 miles southwest of Chicago; on IL 97, 2 miles south of Petersburg and 20 miles northwest of Springfield
Open: Daily, 9:00 A.M. to 5:00 P.M., April through late October; 8:00 A.M. to 4:00 P.M., rest of year; closed holidays except Memorial Day, Labor Day, and July 4
Admission: Free; suggested donation: adults, $2.00; youths 17 and under, $1.00
Restaurants: River Ridge Restaurant; Hilltop concession stand
Shops: Hilltop Bookstore; Lincoln League Craft Shop
Facilities: Visitor Center with orientation film and exhibits; picnic areas; Talisman river boat trip; the Great American People Show outdoor drama; campgrounds; special events

WHERE TO STAY

Inns/Bed & Breakfasts: The Oaks, Petersburg 62675, (217) 632-4480; Bit of Country, Petersburg 62675, (217) 632-3771; Connie's B&B Inn, 1001 S. 6th St., Springfield 62703, (217) 527-1400
Motels/Hotels: Springfield Hilton, 700 E. Adams St., Springfield 62701, (217) 789-1530, (800) 272-8600; Springfield Renaissance Hotel, 701 E. Adams St., Springfield 62701, (217) 544-8800, (800) 228-9898; Capital Plaza, 418 E. Jefferson St., Springfield 62701, (217) 525-1700, (800) 448-3635; Best Western Sky Harbor Inn, 1701 J. David Jones Pkwy, Springfield 62702, (217) 753-3446, (800) 528-1234; Hampton Inn, 3185 S. Dirksen Parkway, Springfield 62703, (217) 529-1100, FAX: (217) 529-1100, ext. 170; McHenry's, Petersburg 62675, (217) 632-2992
Camping: Lincoln's New Salem State Park, RR 1, Box 244A, Petersburg 62675, (217) 632-4000

OVERVIEW

The village of New Salem is indelibly linked in the nation's memory to the Illinois years of Abraham Lincoln, the sixteenth president of the United States. Lincoln engaged in business, first sought political office, and decided to become a lawyer during the six years he lived in this crude frontier village. From New Salem he moved to nearby Springfield as a lawyer and state legislator, to Washington as a congressman, back to Springfield, and then finally to Washington to the nation's presidency.

New Salem Village is a reconstruction of the town, which had completely disappeared, as it looked when Lincoln lived there. With the exception of the Onstot Cooper Shop, all the structures are faithful reproductions which have been built on their original foundations as determined by historical maps, deeds, and documents. The frontier town is arranged along a street with cabins on either side. There are twelve log houses, the Rutledge Tavern, ten workshops, stores and mills, and a school. Historically authenticated flower and vegetable gardens and trees recreate the original village setting.

History
The village of New Salem, which was Abraham Lincoln's home from 1831 to 1837, was founded on the Sangamon River by James Rutledge and his nephew, John M. Camron, a millwright.

Lincoln's connection with New Salem was strictly an accident. In April 1831, Lincoln, then twenty-two years old, and two other young men planned to pole a flatboat loaded with farm produce down the Sangamon River from Springfield to market in New Orleans. Unfortunately, on April 19, their heavily loaded boat became stranded on Camron's dam at New Salem. Thanks to Lincoln's quick thinking, the boat and its cargo were saved from sinking.

Denton Offutt, the merchant whose goods the flatboat was carrying, came ashore with the crew. He thought New Salem had good growth potential and decided to open a store there when he returned from New Orleans. He asked Abe Lincoln to be his clerk. Lincoln agreed and reached New Salem in late July 1831.

Offutt's store did not last long, but Lincoln decided to remain in town. In March 1832, just seven months after his arrival, Lincoln announced his candidacy for the state legislature. During the campaign, he and some friends joined the Fourth Regiment of Mounted Volunteers to assist in the Black Hawk War. Lincoln was elected captain of his company and served until July 10, 1832; that was his entire military career.

After he lost the election on August 6, 1832, Lincoln purchased Rowan Herndon's share in a store owned by Herndon and William Berry. The firm then became known as Berry and Lincoln. In January, Berry and Lincoln moved to a better location at the Warburton Building, now

Lincoln's New Salem, Petersburg, Illinois
A sign hanging from the recreated log structure announces that it is the "First Berry-Lincoln Store" which Abraham Lincoln and William Berry purchased in 1832, soon after Lincoln's defeat as a candidate for the state legislature. Proving to be a better politician than businessman, Abraham Lincoln was elected the sixteenth president of the United States in 1860.
At Lincoln's New Salem, Petersburg, IL.
Photo by Patricia A. Gutek

known as the Second Berry-Lincoln Store. On May 7, Lincoln became
New Salem's postmaster and held that position for three years until the
office was moved to Petersburg. He was also a deputy surveyor for three
years.

He was elected to the Illinois legislation on August 4, 1834, and
reelected on August 1, 1836. On September 9, 1836, he was licensed to
practice law; and on March 1, 1837, he was admitted to the bar. In April,
Lincoln joined the exodus from New Salem to Springfield, where he began
his law career.

Because the Sangamon River could not bear riverboat traffic, New
Salem declined while other towns in the area grew. In May 1836, when
the post office moved to nearby Petersburg, many citizens left the town.
On February 15, 1839, the state legislature subdivided Sangamon County,
creating Menard County, with Petersburg as the county seat. This was the
final blow to New Salem, and most of those residents who had remained
deserted the village.

Interest in the New Salem village site was kept alive by the Old
Salem Chautauqua Association. In 1906, William Randolph Hearst, the
newspaper publisher, purchased the site and conveyed it in trust to the
association. In 1919, the association passed the site to the state of Illinois.
The state legislature appropriated $50,000 for "permanent improvements"
at the site in 1931, and restoration began in 1932. During the Great Depression, the Civilian Conservation Corps restored the Rutledge-Camron
Saw and Grist Mill, the Hill Carding Mill, Miller's Blacksmith Shop, and
the church and schoolhouse. Since then, archaeological research has led
to the reconstruction of outbuildings. A new Visitor Center was opened
in 1992.

TOUR

Start your tour at the **Visitor Center** which opened in 1992. It features an orientation film on Lincoln's life at New Salem and a diorama of
New Salem. The Visitor Center's New Salem Time Walk is a series of
exhibits on Lincoln and New Salem from 1809 to the present. It begins
with Lincoln telling his own story based on an autobiography written for
the 1860 campaign. Events in Lincoln's life at New Salem are told through
stories, pictures, paintings, artifacts, documents, and models.

All New Salem's houses except Samuel Hill's residence had one
story; some had lofts. Usually, they had only one or two rooms. Houses
built before the establishment of Camron's Saw Mill had puncheon floors
made from split logs. With the mill, planks for floors, ceilings, and siding

for houses became available. Fireplaces were made of stone or brick; chimneys, of stone or *cat and clay* (logs and sticks chinked with mud or plaster).

Roofs were made of clapboards or shingles, called *shakes*, secured either by nails or by logs called *weight poles* laid across them. Walls were of logs, notched and fitted together at the corners and chinked with sticks and plaster made of mud and hair. Doors were of frame construction. Houses with leather or wooden hinges and wooden latches and locks predate the blacksmith's arrival at New Salem. After his arrival, fittings were usually made of iron. Houses with wooden latches had buckskin latchstrings, which were tied to the latch and passed outside through a hole above it. When only friends were about, "the latchstring was always out"; but in time of danger, it could be pulled in through the hole. Most buildings had glass windows.

Furniture was brought to the village from former homes, was homemade, or was made in New Salem by Lincoln's contemporary Robert Johnson. There were rush-seat chairs, cord and trundle beds, plain chests of drawers, and corner cupboards for glasses and dishes. For lighting, candles in brass or iron holders were used.

The **Henry Onstot Cooper Shop,** built in 1830, is the only original, restored building at New Salem. It was found in Petersburg in 1922 and returned to its original foundation. It contains displays of barrels and cooper's tools. Nearby is the **Onstot Cabin** where Henry and his family lived.

Behind the cooper shop is the **Trent Brothers' Residence.** Alexander Trent purchased the lot for $50 on August 27, 1832. He owned a grocery and, at one time, the ferry. Alexander Trent served as a corporal in Lincoln's company in the Black Hawk War.

The **Mentor Graham Schoolhouse and Church** is a simple round-log structure. Inside are four half-log benches, a table, and a fireplace. The school was not supported by taxes; it was a subscription school. Tuition ranged from thirty to eighty-five cents a month per pupil, depending on the child's age. Church services were also conducted here. Mentor Graham, who came to Sangamon County in 1828, advised Lincoln to study grammar and assisted him in studying surveying.

The **Isaac Gulihur Residence** is a reproduction of one built in 1832; its owner had served in Lincoln's company in the Black Hawk War. The **Robert Johnson Residence** was built in 1832. A wheelwright and cabinet-maker, Johnson made spinning wheels, wagon wheels, and furniture.

The **Isaac Burner Residence** is a copy of one built on two lots, valued at $10, south of Main Street, in October 1832. In 1836, Burner left New Salem and moved farther west.

In 1831, James and Rowan Herndon arrived at New Salem and opened a store. It was subsequently sold to William Berry and Abraham Lincoln in 1832. The **First Berry-Lincoln Store** didn't stay in this location long, but moved to Reuben Radford's store after buying his stock in January 1833.

The **Lukins and Ferguson Residence** was built by Peter Lukins, who maintained a cobbler's shop.

The **Dr. John Allen Cabin** is one of the better-constructed cabins in New Salem. A Dartmouth graduate, physician, and businessman, Allen was accustomed to comfortable living. He was a Presbyterian, and church meetings were often held in his home.

New Salem (Rutledge) Tavern was originally built as a home in 1829 by James Rutledge, cofounder with John Camron of New Salem. A native of South Carolina, he was a serious and well-educated man who had a library of thirty volumes and founded a debating society attended by Lincoln. Ann Rutledge, Lincoln's alleged fiancée, was one of his ten children.

In 1831, as Sangamon County's population grew, Rutledge converted his home into a tavern and built an addition for guests. Abraham Lincoln lodged in the tavern's loft.

The **Lincoln League Shop** is a craft store in a 1930s stone building that was formerly used as a museum.

The **Rowan Herndon Residence** is a replica of the log cabin built by Rowan and his brother James in 1831. On a visit to James and Rowan, their cousin, William H. Herndon, met Lincoln. They were law partners from 1843 until the president's death, and William Herndon eventually became Lincoln's biographer.

The **New Salem Saw and Grist Mill** was built in 1828. The mill drew trade from miles around, and its prosperity inspired some of its customers to settle in New Salem and open businesses of their own.

Clary's Grocery, a simple log cabin warmed by a fireplace, was opened in 1829 by William Clary. The grocery was a convenient place to visit, have a drink, and stock up on supplies while having grain ground at the mill. By 1832, William Clary sold his store to Alexander Trent and moved to Texas.

Denton Offutt's Store, on the bluff above the river, opened in September 1831, with Abraham Lincoln as Offutt's clerk. This general store sold dry goods, furs, seeds, tallow, lard, bacon, cheese, butter, honey, eggs, hops, vegetables, firearms and ammunition, saddles, tools, and liquor.

The **Second Berry-Lincoln Store,** built in 1831, is a frame structure, which is unusual for New Salem. Its one large room was the store; the rear lean-to served as a storeroom and, for a time, as Lincoln's bedroom.

The business was not a success. New Salem's fortunes were declining, and William Berry consumed much of the store's liquor. Berry had obtained a tavern license so that he could sell liquor by the drink. Lincoln disapproved of the liquor license and dissolved the partnership, selling his share to Berry. Because Lincoln had borrowed money to buy the business, its failure left him in debt as well as unemployed.

The **Hill-McNeil Store** was opened in 1829 by Samuel Hill and John McNeil McNamar. This store, one of the few New Salem buildings to have a porch, was once the center of village social and busines life. It was also used as an election polling place.

The **New Salem Post Office** was located in Hill's store because Hill was the postmaster. After some complaints about his service, he was replaced by Abraham Lincoln on May 7, 1833. Lincoln remained postmaster until May 30, 1836, when the office was relocated in Petersburg. Lincoln developed his lifelong habit of reading daily newspapers when as postmaster he had easy access to them.

Martin Waddle's Residence, built in 1832, has puncheon floors, wooden hinges and locks, and small windows. Waddle was a hatter, and the original iron kettle used in his trade hangs on the east side of the house.

Samuel Hill's Residence is New Salem's only two-story house. Other unusual features are its porch, front and rear doors, outside cellar entrance, and a sliding window.

Dr. Francis Regnier's Office was bought for $20 in 1832. The son of a French physician, Dr. Regnier was an eccentric and witty young man who lived and worked in the office's single room for four years.

A large, two-story log building, **Hill's Carding Mill and Storehouse** was built by Samuel Hill in 1835. The mill's cogs were made of hickory wood, and a yoke of oxen, hitched to a forty-foot wheel, supplied the power by walking on a treadmill. Carding began in May, with some people paying cash for it while others left a percentage of their wool as payment.

Joshua Miller bought the lots for **Miller's Blacksmith Shop** on November 17, 1832, for $25. At his anvil, he forged shoes for oxen and horses, implements and household fittings. Miller was also a wagonmaker.

Joshua Miller and John Kelso, who married sisters, built the **Miller-Kelso Cabin,** the only double house in New Salem. Its iron fittings and an unusual sliding window were made by Miller, the blacksmith. Jack Kelso, known as the village philosopher, preferred fishing and poetry to work. To supplement their income, Mrs. Kelso took in boarders. Abraham Lincoln was one of them, and he became an avid listener as Kelso quoted Shakespeare and the Scottish poet Robert Burns.

During the summer and fall, special events include a quilt show in June, a summer festival in July, prairie story-telling days in August, a traditional music festival in September, candlelight tours in October, and Harvest Feast in November.

The **Talisman,** a replica of the steamboat that plied the Sangamon River in Lincoln's day, provides boat trips daily except Mondays during the summer. (217) 632-7681. Admission charged.

The Great American People Show presents dramatic productions that chronicle the life of Abraham Lincoln in an outdoor amphitheater from mid-June through late August. The Great American People Show, Box 401, Petersburg 62675, (217) 632-7755. Admission charged.

SIDE TRIPS

After New Salem, a logical next stop is **Lincoln's home** in Springfield. The young lawyer, his wife, Mary, and their son moved to this charming house in 1844, when Lincoln was serving as a state legislator. Three more sons were born in Springfield, necessitating an extensive remodeling of the second floor to accommodate the growing family. They lived in the house, the only one Lincoln ever owned, for seventeen years. Lincoln left Springfield for Washington in 1861 after being elected President.

The **Lincoln Home National Historic Site,** at the corner of Eighth and Jackson streets, is set in a four-block area purchased by the National Park Service. The exteriors of many of the Victorian houses which were the homes of the Lincoln family's neighbors have been restored to the 1860s. The brick streets are closed to traffic, so that Lincoln's restored home is in its appropriate mid-nineteenth-century neighborhood setting.

A recent refurbishing of the Lincoln Home included historically correct decorating as ascertained from period documents and physical evidence uncovered in the house. The Lincoln's reproduction wallpaper and carpeting exemplifies the Victorian love of mixing bold patterns and colors. There are two formal parlors, a sitting room, a dining room, and a kitchen on the first floor. Much of the furniture was owned by the Lincoln family. In Abraham Lincoln's bedroom upstairs is the bed that was specially made to accommodate his six-foot-three-inch frame. Open 8:30 A.M. to 5:00 P.M. daily except major holidays. Free. (217) 492-4150. Lincoln Home Visitor Center is at 426 S. 7th St.

The **Great Western Depot** where Abraham Lincoln boarded a train for Washington, D.C., for his presidential inauguration has been restored to the mid-1800s. The brick, three-level train station has both a gentlemen's and a ladies' waiting room on the first floor. The balcony displays photographs of Lincoln's family, friends, neighbors, law partners, and political associates. On the third floor, a film is shown which depicts Lincoln's train route from Springfield to Washington as well as the parallel trip of Confederate President Jefferson Davis to Montgomery, Alabama. Excerpts from the speeches the two men made along the way are used to narrate this film. It begins with Lincoln's moving farewell speech to the hundreds of Springfield well-wishers who gathered at the train station to bid him farewell. The Lincoln Depot is open daily, 10:00 A.M. to 4:00 P.M., from April through August. Free.

Beautifully restored is the 1840 **Lincoln-Herndon Law Offices,** at Sixth and Adams streets, the only surviving structure in which Lincoln had a law office. Guided tours are given of the law offices on the third floor which Lincoln shared with William Herndon. Lincoln practiced law here from 1843 to 1852. On the second floor is the restored federal courtroom. Open daily, 9:00 A.M. to 5:00 P.M. Free.

The beautiful **Old State Capitol** is on the square in downtown Springfield between 5th and 6th streets and Washington and Adams streets. This restored Greek Revival building is an architectural showpiece, with curving stairways, a high cupola, and magnificent senate and house chambers. Attention to detail is evident throughout; the brass is polished, the clocks are wound, and the guides are knowledgeable. The desks in the legislative chambers are reproductions; the other furniture dates from the period, but only nine pieces are original to the Capitol.

The cornerstone of the Capitol was laid in 1837, and construction was completed in 1854, although the sessions were held there from 1840. Lincoln, a representative in the General Assembly from 1834 to 1841, was instrumental in moving the capital from Vandalia to Springfield. An original copy of the Gettysburg Address in Lincoln's handwriting is displayed in a safelike enclosure on the first floor. Admission is free. Open daily. 9:00 A.M. to 5:00 P.M., (217) 785-7961.

Lincoln's Tomb is located in Oak Ridge Cemetery on North Walnut Street. This impressive monument consists of a 117-foot granite obelisk reached by a double stairway leading to a circular entrance bay. Statuary groups representing Civil War troops are at each corner of the obelisk. It is the burial place of our sixteenth president, his wife, and three of their four sons. Tours through the tomb are narrated by guides. Open daily, 9:00 A.M. to 5:00 P.M. Admission is free. For information, call (217)782-2717.

The **Illinois State Capitol,** built between 1868 and 1889, offers free guided tours on weekdays from 8:00 A.M. to 4:00 P.M. For information, call (217)782-2099. The **Governor's Mansion** (1855), located at 5th and Jackson Streets, is the third-oldest continuously occupied governor's mansion in the nation. Tours are given Tuesday and Thursday, from 9:30 A.M. to 11:00 A.M. and from 2:00 P.M. to 3:30 P.M. Admission is free. For information, call (217)782-6450.

HISTORIC NEW HARMONY

Restoration of an 1814 to 1860 Harmonist religious
community and Owenite utopian community; State Historic
Site; NR, NHL

Address: P.O. Box 579, New Harmony, IN 47631

Telephone: (812) 682-4482, (812) 682-4488

Location: In the southwest corner of Indiana, near the Illinois and Kentucky borders; on the Wabash River, at the intersection of IN 66 and IN 68

Open: Daily, 9:00 A.M. to 5:00 P.M., April to October, and weekends in March, November, and December; Atheneum open but no tours given in January, February, and weekdays in March, November, and December

Admission: Introduction Tour: $3.00;
Story Tour: adults, $8.00; seniors, $7.00; children, $4.50;
Short Story Tour: adults, $6.00; children, $4.50;
Arts and Sciences Tour: adults, $6.00; children, $4.50

Restaurants: Red Geranium; Bayou Grill; Country Cottage Restaurant & Confectionery; The Main Cafe; Yellow Tavern

Shops: Museum Shop in the Atheneum; Red Geranium Book Store; Antique Showrooms; Golden Raintree Books; Harmony Pottery; Weathervane Shop; Harmonie Haus; mudpies; earthcare at the depot; Harmonie Weaving Institute

Facilities: Atheneum, a visitors center with orientation film; guided tours; partially wheelchair accessible; New Harmony Inn

WHERE TO STAY

Inns/Bed & Breakfasts: The Old Rooming House, 916 Church St., New Harmony 47631, (812) 682-4724; Harmonie B&B, 344 W. Church St., New Harmony 47631, (812) 682-3730

Motels/Hotels: The New Harmony Inn, 506 North St., P.O. Box 581, New Harmony 47631 (812) 682-4491; Executive Inn, Box 3246, 600 Walnut St., Evansville 47731, (812) 424-8000; Four Seasons Motel, Hwy. 62 West, Mt. Vernon 47620, (812) 838-4821; Best Western Windsor Oaks Inn, 2200 S. Court St., Grayville, IL 62844, (618) 375-7930

Camping: Harmonie State Park, RR 1, Box 5A, New Harmony 47631, (812) 682-4821

Overview

The first historic communal site we ever visited was New Harmony, Indiana, in 1966. Brought there by a need to work in its archives, we were enchanted by the tiny historic town we entered that summer evening at dusk. We had paid twenty-five cents to cross the toll bridge over the Wabash River—a quarter to enter utopia. Our finest investment, that twenty-five cents opened a world filled with fascinating communal groups, historic villages, and outdoor museums that we have never tired of.

New Harmony was a town created out of the wilderness in 1814 by Lutheran Separatists from Germany who called themselves the Harmonie Society. Led by George Rapp, these incredibly industrious people built 150 sturdy structures their first year in Indiana. Skilled craftsmen and good farmers contributed to the economic success of the Harmonists who had adopted a communal lifestyle. The first of the two fascinating groups to live in New Harmony, the Harmonists were responsible for the physical layout and structures of the town. The second group, secular utopians led by a Welshman, Robert Owen, contributed much of the cultural and intellectual legacy of New Harmony.

Because the town did not experience significant growth and development from the mid-nineteenth century to the mid-twentieth century, it had remained pretty much intact. A variety of agencies became interested in the restoration of the town's historic structures. We have watched the continuing restoration of New Harmony on subsequent visits. Now the two primary agencies which own many of New Harmony's historic properties, the state of Indiana and Historic New Harmony, are a unified program of the University of Southern Indiana and the Division of State Museums and Historic Sites. The unified program allows the two organizations to offer a joint tour program of the historic sites.

History

New Harmony, on the banks of the Wabash River in southern Indiana, is both a restoration and a living community. It is noteworthy as the location of two utopian communities, the Harmonists, from 1814 to 1824, and the Owenites, from 1824 to 1828. The first community, religious in origin, was established by German pietists led by George Rapp (1757–1847), a dissenter from the more formal Lutheran church. In 1803, the patriarchal and charismatic Father Rapp led his flock from their native Württemberg in Germany to western Pennsylvania, where they established the town of Harmonie. In 1814, the Harmonists left Pennsylvania in search of a more congenial location to cultivate grapes and other crops.

Historic New Harmony, New Harmony, Indiana
New Harmony, the site of a nineteenth-century Harmonist religious community
and an Owenite utopian community, is glimpsed from the contemporary
Athenaeum which serves as the Visitors' Center.
At Historic New Harmony, New Harmony, IN.
Photo by Patricia A. Gutek

Rapp selected southern Indiana for his new community, which he also called Harmonie, now known as New Harmony. Its location on the Wabash provided excellent transportation to markets.

The Harmonists created a thriving agricultural community of 800 residents who cultivated some 20,000 acres. They remained in New Harmony until 1824, when Father Rapp sold the community to Robert Owen, the British industrialist and utopian socialist. The Harmonists then returned to western Pennsylvania, where they founded Economy, their third community. Travelers can retrace the Harmonist experience in the United States by exploring the three restored villages: Harmony, Pennsylvania; New Harmony, Indiana; and Old Economy, at Ambridge, Pennsylvania, a suburb of Pittsburgh (see page 000). Under Rapp's paternalistic rule, New Harmony prospered. The Harmonists were renowned for their industriousness, frugality, and productivity. The town, consisting of 180 solidly constructed buildings, comprised factories, granaries, mills, private homes, schools, and dormitories. Rapp, an astute businessman, diversified the community's agricultural economy to include manufacturing. Its many products, including beer, whiskey, and wine, found ready markets in the frontier towns and farms of Illinois and Indiana.

Rapp sold New Harmony to Robert Owen for $150,000 in 1824 because he believed the establishment of a new communitarian village would rekindle his followers' enthusiasm. Owen brought a very different type of utopian vision to the town.

At the time of the purchase, Owen (1771–1858) was famous for his reform at the mill town of New Lanark in Scotland, where he improved the working and living conditions of the employees. Owen saw himself as the prophet of a new society based on common property. Feeling constrained by England's traditional class structure and customs, he sold his New Lanark mills and came to the United States, where he purchased New Harmony. At a joint session of the U.S. Congress, attended by the president and the cabinet, Owen announced his plan to create a model community and urged interested individuals to join him at New Harmony.

Owen formed an ill-defined partnership with William Maclure, an amateur geologist and philanthropist. Maclure, who took responsibility for the educational phase of the experiment, brought with him an illustrious group of scientists and educators. He sought to combine basic research in the natural sciences with the educational methods devised by the Swiss reformer Johann Heinrich Pestalozzi (1746–1826), who espoused the power of education as a tool of social regeneration. Maclure hoped to turn New Harmony into a scientific and educational center, a kind of nineteenth-century think tank. Among the scientific notables who joined Owen's New Harmony experiment were Thomas Say, a pioneer natural scientist; Charles-Alexandre Lesueur, a naturalist and artist; and Gerard Troost, a chemist and mineralogist.

Maclure, who wanted to introduce a scientifically based, practical education to the United States, persuaded a group of Pestalozzian teachers to staff New Harmony's schools. The ill-sorted intellectuals, educators, scientists, and farmers who joined Owen and Maclure at New Harmony devoted more time to debates than to working. Internal dissension brought disharmony to New Harmony, and Owen's communal experiment ended with his return to England.

The Owenite legacy became a part of Indiana's history. Owen's sons made significant political and educational contributions to the state. Robert Dale Owen, his eldest son, served in Congress; David Dale Owen headed the U.S. Geological Survey; Richard Dale Owen became Purdue University's first president. For more than a decade after the experiment's end, Maclure's scientists and educators continued their research, publication, and teaching.

Today, New Harmony has many of the qualities that Owen and Maclure wanted to see during their own lives. Its restored buildings illustrate the Harmonist and Owenite heritage. Its exhibits highlight science and education. To stroll New Harmony's quiet streets at twilight is to walk with Father Rapp, Robert Owen, William Maclure, and those who sought to create a utopia on America's frontier.

TOUR

New Harmony is a living rural town with a population less than one thousand. The historic properties are not fenced in but are interspersed among private homes and businesses. Begin your tour of New Harmony at **The Atheneum** which serves as the Visitors' Center. Guided tours originate there.

The Atheneum is a shining white building of contemporary design completed in 1979; its architect was Richard Meier. It contains exhibit areas, conference facilities, and a display of books and publications about New Harmony, as well as a scale model of the 1824 town and an orientation film.

The **David Lenz House** (1822), a Harmonist frame home, illustrates the sturdy and innovative architecture of the Harmonist period. It has been restored and furnished with Harmonist-era artifacts by the National Society of Colonial Dames of America.

Harmonist building frames, fastened with mortise and tenon joints, were locked in place with wooden pegs. Rafters were self-supporting. The energy-conscious Harmonists insulated their homes with *Dutch biscuits,* a wooden board wrapped with mud and straw. Note the centrally located chimney, which was used for both cooking and heating, and the small windowpanes, which resisted wind while providing a source of light. Of interest is the Christian door, a symbol of the Harmonists' religious faith; the upper panels form the cross, and the lower ones represent an open Bible. Among the furnishings are Harmonist-style chairs; a pie safe typical of southern Indiana; a small Shaker table; and a Harmonist-style bed and chest.

The **West Street Log Cabins** are replicas of early Harmonist buildings built between 1814 and 1819. In the Potter's Shop is a broom making machine. The Eigner Cabin is furnished as an early Harmonist home.

Robert Fauntleroy House, a Harmonist frame home, was built in 1822 and enlarged by Robert Fauntleroy, the husband of Robert Owen's daughter, Jane, in 1840. Its furnishings are from the Victorian period.

The **Workingmen's Institute and Library,** built in 1894, has archives and collections on the Harmonists and Owenites that attract scholars and authors. There are also extensive collections on Maclure and his scientific and educational associates. The building also houses the **New Harmony Public Library,** a small **art gallery,** and a local **history museum.**

The institute, established in 1838 by William Maclure, was designed as an educational center for working men and women. From 1830 to 1860, the institute's School Press published pioneering scientific books by a number of Maclure's scientific associates, including Say and Lesueur. Be sure to see the portraits of William Maclure and Joseph Neef, a Pestalozzian teacher.

Murphy Auditorium (1913) was extensively restored and renovated in 1975. Funds for its original construction were provided by Dr. Edward Murphy (1813–1900), a New Harmony physician. Today, it is used for lectures, concerts, and other educational and artistic performances and professional summer theater.

Lichtenberger Store (1901) now houses the **Maximilian-Bodmer collection** of hand-colored lithographs called *Travels in the Interior of North America, 1832–1834.* These drawings and sketches were made by the Swiss artist Karl Bodmer (1809–1893), who accompanied the German nobleman Prince Alexander Philip Maximilian on an expedition through the American frontier wilderness. Especially noteworthy are Bodmer's drawings of Indians, animals, and frontier scenes.

George Keppler House (1822), a Harmonist residence, contains exhibits on New Harmony as a geological research center. It features the surveys of David Dale Owen (1807–1860).

In the 1830 **Owen House** is a decorative arts display of the 1830s and 1840s which includes Chippendale, Sheraton, and Empire furniture. The Jaquess parlor and entry are stencilled and there are folk art works by Jacob Maentel.

The 1829 **John Beal House** is a one-story frame building of waddle and daub construction. Exhibits here focus on Owenite educational and scientific figures including William Maclure, Gerard Troost, Joseph Neef, Thomas Say, Charles-Alexandre Lesueur, and Marie Fretageot.

The 1822 **Scholle House,** a brick residence, was the home of Harmonist shoemaker Mattias Scholle. It houses changing exhibits of regional art and history.

The **Victorian Period Doctor's Office** displays a collection of medical equipment and tools donated by Mead Johnson Foundation. There is also an apothecary shop.

Thrall's Opera House, restored in 1969 by the state of Indiana, is used for theatrical performances, conferences, and lectures. Originally a Harmonist dormitory built in 1824, it was converted into an opera house in 1856.

Solomon Wolf House (1823), a Harmonist brick residence, now houses an electronic scale model of New Harmony in 1824, the year of the Harmonist departure and the Owenite arrival. The model's sound and light show provides an excellent overview of New Harmony's rich but complicated history.

Dormitory Number 2 (1822), one of New Harmony's earliest restorations, is a fine example of Harmonist architecture. It was put to significant use by both Harmonists and Owenites. The Harmonists used it as a dormitory for single persons. In the Owenite period, it was the location of Joseph Neef's Pestalozzian School. Neef, once a noncommissioned officer in Napoleon's army in Italy, was trained by Pestalozzi, the Swiss educational reformer, at Burgdorf in Switzerland. Neef came to the United States under Maclure's patronage to introduce the Pestalozzian educational method, which was based on object lessons. Dormitory Number 2 contains exhibits on education and printing.

Roofless Church (1959), built and maintained by the Robert Lee Blaffer Trust, commemorates New Harmony's spiritual meaning. Although recently created, the Roofless Church, which was designed by architect Philip Johnson, incorporates many symbols of New Harmony's religious past, especially from the Harmonist era. The concept of rooflessness unites earth and sky; the rectangular brick wall recalls the egalitarian spirit of the Harmonist cemetery. Within the domed tabernacle is the sculpture *Descent of the Holy Spirit* by the contemporary artist Jacques Lipschitz.

The Roofless Church and the nearby **Tillich Park** which is a memorial to and the burial place of the theologian Paul Johannes Tillich were projects of Jane Blaffer Owen, the wife of an Owen descendant. She also built the New Harmony Inn and the Red Geranium Restaurant.

The graves in the **Harmonist cemetery** are unmarked, exemplifying the Harmonist principle of equality. Members of Rapp's society would remain equal in death as they had been in life. The wall surrounding the cemetery was built with bricks from the Harmonist church, which was taken down in the 1870s.

The hedge **labyrinth,** a fascinating maze located eight blocks south of the town, is a recreation of the one designed by the Harmonists. **Maple Hill Cemetery,** half a mile south of New Harmony, contains the burial sites and monuments of many New Harmony notables, including David Dale Owen and Joseph Neef.

Lining New Harmony's streets are golden rain trees (*Koelreuteria paniculata*), supposedly introduced to the area by the naturalist Thomas Say. The trees bear bright yellow flowers in June that become long seedpods by the fall.

Several buildings of historical significance are privately owned and not open to the public. However, visitors will want to take note of them.

Rapp-Maclure-Owen Mansion (1844), the town's dominating structure, located prominently on the corners of Church and Main streets, was restyled and rebuilt by Alexander Maclure, the brother of William Maclure. The white one-story Greek Revival residence was built on the foundation of the residence of New Harmony's founder, George Rapp. From 1850 to 1860, it was David Dale Owen's residence. On the grounds is the tomb of Thomas Say, called the founding father of American zoology, who died in New Harmony in 1834. **Footprint rock** was found by George Rapp; he claimed it bore an angel's footprint.

The vine-covered **granary** (1819), a large stone and brick building, was erected by the Harmonists to store grain and supplies. In 1843, David Dale Owen housed his third geological laboratory here.

The **Owen Geological Laboratory** (1859) is an imposing stone building with a turret. It was designed and built by David Dale Owen.

Joseph Neef House (1822), a Harmonist frame and brick family dwelling, became the home of Joseph Neef.

CONNER PRAIRIE

Recreation of an 1836 Indiana pioneer village

Address: 13400 Allisonville Road, Noblesville, IN 46060-4499
Telephone: (317) 776-6000; 24-hour information line: (317) 776-6004
Location: In central Indiana, six miles north of Indianapolis, four miles south of Noblesville
Open: Tuesday to Saturday, 10:00 A.M. to 5:00 P.M., Sunday, 12:00 noon to 5:00 P.M., May through October; Wednesday to Saturday, 10:00 A.M. to 5:00 P.M., Sunday, 12:00 noon to 5:00 P.M., April and November
Admission: Adults, $8.00; seniors, $7.25; children 6 to 12, $5.00
Restaurants: Governor Noble's Eating Place; Snacks on the Common; Bakery
Shops: Museum Shop
Facilities: Museum Center with Weaver Gallery, theater, and orientation film; special events; hands-on crafts area; Earlham College museum

WHERE TO STAY

Motels/Hotels: Courtyard by Marriott/Castleton, 8670 Allisonville Rd., Indianapolis 46250, (317) 576-9559, FAX: (317) 576-0695; Guest Quarters Suite Hotel, 11355 N. Meridian St., Carmel 46032, (317) 844-7994, FAX: (317) 844-2118; Holiday Inn-North, 3850 De Pauw Blvd., Indianapolis 46268, (317) 872-9790; FAX: (317) 871-5608; Waterfront Inn, 409 W. Jackson St., Cicero 46034, (317) 773-5115, (800) 876-3936
Camping: Mounds State Park, Anderson 46013, (317) 642-6627; Riverbend Campground, 21695 State Rd., 37N, Noblesville 46060, (317) 773-3333; Kamper Korner, 1951 W. Edgewood Ave., Indianapolis 46217 (317) 788-1488

OVERVIEW

Conner Prairie's outdoor museum is a recreated pioneer village composed of early Indiana buildings moved to what had been the Conner farm. William Conner's restored 1823 mansion is also at Conner Prairie. The museum takes its name from this early settler who established a trading post on the White River near present-day Noblesville in 1802. Also on the museum's 250 acres is the Museum Center and the Pioneer Adventure

Area, where visitors can try nineteenth-century activities like candlemaking, spinning, and weaving.

Conner Prairie is known for its first-person interpretation. Costumed interpreters recreate life in 1836 by taking on the identities of historic figures, speaking and behaving as if they were that person in 1836. Although this surprises visitors at first, they adjust quickly to conversing as if they had stepped 150 years back in time. Children find it especially delightful.

HISTORY

Conner Prairie commemorates the life and times of William Conner, a pioneer who played an influential role in the early history of the state of Indiana. Conner was born December 10, 1777, in Ohio. His mother was born in a Delaware-Moravian settlement in Ohio. Moving to Indiana in 1802, he established a trading post at White River. Because he spoke their language, Conner gained the trust of the Delaware Indians who inhabited this heavily forested region of Indiana. His fur-trading business thrived. Conner married Mekinges, daughter of the Delaware Chief Anderson; they had six children.

When Indiana became a state in 1816, the state owned two-thirds of the land. Conner, who had occasionally served as a scout and an interpreter at American Indian councils for William Henry Harrison, then governor of the Northwest Territory, helped negotiate the 1818 Treaty of St. Mary, Ohio. With that treaty, Indiana's native tribes, including Delawares, relinquished their rights to a large piece of central Indiana land referred to as the "New Purchase." In 1820, as part of the agreement, a large group of Delawares, including Mekinges and the six Conner children, moved west across the Mississippi.

Conner stayed on, and as permanent settlement began around his trading post, he quickly adapted his business to supply the settlers' needs. In 1823, he replaced his log house with a brick Federal-style building on a bluff overlooking a 200-acre prairie planted with grain. In addition to being a home for Conner, who had remarried, the house served as the county's first post office. For a while, the Hamilton County Circuit Court held sessions there.

Conner and his second wife, Elizabeth Chapman, had ten children, seven of whom were born at the prairie. The other three children were born in Noblesville, where Connor moved in 1837. Conner went on to

Conner Prairie, Noblesville, Indiana
A costumed interpreter performs domestic chores at the Golden Eagle, an inn
operated by the Zimmerman family. At Conner Prairie, Noblesville, IN.
Photo by Patricia A. Gutek

become a prominent Indiana citizen and was elected to the state legislature
three times.

The property at Conner Prairie eventually passed out of family hands
and fell into disrepair. In 1934, Eli Lilly, a grandson of the founder of the
pharmaceutical house of that name, purchased the Connor homestead. He
and his wife, Ruth Lilly, began renovating the house and furnished it with
authentic period pieces.

To recreate William Conner's early life, Lilly purchased several log
buildings in Brown County and relocated them at Conner Prairie, which
became a private museum depicting the life of an early Indiana settler.

In 1964, the Lillys gave the museum and surrounding grounds to
Earlham College to be operated as a living outdoor museum, open to the
public. Earlham added a village area to the settlement in the 1970s.

TOUR

Begin your tour at the **Museum Center** where you can view an audio-visual presentation on Indiana pioneer days. The Weaver Gallery has changing exhibits on facets of life in the nineteenth century.

There are three areas to explore at Conner Prairie: the **1836 Village of Prairietown,** the **Conner Estate,** and the **Pioneer Adventure Center.** Settings are pleasant and pastoral; winding paths keep most buildings hidden from view. In the **1836 Village,** Conner Prairie guides play the parts of people who might have lived in the settlement in 1836. They have names, ages, occupations, families, and pasts. When you walk into a house, you are entering a particular person's home; and that person greets you and tells you about himself or herself in a natural, conversational way.

The **Golden Eagle,** a frame two-story inn, is run by Mrs. Zimmerman and her children. While the women took tea in the first-floor ladies' parlor, the men discussed politics and business in the barroom.

The **Fenton Cabin** is home to a weaver, who has his loom set up in the one-room log house. A bed and a spinning wheel are the other simple furnishings.

Samuel Hastings fought with General William Henry Harrison at Tippecanoe in 1811. He then became a farmer, but after some lean years, he lost his farm. In 1836, he was a pauper maintained by the county. His cabin is furnished so sparsely that there is not even a bed, only a mattress on the floor. **Hastings' Cabin** is a heartrending but undoubtedly realistic picture of the conditions in which some people in that era lived.

The two-room **McClure House** is more sumptuously furnished, with a rope bed, cradle, trunk, spinning wheel, clock, and chest of drawers. Owned by a carpenter Daniel McClure and his wife Hannah, the carpentry shop, complete with a foot-pedaled lathe, stands behind the house.

The large frame **Campbell House,** built in the early Greek Revival style, reflects the income and position of the doctor and his wife, Harriet. The parlor is attractively decorated with wallpaper, a piano, clock, mirror, and a velvet couch. While Mrs. Campbell serves tea to two other women in the parlor, she complains about leaving the sophistication of Lexington, Kentucky, for the roughness of the Indiana frontier. Nevertheless, Mrs. Campbell's kitchen has an iron stove—in 1836 a real innovation in cooking. Dr. Campbell's office is in back of the house; there he leisurely discusses modern medical treatments such as the use of leeches and bleeding.

In the one-room log **schoolhouse,** students attend school in November, December, and January, six days a week from 7:00 A.M. to 4:00 P.M. They study phonics and Noah Webster's spellers; because of a scarcity of books and writing materials, they recite most of their lessons. The schoolmaster is paid three cents per student per day, room and board, and vegetables for his pigs.

The **Whittaker House** is the home of the storekeeper and his wife. Mrs. Whittaker has a wild-goose-chase quilt on her bed, and you'll find her at work on another quilt, which is set up on a quilting frame.

As with all communities, sometimes there is something special happening. When you visit Prairietown, there might be a wedding, a funeral, a Literary Society meeting, political speakers, a camp meeting, a court session, a Temperance Society meeting, or a visiting phrenologist.

Shelves of dry goods, china, and clothes can be found in the one-story frame **general store.** "Spirits" are kept in the store's back room. The storekeeper uses a daybook for his accounts.

In the **blacksmith shop,** Ben Curtis and his apprentice are busy at a well-equipped forge but are not too preoccupied to talk politics. The **Curtis Home,** which Ben shares with his wife and young children, is a two-story frame. The furnishings, which include a beautiful corner cabinet, a couch in the parlor, a dry sink, and a spinning wheel, indicate that the blacksmith's business is fairly prosperous. The **apprentice's domicile,** on the other hand, is a simple log house.

The **Baker House,** a simple structure, reflects the status of the Baker brothers, the settlement's potters. They make their wares in the potter's shed and fire them in a kiln, which is housed in a separate building.

The **Conner Estate** is the nucleus around which Conner Prairie developed. William Conner's house, built in 1823, is a brick Federal-style mansion on a bluff overlooking the 200-acre prairie.

Although it was restored by Eli Lilly in the 1930s, wear and tear on the house from visitors took its toll. Using improved restoration investigative techniques, in 1992, a thorough re-restoration of the Conner mansion was undertaken to return it to a more historically correct 1823 appearance. An exhibit on the re-restoration process complete with blueprints and drawings is in the nearby Barn. Changes involved reproducing original wallpaper, returning painted surfaces to their original colors, reconstructing woodwork, and changing the function of rooms. It is furnished with pieces owned by Conner and comparable period pieces. The log outbuildings, moved to the site from Brown County, are typical of this period in Indiana. They include the **springhouse,** used for storing perishable foods; the **still,** where corn is distilled into whiskey; and the **loom house,** where textiles were woven.

Inviting hands-on participation, the **Pioneer Adventure Center** focuses on the crafts and chores of 1836. Visitors are invited to try weaving, cooking, spinning, quilting, candle dipping, soap making, blacksmithing, woodworking, and gunsmithing. Children can amuse themselves playing nineteenth-century games.

Special events include an art, craft, and antique show in March, a Memorial Day hot air balloon event, a Fourth of July celebration, Symphony on the Prairie on July and August weekend evenings, a cross stitch exposition in July, Headless Horseman hayride in late October, a Christmas candlelight walk, and a Festival of Gingerbread in December.

SIDE TRIPS

The Indianapolis area offers many features attractive to visitors. The **Children's Museum,** 3000 North Meridian Street, (317) 924-5431, is open Monday to Saturday, 10:00 A.M. to 5:00 P.M., and Sunday from 12:00 noon to 5:00 P.M. It is closed Mondays, Memorial Day to Labor Day. Admission charged.

Indianapolis is also the location of the **President Benjamin Harrison House,** 1230 North Delaware Street, (317) 631-1898. Open Monday to Saturday, 10:00 A.M. to 4:00 P.M.; Sunday, 12:00 noon to 4:00 P.M. Admission charged. The **James Whitcomb Riley House,** 528 Lockerbie Street, (317) 631-5885, is open Tuesday to Saturday, 10:00 A.M. to 4:00 P.M.; Sunday, 12:00 noon to 4:00 P.M. Admission charged.

AMANA COLONIES

German Inspirationist communal religious colonies from 1855 to 1932; NR

Address: Amana Heritage Society, P.O. Box 81, Amana, IA 52203; and/ or Amana Colonies Convention & Visitors Bureau, P.O. Box 303, Amana, IA 52203

Telephone: Heritage Society: (319) 622-3567; Visitors Bureau: (319) 622-3828; (800) 245-5465

Location: In southeast Iowa, 100 miles east of Des Moines; 21 miles southwest of Cedar Rapids, 15 miles northwest of Iowa City; off I-80, exit 225, then north on US 151 to US 6; five colonies are on Hwy. 220 and two colonies are on US 6

Open: Village shops, restaurants, and accommodations are open year-round; Museum of Amana History: Monday to Saturday, 10:00 A.M. to 5:00 P.M., Sunday, 12:00 noon to 5:00 P.M., mid-April to mid-November; Communal Kitchen and Cooper Shop Museum: Monday to Saturday, 9:00 A.M. to 5:00 P.M., Sunday, 12:00 noon to 5:00 P.M., May to October; Communal Agricultural Exhibit: Monday to Saturday, 10:00 A.M. to 5:00 P.M., May to September

Admission: Museum of Amana History: adults, $2.50; children, $1.00; Communal Kitchen and Cooper Shop Museum: adults, $1.50; children, $.75; Communal Agricultural Exhibit: adults, $1.00; children, $.50; combination tickets and group rates available

Restaurants: Amana: Ronneburg Restaurant, Ox Yoke Inn, Amana Barn Restaurant, Brick Haus Restaurant, Colony Inn, Colony Cone; South Amana: Colony Market Place Restaurant; Homestead: Homestead Kitchen, Bill Zuber's Restaurant; Middle Amana: Pizza Factory & Grill; Little Amana: Little Amana Bratwurst Haus, Seven Villages Restaurant

Shops: Antique, craft, wool, furniture, meat, wine and cheese stores throughout the Amana colonies

Facilities: Seven related villages with museums, shops, and restaurants

WHERE TO STAY

Inns/Bed & Breakfasts: Noe House Inn, Amana 52203, (319) 622-6350; Baeckerei, South Amana 52334, (319) 622-3597, (800) 484-1031; Babi's, South Amana 52334, (319) 662-4381; Rawson's, Homestead 52236, (319) 622-6035; Die Heimat Country Inn, Homestead

52236, (319) 622-3937; Dusk to Dawn, Middle Amana 52307, (319) 622-3029; Art Werks, High Amana 52203, (319) 622-3794
Motels/Hotels: Guest House Motel, Amana 52203, (319) 622-3599; Amana Holiday Inn, Box 187, Amana 52203, (319) 668-1175, FAX: (319) 668-2853; Day's Inn, Little Amana 52361, (800) 325-2525
Camping: Amana Colonies RV Park, Amana 52203, (319) 622-6262

OVERVIEW

Established by German immigrants who left the Old World to find religious freedom in the New, the Amana Colonies are a testament to America's ethnic and religious diversity. The seven Amana colonies—Amana, West Amana, High Amana, Middle Amana, East Amana, South Amana, and Homestead—were founded in 1855 by members of a predominantly German religious sect, somewhat akin to the Pietists, who called themselves "the true Inspirationists." These colonies, which attract thousands of visitors each year, do not fit precisely the definition of a museum village. They are living communities, but they have also retained a rich heritage that makes them worth visiting for those who wish to experience the cultural, ethnic, and religious diversity that is America's past. The German religious sect who settled the Amana Colonies is a distinct religious group and should not be confused with other small denominations such as the Amish and the Shakers.

The Amana Heritage Society has restored building museums in three colonies which together constitute an outdoor museum. Although many original Amana buildings are private residences, many others are used as bed and breakfasts, craft shops, restaurants, and food stores. Although technically speaking these buildings are not restored, neither have they been greatly altered. The towns' layouts remain unchanged from their original plans with the possible exception of Amana, which is the most heavily visited by tourists. The seven Amana Colonies constitute a very unique museum village, with fine collections of original furnishings and artifacts displayed in the restored museum builings.

Today, the Amanas are bustling with tourists shopping for the sturdy Amana woolens, handicrafts, and food or eating hearty German family-style dinners in the local restaurants. Of course, shopping and dining are part of a visit to the Amanas, but a traveler should take the time to study and tour the colonies.

HISTORY

The Amana story began in southwestern Germany in 1714, when two *Werkzeuge* ("inspired ones"), Johann Friedrich Rock, son of a Lutheran

Amana Colonies, Amana, Iowa
Unlike other Christian churches with steeples and crosses, Inspirationist churches,
like this one in South Amana, resemble elongated brick houses. The bell was rung
to announce services. Colonists attended as many as eleven religious
services per week. At Amana Colonies, Amana, IA.

Photo by Patricia A. Gutek

minister, and Eberhard Ludwig Gruber, a Lutheran clergyman, began to
receive what they believed to be divinely inspired messages. Rock, Gruber,
and their followers were convinced that as in the days of the Old Testament prophets, God revealed His truths to certain inspired persons. The
importance that the group gave to divine inspiration led to the name that
they later took as a separate church: the Community of True Inspiration.

The Inspirationists, like the Harmonists of New Harmony, Indiana
(see page 237), and the Separatists of Zoar, Ohio (see page 286), were
seeking a simple and direct religious experience that they found lacking in
the more formal Lutheran church. Because they deviated from orthodox
doctrine, refused to bear arms, and wanted to educate their children in
their own religious beliefs, the Inspirationists were persecuted in Prussia

and the other German states. Despite their oppression, they survived and kept their faith alive. In 1817, the small group of believers was reinvigorated by a revival led by Christian Metz and Barbara Heinemann, two principal leaders in a new generation of "inspired ones." In 1842, they began to emigrate to the United States in search of religious freedom.

They first established communities near Buffalo, New York. After spending a decade in New York, the Inspirationists decided to relocate their communities in the fertile Iowa plains. In 1855, Amana, the first colony, was founded; West Amana, South Amana, High Amana, East Amana, Middle Amana, and later, Homestead, on the railroad line to Iowa City, followed.

The Amana Colonies were established as communal societies, where work was shared and property was held in common. Members lived together and went out to work in the fields, pastures, and mills. The Amanas were governed by a Grand Council of Thirteen Elders; each colony also had a Village Elders Committee as its local government. The committees made the major decisions for the colonies and also assigned the occupations of the members.

Agriculture was the basis of the Amanas' economy. The Inspirationists' landholdings increased from their original 3,000 acres, purchased in 1855, to an unbroken tract of 25,659 acres by 1932. Land, including the village yards, was intensively cultivated; the chief crops were corn, oats, wheat, hay, and potatoes. A distinctive feature still found in the Amanas is the practice of growing grapes on vine-covered trellises mounted on the facades of buildings; this practice not only provides grapes for the delicious Amana wines but also is a natural form of insulation.

In addition, each village had crafts and industries. Each colony had a blacksmith's shop, cabinetmaker's shop, general store, post office, bakery, dairy, wine cellar, and sawmill. The major industry in Amana and Middle Amana was the manufacture of woolen cloth, and the Amanas today continue to be known for their high-quality wool textiles.

Each colony's building plan emphasized internal order and utility. Most of the Inspirationists lived in communal houses without kitchens. Their homes were made of sandstone, brick, or unpainted wood. The usual plan for these houses was a central hall, with two suites, each with two rooms, on each floor. Cooking was done in communal kitchen houses by crews of ten women, directed by a *Küchenbas* ("kitchen boss"). Meals were served in these large houses to thirty or forty people at a time. The kitchen houses, located on the village's main street, were the heart of the community.

Although the Inspirationists were, and still are, intensely religious people, often attending eleven services each week, many visitors have difficulty in locating the colonies' churches. Unlike other Christian churches, with their steeples and crosses, the stone or brick churches of the Inspirationists are similar to elongated houses, with elders' residences built at the ends.

Each church has two or more meeting rooms, the largest of which was used for the general service. These rather austere rooms are furnished with wooden benches on plain wooden floors; walls are painted a light blue. The general worship service consists of readings from the Bible and the testimonies of *Werkzeuge* and hymn singing.

The Amanas developed an educational system that enhanced the occupations of communal life. Children were sent to the *Kinderschule* ("children's school") from age two to age seven. The *Kinderschule*, which was somewhat like a kindergarten, left mothers free to work while their youngsters were cared for by the women who were assigned to the schools. From ages seven to fourteen, children attended the colonies' schools, which followed a conventional curriculum that stressed reading, writing, and arithmetic.

In 1932, when the United States was being economically ravaged by the Great Depression, the Grand Council, after much debate, proposed the reorganization of the Amanas on the basis of private ownership, with each family receiving shares of common stock. The proposal was voted on in a referendum, and more than 90 percent of the community members approved the change. Several factors appear to have motivated the Amanas' decision to privatize: a belief that private initiative might improve the colonies' economic condition; social and technological changes in American life that reduced the feasibility of separatist communities; and discontent among many young people, particularly women, who felt that the communal system restricted freedom of choice. Although the Amanas have advanced into the twentieth century along with the rest of the nation, the descendants of the earlier settlers continue to adhere to many of the values and practices of their forebears.

TOUR

As you tour the Amana Colonies, try to visualize them both as a whole and as separate communities. The seven colonies together form a way of life that originally was organized according to Inspirationist religious beliefs and the transplanted traditions of nineteenth-century rural Germany. Each colony should also be viewed as a close-knit agricultural village with its own stores, shops, wineries, and restaurants that reflect the Amana ethnic tradition.

The **Museum of Amana History,** located in the village of Amana, is maintained by the Amana Heritage Society, a not-for-profit organization dedicated to maintaining Amana's cultural heritage. Three nineteenth-century buildings constitute the Museum of Amana History: the 1864 **Noe House,** the 1870 **Schoolhouse,** and the **Washhouse/Woodshed.** The Noe House, which has been restored to the communal period, was originally a communal kitchen and later a doctor's residence. Artifacts, tools, utensils, and lithographs that belonged to Amana families are used to trace the history and development of Amana. The Amana Schoolhouse was an active school from 1870 to 1955. It contains the Christmas Room, a *Kinderschule,* a *Strickschule,* and a toy exhibit. A film on the history of Amana is shown in the Schoolhouse auditorium, and the Museum Store is located here. Audio programs in the Washhouse/Woodshed give background information on exhibits of tools and garden implements.

Amana, the busiest of the seven colonies, has many bakeries, meat shops, wine and cheese stores, antique and craft stores. Don't miss the Amana Furniture and Clock Shop, a workshop and display room of handcrafted walnut, cherry, and oak furniture; the Amana Woolen Mill featuring famous Amana woolen goods including clothes, blankets, and fabrics; Amana General Store, an original store built in 1858; the Millstream Brewing Co., Iowa's oldest brewery and four wineries; and Amana Meat Shop & Smokehouse, an old-fashioned butcher shop featuring ham, bacon, and sausages.

The Amana Heritage Society's **Communal Agriculture Exhibit** is in South Amana. Housed in an 1860 oxen barn are agricultural implements including equipment for planting, plowing, harvesting, haymaking, and livestock management. An exhibit focuses on the system of communal farming in each village which had its own cropland, pasture, timber, farm boss, and farm labor crew. Trades related to agriculture including blacksmithing, harnessmaking, and wagonmaking are highlighted. Also in South Amana is the **Barn Museum** which has a large collection of miniatures built by Henry Moore.

The Communal Kitchen and the Cooper Shop in Middle Amana are also maintained by the Amana Heritage Society. Homes in the colonies did not have kitchens. Amana had as many as sixty communal kitchens where meals were prepared for thirty to forty people three times a day. Amana's only intact communal kitchen, the 1863 Ruedy Kitchen, with its large brick hearth, dry sink with wooden tubs, cooking implements, and dining room with long tables has been preserved as it appeared in 1932, the year the society dissolved. The Cooper Shop, built around 1863, is the only one remaining in the colonies. Original coopering tools as well as buckets, tubs, and barrels are displayed. Also in Middle Amana is Hahn's Hearth Oven Bakery which still bakes breads and pastries in an original wood-burning oven, and Amana Refrigeration, Inc., the appliance company which began as a colony industry.

In High Amana, visit the **Amana Arts Guild Center** which is an art gallery and museum shop featuring early Amana art, folk art, and crafts. There is also an **Old Fashioned High Amana Store,** a gift store whose interior has not changed in 100 years.

Homestead has the **Ehrle Brothers Winery,** the oldest, original winery in the Amana Colonies. There are also one- and three-mile nature trails.

SIDE TRIPS

Travelers may wish to visit the **Herbert Hoover National Historic Site.** The two-room birthplace cottage, the Hoover Presidential Library, a one-room school, a Quaker meetinghouse, a reconstructed blacksmith shop, a visitors center, and the gravesites of President and Mrs. Hoover are in a well-landscaped 186-acre park located 10 miles east of Iowa City on I-80. The house, restored to its 1871 appearance, was the birthplace and boyhood home of Herbert Hoover from 1874 to 1884. Hoover, the thirty-first president of the United States, served from 1929 to 1933. Open daily, 8:00 A.M. to 5:00 P.M.; closed New Year's Day, Thanksgiving, and Christmas. For further information, write Herbert Hoover National Historic Site, P.O. Box 607, West Branch, IA 52358; phone (319) 643-2541.

HENRY FORD MUSEUM & GREENFIELD VILLAGE

Recreation of an American village from colonial times to the modern era and indoor museum of American technology; NR

Address: P.O. Box 1970, 20900 Oakwood Blvd., Dearborn, MI 48121-1970

Telephone: (313) 271-1620, (800) 835-5237, TDD: (313) 271-2455

Location: In southeast Michigan, 12 miles west of Detroit; on Oakwood Boulevard, just west of the Southfield Freeway (MI 39) and just south of Michigan Avenue (U.S. 12)

Open: Greenfield Village: mid-March through January 1, daily, 9:00 A.M. to 5:00 P.M.; Henry Ford Museum: daily, 9:00 A.M. to 5:00 P.M.; Museum and Village closed Thanksgiving and Christmas

Admission: Combination Ticket for Henry Ford Museum & Greenfield Village: adults, $20.00; children 5 to 12, $10.00; Greenfield Village only: adults, $11.50; senior citizens, $10.50; children 5 to 12, $5.75; Henry Ford Museum only: adults, $11.50; senior citizens, $10.50; children 5 to 12, $5.75; narrated carriage tour: $4.00 per person; narrated bus tour: $3.00 per person

Restaurants: Village: Eagle Tavern, Taste of History, Mainstreet Lunch Stand, Picnic Lunch Stand; Museum: American Cafe, Corner Cupboard

Shops: Village: Greenfield Village Store; Museum: Museum Store; The Plaza Store; American Life Collection Gallery

Facilities: Education programs; research center; theater; partially handicapped accessible; carriage tours; Suwanee Steamboat; train; carousel; 1931 bus; winter sleigh rides

WHERE TO STAY

Motels/Hotels: Marriott-Dearborn Inn, 20301 Oakwood Blvd., Dearborn 48124, (313) 271-2700, FAX: (313) 271-7464; Best Western Greenfield Inn, 3000 Enterprise Drive, Allen Park 48101, (313) 271-1600, FAX: (313) 271-1600, ext. 7189; Hampton Inn, 20061 Michigan

**Henry Ford Museum & Greenfield Village,
Dearborn, Michigan**
Orville and Wilbur Wright operated the Wright Cycle Co., a bicycle business, in
Dayton, Ohio. Moved to Greenfield Village, the 1870 building has been restored
to 1903—the year the brothers made their first successful flight. At Henry Ford
Museum & Greenfield Village, Dearborn, MI.

Photo by Patricia A. Gutek

Ave., Dearborn 48124, (313) 436-9600, FAX: (313) 436-8345; The
Ritz-Carlton, Dearborn, 300 Town Center Dr., Dearborn 48126,
(313) 441-2000, FAX: (313) 441-2051
Camping: Detroit/Greenfield KOA, 6680 Bunton Rd., Ypsilanti 48197,
(313) 482-7722; Wayne County Fairgrounds, 10871 Quirk Rd.,
Belleville 48111, (313) 697-7002

OVERVIEW
Get ready for something different when you visit Henry Ford Museum & Greenfield Village. There's no other museum village like it. For
one thing, it's bigger. Together, Henry Ford Museum & Greenfield Village

comprise the largest indoor/outdoor museum complex in the country. Secondly, most museum villages focus on the history of a particular region, but Greenfield Village has no regional focus. Not restored to a particular year or era, its exhibits portray aspects of American history from colonial to modern times.

What this outdoor museum does focus on is people. Many of Greenfield Village's people are Americans who are highly divergent thinkers. They are the inventors, political figures, scientists, or educators who are responsible for technological progress and social change in the United States. As a memorial to those exceptional Americans who were instrumental in changing America from a primarily rural, agricultural nation to an industrial, urban nation, Henry Ford has gathered their homes, laboratories, and businesses from all over the country to form a section of his American village. Buildings have been restored and furnished as they were when occupied by people named Edison, Ford, Wright, Heinz, Firestone, and Webster.

Other historic buildings in Greenfield Village help tell the story of everyday Americans who also contributed their labor to the building of this great nation. The emphasis in this museum village is on the American tradition of ingenuity, resourcefulness, and innovation.

Henry Ford Museum is an immense indoor museum displaying a vast variety of historical artifacts in the fields of American agriculture, industry, domestic life, and the decorative arts.

HISTORY

Henry Ford Museum & Greenfield Village is the brainchildren of one man: Henry Ford. The automobile magnate who developed the mass-produced automobile, Ford was a self-made industrialist. He regarded America as a land of opportunity and became interested in preserving its heritage.

He began collecting machines and instruments that had been significant but were now outmoded. Once he started, his collection grew rapidly as he enlisted the aid of friends and employees. By 1925, Ford's collection had completely filled the old Dearborn tractor factory.

Soon Ford turned to collecting buildings. His plan was to create both a museum and a village. His vision included showing change from era to era. He wished to show common household items from the hand-crafted era through the machine stage into the rapid changes of industrialization.

Much of Ford's collection focuses on his personal heroes. Among his acquisitions was the group of buildings associated with Thomas Edison's electric light, plant breeder Luther Burbank's office, an Illinois courthouse where Abraham Lincoln practiced law, Noah Webster's house, the Wright brothers' shop, and his own childhood home and first school.

In the early 1920s, Ford conceived of a museum that would preserve the American past. He set aside a tract of land at Dearborn, Michigan, for his museum's buildings and exhibits.

A fourteen-acre museum building was designed by architect Robert O. Derrick who based his design of the central portion of the structure's facade on Philadelphia's Independence Hall and either end on Independence Square's Congress Hall and Old City Hall. Twenty-eight buildings were arranged in the village. On October 21, 1929, the fiftieth anniversary of the electric light, Henry Ford Museum & Greenfield Village was dedicated to Thomas Edison.

Ford continued to acquire large numbers of structures and historic objects in the years following the dedication of the museum. There are now eighty-five buildings on the eighty-one-acre village site.

Henry Ford Museum & Greenfield Village is visited annually by more than a million people. Its Americana collection ranks with the finest in the country. Of particular merit is its transportation collection.

Tour

Greenfield Village is very large, with well-laid-out streets, attractive landscaping, and beautifully restored original buildings. Its sheer scope and volume prevent us from anything more than just listing what is in the collection; detailing the background and contents of each exhibit would require a separate book. This pleasant, huge, and varied museum complex is well worth a two-day visit by the entire family so that the wealth of exhibits can be savored and enjoyed.

Greenfield Village has more then eighty historic homes, workplaces and community buildings on eighty-one developed acres, ranging from colonial times to modern times. Many original commercial, religious, and social structures have been moved to the village from American small towns. Standing at the head of the Village Green is the **Martha-Mary Chapel,** a small church built from the bricks of the childhood home of Clara Bryant, Henry Ford's wife. Also on the green is a two-story white inn, the **Eagle Tavern** (1831), moved from Clinton, Michigan. It has been restored to the 1850s, and is now used as a restaurant serving fare from that period. The **Scotch Settlement School,** the little red schoolhouse from Dearborn township which Henry Ford attended as a child, and the **Town Hall** which serves as an information center face the green.

Additional community buildings include the 1892 **Cohen Millinery Shop,** the 1859 **Smiths Creek Depot,** the 1854 **Elias Brown General Store,** the 1839 **Dr. Howard's Office,** the 1878 **Grimm Jewelry Store** which was moved from Detroit, the **Phoenixville Post Office** which has been restored to 1905, and the 1840 Illinois **Logan County Courthouse** in which Abraham Lincoln practiced law.

The village's historic homes span a period of three centuries and include buildings connected with famous Americans. The **Edison Homestead,** from Vienna, Ontario, Canada, was the home of Thomas Edison's grandparents. Thomas Edison spent many boyhood summers there. The 1870 **Wright Brothers' Cycle Shop and Home** have been restored to 1903—the year the brothers made their first successful flight. The late-nineteenth-century, two-story, frame house from Dayton, Ohio, was the childhood home of Wilbur and Orville Wright. It reflects the period in which the Wright brothers were developing their flying machine in the adjacent **Wright Cycle Co. Shop.**

The **Heinz House** was the childhood home of Henry John Heinz and the original headquarters of the Pennsylvania-based H.J. Heinz Co. It features an exhibit that illustrates the development of brandname products and provides more than a century of product promotion history including distinctive advertising, packaging, and promotional specialties.

The **Firestone Farm** from Columbiana County, Ohio, was the birthplace of industrialist Harvey Firestone. The working farm, which is set in the 1880s, features crops and animals appropriate to that period.

Henry Ford was fond of the *McGuffey Readers* which were used by generations of American children in learning to read. He acquired the 1780 **Birthplace of William McGuffey,** the educator who wrote the *McGuffey Readers,* and moved it from Washington County, Pennsylvania. Nearby is the recreated **McGuffey School.** The **Luther Burbank Birthplace** was built in Lancaster, Massachusetts, around 1820. Burbank was born in the house in 1849. From New Haven, Connecticut, the **Noah Webster House** was home to the man who compiled the first American dictionary in 1828.

The **Henry Ford Birthplace** is a simple, two-story, white, clapboarded farmhouse built by Henry's father, William, in Dearborn in 1863. Ford restored the house to its appearance during his childhood. The **Bagley Avenue Brick Shed** is a replica of the shop where Ford built his first car.

Exhibits which focus on the family lives of enslaved and freed African Americans in America are the **Hermitage Slave Houses** and **Mattox**

House. The Slave Houses are brick, one-story, sixteen-foot-square structures which were originally constructed on the Hermitage Plantation near Savannah, Georgia, between 1820 and 1850. Mattox House is a one-and-one-half story, two-room frame farmhouse built about 1879 in Bryan County, Georgia. It was the home of Amos Morel, a formerly enslaved African American who was freed by the Emancipation Proclamation. This house has been restored to the 1930s when Morel's grandson, Amos Mattox, and his wife ran the farm.

Edison's Menlo Park Compound contains the restored and reconstructed buildings connected with Thomas Edison's invention of the electric light bulb. Edison's Research Laboratory, Machine Shop, Library and Office Building, and Carpenter's Shop were moved from Menlo Park, New Jersey. Edison developed 420 of his more than 1,000 patented inventions in the New Jersey laboratory. The lab is restored to the way it looked on October 21, 1879, when the first successful incandescent lamp was tested. On the second floor of the laboratory are many of Edison's inventions, including the phonograph, mimeograph, telephone transmitter, and radio tube.

Many of Edison's assistants lived in Sarah Jordan's Boardinghouse, restored to 1879, which is now adjacent to the laboratory. The boardinghouse was one of the first homes to be lit by electricity; heavy electrical cords lead to it from the laboratory. Two other Edison laboratories from West Orange, New Jersey, and Fort Myers, Florida, are in the Edison Area.

The Crafts and Manufactures area focuses on America's transition from an agricultural society to an industrial power. Included are the Tripp Up-and-Down Sawmill (1855), Armington and Sims Machine Shop and Foundry, Richart Carriage Shop (1851), Loranger Gristmill (1832), Plymouth Carding Mill (1850), the pottery, printing office, tin shop, glass house, and textile building.

Glass, pottery, printing, tin, and textile demonstrations are given regularly. A 1901 Chessie System Railroad Turntable from Petoskey, Michigan, has recently been installed so that Greenfield Village's railroad equipment can change direction.

You'll need at least two days in Dearborn because it takes another day to go through the twelve-acre Henry Ford Museum. Ford's outstanding collections in transportation, industry, domestic life, communication, and agriculture converge around the sweeping changes that transformed America from a rural, agrarian society into a highly industrialized nation. "Made in America" is a major exhibit of eighteenth-, nineteenth-, and twentieth-century machines that produced power and goods, along with

1,500 industrial artifacts, audio-video presentations, hands-on activities, operating machines, and films.

"The Automobile in American Life," another major exhibit, is divided into six sections: the automotive landscape, tourism, automotive design, symbolism, advertising, and the evolution of the automobile. Displayed are more than 100 historically significant vehicles plus some of the businesses spawned by the automobile including a wonderful 1940s Texaco service station, a 1941 tourist cabin, a 1946 diner, and a 1950s drive-in movie.

The Innovation Station, one of the museum's newer installations, is a giant learning game which provides a hands-on encounter with defining and solving problems. Participants use stationary bicycles, hand cranks, and a stair stepper to make the power needed to distribute brightly colored plastic balls through a network of tubes and sorting devices into receiving bins. As problems occur, the players, as many as thirty at a time, must use teamwork and innovation to reach solutions.

The Domestic Life exhibit of American furniture and decorative arts includes antique furniture, clocks, watches, pottery, toys, silver, pewter, stoves, sewing machines, kitchen utensils, and appliances dating from the seventeenth century to the present.

Henry Ford was a collector with sometimes eccentric taste. Among his exhibits are the rocking chair from Ford's Theater in which Abraham Lincoln was seated when he was shot by John Wilkes Booth on April 14, 1865, as well as Lincoln's shawl and the play program; the Lincoln presidential limousine in which President John F. Kennedy was riding in Dallas when he was shot on November 22, 1963; and Thomas Edison's last breath in a glass vial obtained by his son when his father was on his death bed as requested by Henry Ford.

SIDE TRIPS

Fair Lane is the Henry Ford Estate built in 1915 for more than two million dollars. Located on the Rouge River, Fair Lane has its own six-level power plant connected to the mansion by a tunnel that made it self-sufficient in power, heat, light, and ice. The estate is on a seventy-two-acre site with gardens and trails on the University of Michigan, Dearborn campus. The powerhouse, boathouse, and gardens have been restored and tours are given of the house and grounds. Located on Evergreen Road in Dearborn, one mile from Henry Ford Museum & Greenfield Village. Daily, April to December; Sunday to Friday from January through March. Admission charged. (313) 593-5590.

Historic Fayette Townsite

Restoration of a nineteenth-century iron-smelting village; NR

Address: Fayette State Park, 13700 13.25 Garden Lane, Garden, MI 49835
Telephone: (906) 644-2603
Location: On Michigan's Upper Peninsula, on Lake Michigan side, on the Garden Peninsula 17 miles south of US 2
Open: Daily, 9:00 A.M. to 5:00 P.M., May to mid-October, 9:00 A.M. until 8:00 P.M., during the summer
Admission: State Park: $3.50 per car; no separate admission to Historic Fayette Townsite
Facilities: Visitor Center; guided tours; tour boat cruises; carriage tours; state park has a swimming beach, hiking trails, campground, picnic area, fishing, scuba diving, and boating

Where to Stay

Cottages/Cabins: Lone Eagle Resort, Box 3272-A, Star Route, Manistique 49854, (906) 341-8102; Mountain Ash Resort, RR 2, Box 2490, Indian Lake, Manistique 49854, (906) 341-5658; Burson's Delta Resort, Box 3173 St. Rt., Manistique 49854, (906) 573-2779; Hovey's Bear Trap Resort, RR 1, Box 1273, Manistique 49854, (906) 341-6553
Bed & Breakfasts: The Summer House, State St., Garden 49835, (906) 644-2457; Marina Guest House, 230 Arbutus, Manistique 49854, (906) 341-5147; Historic House of Ludington, 223 Ludington St., Escanaba 49829, (906) 786-4000; Celibeth House, Rt. 1, Box 58A, Blaney Park 49836, (906) 283-3409
Motels/Hotels: Best Western Breakers Motel, P.O. Box 322, Manistique 49854, (906) 341-2410; Manistique Motor Inn Budget Host, Rt. 1, Manistique 49854, (906) 341-2552, (800) 666-5552
Camping: Fayette State Park, 13700 13.25 Lane, Garden 49835, (906) 644-2603; Indian Lake State Park, Rt. 2, Box 2500, Manistique 49854, (906) 341-2355; Woodstar Beach Campground, 2674 Rt. 2, Manistique 49889, (906) 341-6514

Overview

A local newspaper reporter who interviewed us for an article about the first edition of this book asked us if we had ever been to the outdoor museum in Michigan's Upper Peninsula—Historic Fayette Townsite. We hadn't, nor had we even heard about it. Soon afterward, we visited Fayette, a restored, nineteenth-century, iron-smelting town picturesquely set on Snail Shell Harbor with its dramatic limestone cliffs and surrounded by lush forests. Glistening white sailboats which had sailed in from Big Bay de Noc were docked at the harbor on that sunny August day. Grateful for the suggestion, we have corrected the omission in this second edition.

The Jackson Iron Company operated an iron furnace on Michigan's Upper Peninsula from the late 1860s until 1891. Jackson's employees, most of whom were young European or Canadian immigrants, and their families formed a community of 500 people in the isolated area. Buildings in the town were built and owned by the company. After the iron furnace closed in 1891, the town of Fayette was abandoned by the Jackson Iron Company though local residents continued to utilize the structures until the 1950s when the state of Michigan acquired the property.

More than twenty original Fayette structures still stand. Some are furnished, others serve as museums with exhibits while others are being stabilized. Restoration is ongoing and is aided by archaeological research. Although the townsite is relatively large, only several buildings have been restored. Fayette is a combination museum village and ghost town. Today, this area of Michigan is a popular summer recreational area that draws many tourists. In addition to swimming and sailing, visitors can glimpse a 100-year-old company town which illustrates a chapter in Michigan's industrial past. And, for a unique touch, you can arrive by boat and tie up at the harbor.

HISTORY

Jackson Iron Company, originally named Jackson Mining Company, was formed in 1845 to mine copper but a year later was mining iron ore in the Upper Peninsula's Marquette County. In 1864, the company purchased land on the Garden Peninsula to build a blast furnace for the production of charcoal iron. This site was selected because of the availability of the products needed to produce pig iron: iron ore, limestone which was used as a flux to remove the iron's impurities, and hardwood trees which would be cut and then burned into charcoal to be used as fuel in the furnaces. The Garden Peninsula's deep harbor facilitated shipping. Iron ore could be transported by rail from the Jackson mines seventy miles away at Negaunee to Escanaba, a Lake Michigan port, and then towed by barge across Bay de Noc to the Jackson furnace. Limestone could be quarried from the bluff along the eastern shore of the harbor. The maple and beech forests on the Garden Peninsula would provide the hardwood which would be processed into charcoal.

Fayette Brown was the company manager, and the townsite was named for him. A blast furnace and casting house were constructed in 1867 as well as a large dock and eight charcoal kilns. A second furnace stack and casting house were built in 1870. Unlike earlier blast furnaces, Fayette's furnaces were powered by steam rather than water and were hot blast instead of cold as the air blown into them was preheated. During its twenty-four years of operation, Fayette's blast furnaces produced 229,288 tons of iron. Finished pig iron was shipped from Fayette's Snail Shell Harbor to major Great Lakes ports. Most of the iron was converted to industrial application including steel for railroad rails as the railroads expanded across America.

Fayette was, by necessity, a company town. Since Michigan's Upper Peninsula was isolated and relatively unpopulated, the company built employee housing as well as businesses, including a butcher shop, a general store, and a barber shop. They also hired a doctor, had a school for the children of the employees, and a Catholic church. At its peak, Fayette was a community of about 500 people, including a superintendent, foreman, furnace laborers, and their families. About eighty percent of the workers were young immigrants including French Canadians, Belgians, Irish, Germans, Scandinavians, and Bohemians. Employees worked hard under hot, noisy, and often dangerous conditions for $1.00 to $1.50 a day. Expenses incurred for rent, medical attention, or purchases were deducted from a worker's monthly earnings. Community recreation included baseball games, horse races, dances, band concerts, and holiday parties.

After nearly two-and-a-half decades of operation, the company's nearby reserves of uncut woodland dwindled and it became necessary to obtain supplies of wood from greater distances. Added transportation costs occurred simultaneously with a drop in the market price of charcoal iron due to improvements in the quality of cheaper coke iron. The Jackson Company was faced with remodeling and updating its operation or going out of business. Deciding that a new investment would not guarantee profitability, the Jackson Iron Company closed its smelting operation at Fayette in 1891. Most workers left to find employment elsewhere, though a small number stayed and became farmers, commercial fishermen, or hotel workers.

Fayette became a state park in 1959 and in the mid-1970s, the Bureau of History of the Michigan Department of State, in cooperation with the Parks Division of the Department of Natural Resources, began a new era of stabilization and restoration of the site.

Tour

Whether you arrive by water or land, begin your tour at the **Interpretive Museum** or **Visitor Center** which displays a scale model of the 1880s townsite. Other exhibits include a chronological timeline of the Jackson Iron Company, women's clothing, shipping, types of restoration work, and the progression of ore from the mines to general use. It also houses an exhibit on the furnace workers who lived at Fayette, many of whom were from Europe. 1880 census data were used as a source of information on these hardworking people.

Most of the restored buildings are weathered, gray frames as is the three-story **Hotel.** Originally named the Fayette House, it was built in the late 1860s to accommodate traveling salesmen and summer visitors, most of whom arrived by boat. Unmarried furnace workers occupied the third floor. The hotel was remodeled and enlarged in 1882. Company owned, the hotel was leased to proprietors for $1,000 a year. The hotel continued to operate after the furnace closed as the area was a popular tourist destination. The furnished lobby can be seen on the first floor.

Originally used as a granary, the **Town Hall** is a two-story, weathered, gray building. The second-floor was used as a Music Hall while on the first floor were a barber shop, apothecary, and butcher shop. The Butcher Shop's meat was stored in an insulated cooler. An overhead cable system conveyed blocks of ice, which were cut from the frozen lake and stored in a icehouse, up the hill from the butcher's shop.

More than twenty New England saltbox-style houses were built for the supervisory employees of Jackson Iron Company. Nine houses remain and the stone foundations of the others are visible. One **Supervisor's Home** is furnished with Victorian furniture, while another has interpretive panels.

The **Company Offices** housed Jackson Iron Company's superintendent and bookkeeper. Reflecting his important position, the Superintendent's Office has a large rolltop desk, a leather swivel chair, a safe, an iron stove for heating, and a corner sink with hot and cold water. Victorian influence is seen in the interior paint scheme which is brown with navy and red trim.

Machinists maintained industrial equipment in the one-story, limestone and red-brick **Machine Shop.** It is set up to show various aspects of life at Fayette, including the furnace operation, a woman's daily life, school, and machinery operations and repair.

Forming the heart of the industrial village is the **Furnace Complex,** which consists of large, impressive, limestone, stabilized ruins. In 1993, the state park repointed, repaired, and reroofed the entire Furnace Complex. The first blast furnace was built in 1867 and the second in 1870. Adjacent to each furnace was a Casting Room. After smelting, molten iron was released through a tap hole near the bottom of the furnace. It flowed down channels into sand molds called pigs in the sand floor of the Casting Room. In the upper level of the furnace complex are the brick remains of the hot blast ovens and the walls of the boiler and blower rooms. After measured amounts of charcoal, ore, and limestone were dumped into the furnace, blast ovens heated air, which was forced into the furnaces by steam-powered blowers to make the charcoal burn.

Charcoal, the fuel used in the furnaces, was made in kilns. By about 1875, sixty kilns operated at or within ten miles of Fayette. One of the red-brick, beehive-shaped **Charcoal Kilns** has been reconstructed. In a carefully controlled procedure that took eight days, thirty-five cords of hardwood would be burned to produce 1,750 bushels of charcoal. The restored **Lime Kiln** was used to heat limestone quarried from the bluffs. After lime was produced, it was used in mortar for masonry and for plastering interior walls.

The **Doctor's House** was the home of the company doctor, Dr. Curtis J. Bellows. It is a two-story limestone and frame house. Bellows was a Civil War veteran from Ohio who practiced medicine at Fayette until his death in 1882. Upstairs, there is a furnished sitting room and kitchen.

The most impressive home at Fayette was the **Superintendent's House.** Situated on a bluff overlooking the harbor, the eleven-room, frame house had a wrap-around porch and a wallpapered privy. The downstairs of the Superintendent's House is open with panel displays explaining the residence and its occupants.

Recently, the **Company Store** has been stabilized.

SIDE TRIPS

Michigan's Upper Peninsula is a nature lover's paradise, much of it preserved as national or state parks. Pictured Rocks National Lakeshore is a forty-two-mile section of Lake Superior shoreline. P.O. Box 40, Munising 49862, (906) 387-3700. Hiawatha National Forest has 879,000 acres of woods and lakes including shoreline of Lake Huron, Lake Michigan, and Lake Superior. 2727 N. Lincoln Rd., P.O. Box 316, Escanaba 49829, (906) 786-4062.

STUHR MUSEUM OF THE PRAIRIE PIONEER

Recreation of a late-nineteenth-century Nebraska railroad town

Address: 3133 W. Highway 34, Grand Island, NE 68801

Telephone: (308) 385-5316; FAX: (308) 385-5028

Location: Grand Island is in southeast Nebraska; Stuhr Museum is four miles north of I-80, exit 312, at jct. of US 281 and US 34

Open: Daily, 9:00 A.M. to 5:00 P.M., May to mid-October; outdoor museum closed rest of year; Main Museum and Fonner Rotunda only: Monday to Saturday, 9:00 A.M. to 5:00 P.M., Sunday, 1:00 P.M. to 5:00 P.M., from mid-October through April

Admission: Adults, $6.00, children 7 to 16, $3.50, May to mid-October; adults, $4.00, children 7 to 16, $2.00, mid-October through April

Restaurants: The Silver Dollar Cafe

Shops: Museum Shop; General Mercantile Emporium

Facilities: Visitor Center; arboretum with picnic areas; special events; crafts demonstrations; partially wheelchair accessible

WHERE TO STAY

Motels/Hotels: Days Inn, 2620 N. Diers Ave., Grand Island 68803, (308) 384-8624; Best Western Island Inn, 2311 S. Locust St., Grand Island 68801, (308) 382-1815; Holiday Inn Midtown, 2503 S. Locust, Grand Island 68801, (308) 384-1330; Riverside Inn, 3333 Ramada Rd., Grand Island 68801, (308) 384-5150, FAX: (308) 384-6551

Camping: Mormon Island State Recreation Area, Grand Island, (308) 381-5649; West Hamilton RV Park, Rt. 2, Box 163A, Doniphan 68832, (402) 886-2249

OVERVIEW

Stuhr Museum of the Prairie Pioneer is designed to preserve and interpret the pioneer heritage of Nebraska's Great Plains between 1850 and 1900. It tells the story of the people of Nebraska from the Plains Indians to the homesteaders and early town builders. The museum also focuses on the railroads that traversed and crisscrossed Nebraska's plains at the end of the nineteenth century and the railroad towns they spawned.

**Stuhr Museum of the Prairie Pioneer,
Grand Island, Nebraska**

Horses graze near the livery stable in Railroad Town, a recreated late-nineteenth-century town. At Stuhr Museum of the Prairie Pioneer, Grand Island, NE.

Photo by Patricia A. Gutek

Stuhr's 200-acre museum complex includes a Main Museum Building devoted to the culture of the prairie pioneers, the Fonner Memorial Rotunda with exhibits on the Plains Indians, a forty-acre crossroads railroad town of the late nineteenth century with sixty buildings, a mid-nineteenth-century pioneer settlement of eight structures, a Pawnee Earth Lodge, an antique farm machinery and auto exhibit, and a railyard exhibit.

HISTORY

Approximately 40,000 Plains Indians—Sioux, Cheyenne, Arapaho, and Potawatomi—were living in central and western Nebraska when white explorers entered the area. The Plains Indians were seminomadic, horse-riding, and buffalo-hunting tribes. Eastern Nebraska was home to farming tribes including the Otoe, Omaha, Pawnee, and Ponca.

In the early nineteenth century, the United States government sent explorers into the Nebraska Territory, which was part of the Lousiana Purchase acquired in 1803. President Thomas Jefferson commissioned Captains Meriwether Lewis and William Clark to explore the west. They mapped eastern Nebraska in 1804, and, in 1806, Lt. Zebulon M. Pike explored central Nebraska. Further exploring expeditions were conducted by Maj. Stephen H. Long in 1819, Lt. John C. Fremont in 1842, and Lt. G.K. Warren in 1855.

Early reports referred to Nebraska as part of the Great American Desert. Because of the erroneous perception that the state was unfit for agriculture, Nebraska's fertile soils remained largely untapped until the late 1880s. Most wagon trains heading west traveled through Nebraska's Platte River Valley on the Oregon Trail, a major trail taken by thousands of pioneers in the 1840s. Brigham Young followed the Platte River westward on the Mormon Trail as he led his people to sanctuary in Utah. Still others followed the Platte westward lured by the discovery of gold in California in 1849 and Colorado in 1859.

To protect these westward moving migrants from hostile American Indians, a string of United States Army posts was established along the trail, including Fort Mitchell, Fort Kearny, and Fort Hartsuff.

Not everyone who traveled through Nebraska regarded it as a desert. Some pioneers recognized its potential agricultural wealth and wanted to settle in Nebraska. In 1854, Congress passed the Kansas-Nebraska Act which opened to settlement the land west of the Missouri River that had previously been reserved for American Indians. The Homestead Act of 1863 allowed homesteaders to claim 160 acres of free land.

In 1867, Nebraska was admitted to the Union as a state. By this time, the railroads were impacting western migration. In that same year, 1867, the Union Pacific Railroad was completed across Nebraska. By the 1880s, the Burlington railway system formed a rail network across the state. Railroads received large land grants from the federal government to subsidize the cost of construction. This land was then sold to pioneers, many of whom were encouraged by the railroads to immigrate from Europe. Because of the growing population along the railroads, towns quickly sprung up to serve the social and economic needs of cattle ranchers and farmers.

Stuhr Museum was developed to preserve the heritage of the pioneers who settled Nebraska's Great Plains using historic buildings and artifacts from throughout the state. The museum was organized in 1960 as a subdivision of the Hall County, Nebraska, government. It is named for Leo B. Stuhr, a Grand Island businessman, farmer, historian, and a son of pioneers, who donated the land and money to begin the museum.

Tour

Begin your tour at the **Main Museum Building** which also serves as the Visitor Center. The orientation film is narrated by Henry Fonda who was born in Grand Island. The Main Building, completed in 1967, was designed by the renowned architect, Edward Durell Stone. In its E. J. Wolbach Hall of History are exhibits on Nebraska's history from 1860 to 1910 along with a scale model of Railroad Town.

The **Gus Fonner Memorial Rotunda,** a structure shaped like a wagon wheel, houses August L. Fonner's collection of Plains Indian and western artifacts. There are arrowheads, spear points, moccasins, beadwork, pottery, baskets, and buffalo-hide clothing as well as exhibits on the horse, chaps, saddles, spurs, lariats, and a western tavern gaming room.

Railroad Town is a recreated prairie community of the 1880s and 1890s comprised of sixty historic shops, offices, and homes relocated from throughout Nebraska.

Dr. Phillipson's Veterinary Infirmary includes two operating rooms: one for horses and the other for dogs and smaller animals. Both are equipped with operating hoists, tables, charts, and surgical equipment. A pharmacy is stocked with drugs and medical apparatus.

The **Schimmer Barn,** a red barn of the 1890s, displays wagons, buggies, sleighs, and harnesses. The **William Siebler Blacksmith Shop** has a forge, anvil, and tools which are used for demonstrations of the blacksmith's craft. Demonstrations are also given at the **C. N. Barber Tinsmith and Carpenter Shop.**

The **Learned Hose Company No. 1** is a firehouse with three large pumps. The **Town Marshall's Office** is furnished with a large desk, cast-iron stove, cot, and clock. Nearby is an outdoor, iron prison cell.

The **U.S. Post Office** is a white frame building from 1865 which was the home of the first postmaster of Grand Island. The original postal equipment is from the Merna Post Office. The **Hardware Store** features cutlery, tools, and utensils of the late 1880s and 1890s.

The **Milisen House,** a large, gray, frame house in the Italianate style of architecture, was built in 1880. It has a distinctive hip roof, ornamental cast-iron roof cresting, and wide overhanging eaves outfitted with decorative brackets. It was the home of Charles Milisen, an engineer for the Union Pacific Railroad who came from Pennsylvania in 1867.

The 1883 **Lesher House** is an example of folk Victorian architecture. Although it appears to be a one-story house, there is an upstairs bedroom. Furnished in the Victorian style, it was illuminated by carbide gas. The parlor and bedroom have elaborately carved woodwork and wainscoting while original stenciling can be seen in the kitchen.

The **Peter's School** is a white, frame, one-room school that contains a teacher's desk, pupils' benches, and books. Town meetings took place in the 1884 **Washington Township Hall.** It now features an exhibit on surveying.

A green frame building houses the **O.A. Abbott Law Office** and the **Kenesaw Bank,** built in 1883. The tellers' stations, desks, and banking fixtures are from the Nuckolls County Bank located in Nelson.

The **A.J. Sousa Shoe Shop** displays shoes, boots, and shoe-making equipment while the **General Mercantile Emporium** is a well-stocked general store. The **Silver Dollar Cafe** is a small restaurant that serves sandwiches and soft drinks. **Eltman's Barber Shop** was the place not only to get a haircut or a shave, but also a hot bath.

The **Platte Valley Independent** was a small-town newspaper that was first published July 2, 1870. In the newspaper office are early printing presses and a linotype machine. **Dr. M. H. Defenbaugh's Office** represents the office and examining room of a small-town doctor. The **Railroad Town Telephone Exchange** features an operating switchboard of the Nebraska Telephone Company.

The **Fonda House,** birthplace of actor Henry Fonda (1905–1982), was built in 1884 in Grand Island. In 1904 the house was rented by Henry's father, William Brace Fonda, and his wife, Herberta. Henry Fonda was born in the house on May 16, 1905. In 1966, Fonda arranged to have the house moved to Stuhr Museum and restored. The green, frame, one-story home includes a parlor, dining room, bedroom, bathroom, and kitchen. The house is furnished as it might have been when the Fonda family lived there.

The **Pioneer Settlement** is a complex of eight 1850s and 1860s log cabins which constitute a "Road Ranch," a place where travelers along the pioneer trails could buy provisions and have their wagons repaired. Buildings include the **Stelk Chicken House,** the **Bockman Barn,** a **corn crib,** the **Schleichardt Blacksmith Shop,** the **Menck Cabin,** the **Schleichardt summer kitchen,** and the **Vieregg Cabin.**

The **Pawnee Indian earth lodge** is a replica of a dwelling of the Pawnee Indians who once lived in Nebraska. It contains clothing, weapons, and tools.

More than 200 pieces of farm machinery and fifteen automobiles are in the **Antique Farm Machinery and Auto Exhibit.**

The **Railyard Exhibit** has an 1890 depot, a 1901 standard-gauge locomotive, miscellaneous railstock, and a railroad museum in a wooden caboose. The **Arboretum** is a wooded area with flower gardens, a small lake, and picnic areas.

Special events include an 1890s Memorial Day, a Spring Festival in mid-June, Trails Day in late June, 1890s Fourth of July, Prairie Transportation Day in mid-July, Hay Day in mid-August, Autumn Festival in mid-September, Antique Engine and Tractor Days in October, and an Old-Fashioned Christmas and Lamplight Walk in December.

HAROLD WARP PIONEER VILLAGE

Recreation of a Nebraska pioneer village of the 1830s

Address: Minden, NE 68959-0068
Telephone: (308) 832-1181, (800) 445-4447
Location: In south central Nebraska, on NE 10, 12 miles south of I-80, exit 279
Open: Daily, 8:00 A.M. to sundown
Admission: Adults, $5.00; children 6 to 15, $2.50
Restaurants: Pioneer Village Restaurant; Snack Bar
Facilities: Motel, campgrounds

WHERE TO STAY

Motels/Hotels: Pioneer Village Motel, Minden 68959, (308) 832-2750, (800) 445-4447, FAX: (308) 832-2750; Ramada Inn, 110 S. 2nd Ave., Kearney 68847, (308) 237-5971; Holiday Inn, Box 1118, 301 S. 2nd Ave., Kearney 68847, (308) 237-3141, FAX: (308) 234-4675

Camping: Pioneer Village Camp Ground, Minden 68959, (308) 832-2750, FAX: (308) 832-2750; Fort Kearny State Historical Park, Kearney 68847, (308) 234-9513

OVERVIEW

The theme of Pioneer Village is the mechanization of the United States from the 1830s onward based on mechanical inventions. While there is a resemblance to Henry Ford's Greenfield Village in Michigan, the exhibits at Pioneer Village follow the chronology of their invention and development. In twenty-eight buildings, some of which are historic Nebraska structures that have been relocated to form a village and others that are contemporary exhibit buildings, more than 50,000 historical artifacts which show the evolution of transportation, communications, and agriculture are displayed.

HISTORY

Pioneer Village was founded in 1953 by Harold Warp, a Chicago plastics manufacturer who invented Flex-O-Glass and other plastic products. Warp was the son of Norwegian immigrants who homesteaded near Minden in the 1870s. The industrialist felt the need to establish the village

Harold Warp Pioneer Village, Minden, Nebraska
Attended by Harold Warp, the Grom School of District 13, Kearney County,
Nebraska, is typical of the one-room country schoolhouses found in rural United
States in the late nineteenth century. At Harold Warp Pioneer Village,
Minden, NE.

Photo by Patricia A. Gutek

when the one-room country school he attended was put up for auction in 1948. He feared that buildings and artifacts from America's past would disappear unless they were preserved.

Pioneer Village has grown from its original ten buildings and 10,000 historical items to its present 28 buildings and 50,000 historical artifacts. Since 1983, Pioneer Village has been administered by a self-supporting, non-profit foundation.

TOUR

Pioneer Village houses its collection of Americana in historical buildings that have been restored and relocated around a village green on the twenty-acre site, and in several large contemporary exhibit buildings.

Exhibits in the **Main Building** show the chronological development of transportation, lighting, guns, and money. The most extensive exhibit, transportation, begins with an 1822 ox cart followed by covered wagons, Conestoga wagons, stage coaches, freighter wagons, a horse-drawn street car, a steam train, an electric trolley car, horseless carriages, and automobiles. The development of the airplane is shown by a duplicate of the Wright Brother's flying machine of 1903; the Glenn Hammond Curtis plane of 1910, which made the first New York-Philadelphia round-trip; and Iowa's first flying machine of 1910. Lighting exhibits range from candles to the electric light bulb.

The **Elm Creek Fort,** a four-room log stockade and cabin built in 1869 as a defense against American Indian attacks, was Webster County's first dwelling and community fort.

The **People's Store,** stocked with merchandise of the 1880s and 1890s, displays high-button shoes, men's shirts, baskets, candle molds, animal traps, crocks, and coffee and tea tins. A potbelly stove sits in the center of the room.

The **Bloomington Land Office** was built of Kansas limestone in Franklin County in 1874. It served as a government land office where homesteaders, many of whom are Scandinavian and German immigrants, filed their land claims after the Homestead Act in 1862. On display are photographs of Harold Warp's parents, John Nelson Warp (1847–1907) and Helga Johannesen Warp (1861–1915), a copy of Mary Washington's (George Washington's mother) will, and an election poster of William Henry Harrison, Whig candidate for president in 1840.

The **Fire House** features fire-fighting equipment from the hand-bucket cart to the modern fire truck, and includes several pumping wagons and an oil-pumping diesel engine from the Teapot Dome oil field.

The **Lowell Depot** of the Burlington & Missouri Railroad was its western terminus during homesteading days. Inside the depot is the Railway Express Agency office, the station master's office with its telegraph equipment, a waiting room, and a storage room. In the railway area are two steam engines: a wood-burning, narrow-gauge Porter (1880) with a caboose, and an 1889 Baldwin locomotive.

The **Country School,** a white frame building with green shutters, is the Grom School of District 13, Kearney County. Attended by Harold Warp, its rescue from the auction block was the impetus which propelled Warp to start Pioneer Village. The school has a corrugated tin ceiling and a potbellied cast-iron stove. On its walls are pictures of George Washington, Theodore Roosevelt, and Abraham Lincoln. There are exhibits on William Holmes McGuffey, author of the *McGuffey Readers,* and Oscar Warp, Harold Warp's brother who was superintendent of schools in Kearney County from 1912–1916.

The **Sod House** is a replica of the temporary dwellings constructed from sod which settlers erected in the often treeless Nebraska plains. Eleven acres of prairie sod were used to make the three-foot-thick walls. The white plaster interior contains a stove, tub, crocks, chairs, beds, and other items used by pioneers.

China, pottery, and cut glass are displayed in the **China Shop.** The **Church,** St. Paul Lutheran, was built in Minden in 1884. The white frame church contains a baptismal font from Denmark and an 1856 Sneltzer pipe organ. Nondenominational services are held on summer Sundays. The 1879 Armitage-Herschel **merry-go-round,** a steam carousel, is operational and can be ridden for five cents.

A number of exhibits relate to the time when horses were the chief means of transportation. The original **Horse Barn** is from the Warp homestead. The **Pony Express Station,** an original log building, was the Pumpkinseed relay station to the Black Hills. The **Pony Express Barn** is an authentically reconstructed building with model horses, saddles, and a twenty-mule-team borax wagon. The smith's craft is demonstrated in the **Blacksmith Shop,** outfitted with forge, anvil, lathes, and tools. The **Livery** houses horse-drawn carriages, harnesses, saddles, buggies, sleighs, wagons, a Wells Fargo stage, and a Concord coach.

The evolution of the automobile is the subject of extensive exhibits and has a great deal of appeal for car buffs. One two-story exhibit building is loaded with **Antique Cars,** another with **Chevrolets and Other Cars,** and a third with **Fords, Studebakers, Motorcycles, Snowmobiles, and Bicycles.**

Since most pioneers were engaged in farming on the prairie, the evolution of farm machinery and implements is the subject of a huge display. There is a large **Antique Farm Machinery Building,** an **Antique Tractor and Truck Building,** and an **Agricultural Building and Steam Tractors.**

The **Home and Shops Building** illustrates the development of household furnishings at thirty-year intervals from 1830 to the present through furnished kitchens, living rooms, and bedrooms. Fully-equipped offices and shops include a music shop, doctor's office, print shop, drug store, and barber shop. The **Home Appliance Building** displays household inventions such as milk separators, refrigerators, stoves, irons, toasters, scales, iceboxes, vacuum cleaners, sewing machines, and washing machines.

The **Hobby House** contains collections of dolls, pitchers, buttons, fans, canes, and other items.

SIDE TRIPS

Fort Kearny State Historical Park, the site of the second Fort Kearny, was erected by the U.S. Army in 1848 to protect the emigrants on the Oregon Trail from American Indians. The military post was abandoned in 1871. There is a reconstructed blacksmith and carpenter shop, a restored 1864 stockade, and an interpretive center and museum with a slide show and exhibits on the history of the fort. Open daily in summer. Also a state recreation area, there is hiking, camping, fishing, and swimming. Kearney 68847, (308) 234-9513. Admission charged.

HALE FARM AND VILLAGE

Recreated early- to mid-nineteenth-century Western Reserve village and restored original farmstead

Address: 2686 Oakhill Road, P.O. Box 296, Bath, OH 44210-0296

Telephone: (216) 666-3711; (800) 589-9703

Location: In northeastern Ohio, between Cleveland and Akron; in Cuyahoga Valley National Recreation Area; 10 miles south of I-80 exit 11

Open: Wednesday to Saturday, 10:00 A.M. to 5:00 P.M.; Sunday, 12:00 noon to 5:00 P.M., last weekend in May through October; some weekends in December, and in February and March for Maple Sugaring—call for hours

Admission: Adults, $7.50; seniors, $6.50; children 6 to 12, $4.50

Restaurants: Gatehouse Restaurant; Snack Bar in Visitor Center

Shops: Museum Shop in Gatehouse Visitor Center

Facilities: Visitor Center with audio-visual orientation program; guided tours; picnic area; craft demonstrations; special events

WHERE TO STAY

Inns/Bed & Breakfasts: Glidden House, 1901 Ford Dr., Cleveland 44106, (216) 231-8900, FAX: (216) 231-2130

Motels/Hotels: Best Western Executive Inn, 2677 Gilchrist Rd., Akron 44305, (216) 794-1050; Red Roof Inn, 99 Rothrock Rd., Akron 44321, (216) 666-0566, FAX: (216) 666-6874; Holiday Inn, 4073 Medina Rd., Akron 44313, (216) 666-4131, FAX: (216) 666-7190; Hilton Quaker Square, 135 S. Broadway, Akron 44308, (216) 253-5970, FAX: (216) 253-2574

Camping: Portage Lakes State Park, Akron, (216) 644-2220; West Branch State Park, Ravenna, (216) 296-3239; Woodside Lake Park, 2256 Frost Rd., Streetsboro 44241, (216) 626-4251; Tamsin Park Camping Resort, 5000 Akron-Cleveland Rd., Peninsula 44264, (216) 650-0579

OVERVIEW

Hale Farm and Village is a high quality outdoor, living-history museum which is partial restoration and partial recreation that depicts life in Ohio's Western Reserve from 1825 to 1850. What is restored is the Hale Farm, an original Western Reserve homestead which was left by a descendent of the original settlers to the Western Reserve Historical Society in the 1950s. In addition to restoring these buildings, the society decided to create a village using original nineteenth-century structures from the Western Reserve. Because the first white settlers in the reserve area were New Englanders, the plan is that of a New England village. Jonathan Hale's farm represents the operation and development of a typical family farm.

The grounds are spacious, the buildings are architecturally interesting, the furnishings and artifacts are authentic, and the interpreters are well informed, making a visit here worthwhile as well as delightful.

HISTORY

Ohio's Western Reserve originally belonged to Connecticut. In 1622, King Charles II of England gave a land grant to the colony of Connecticut which extended all the way to the Pacific Ocean. From approximately the 41st parallel to the 42nd parallel and from sea to sea, the land strip was 50 miles long by 3,000 miles wide. Part of this Connecticut land was also given erroneously to New York and Pennsylvania which caused serious conflict between the colonies. Near the end of the eighteenth century, Connecticut relinquished its rights to the western land with the exception of a three-million-acre area beginning at the western border of Pennsylvania and extending 120 miles along the shore of Lake Erie. Connecticut then sold two-and-a-half million acres of this western land to the Connecticut Land Company and retained one-half million acres to pay its Revolutionary War survivors with land rather than cash. After the Connecticut Land Company surveyed its land in the Cuyahoga Valley, it began selling the Western Reserve property.

The history of the Western Reserve goes back to Ohio's settlement. The Western Reserve's fertile soil attracted a steady stream of migrants from the northeastern states of Connecticut, Massachusetts, Vermont, and New York. These settlers brought with them their township government system and their commitment to education.

Ohio, the first state organized out of the Northwest Territory, adopted its constitution in 1802. One of the most democratic documents of the early nineteenth century, it provided for the election of most officials, eliminated property requirements for voting, and abolished imprisonment for debt.

Although industry developed later in the nineteenth century, agriculture, such as that depicted on the Hale Farm, remained the chief occupation in Ohio's Western Reserve. The family farm was the basic economic

Hale Farm and Village, Bath, Ohio
Outside the 1830 Saltbox House stands the Middletown water pump.
The house was moved from the Western Reserve town of Richfield to
Hale Farm and Village, Bath, OH.

Photo by Patricia A. Gutek

unit, and most farmers raised corn, wheat, cattle, and hogs, especially the
sturdy razorback hog. The region's economic development was advanced
by the construction of the Erie Canal, which linked the Hudson River
with the Great Lakes. Built between 1817 and 1825 at a cost of $8 million,
the canal made it possible for Western farmers to transport their crops to
Eastern markets. By the 1840s, the area's farms were producing surpluses
for sale in the growing Eastern cities. Like many settlers in the Western
Reserve, Hale moved his family from Connecticut to Ohio in 1810.

Hale purchased 500 acres of prime land for $1,250. When the Hale
family arrived at their homestead, they found a squatter who had cleared
land and built a log cabin. Hale gave the man his horse and wagon in
payment for his work and the cabin. They lived in the log cabin until

1826. By then, Hale was more prosperous and built a large brick house modeled on the architecture of New England.

The Hale Farm and Village is a department of the Western Reserve Historical Society, a private, nonprofit organization. Historic preservation and recreation began in 1956 when Clara Belle Ritchie, Jonathan Hale's great-granddaughter, willed the property to the society.

TOUR

Your tour begins at the **Gatehouse** where an orientation film is shown and exhibits on the Hale family are displayed. The museum shop and restaurants are here also.

The Federal-style **Hale House,** original to the property, was built by Jonathan Hale for his wife, Mercy, and their five children. Hale made his own bricks; building the house took him two years. Although by 1827 the house was not finished, the family moved in and lived on the first floor which has been restored to that time. There is a kitchen with a fireplace for cooking, a mother's bench, and a table set with handleless cups. The bedroom has a rope bed with a straw mattress on the bottom and a feather mattress on top, a child's bed, and a crib. A cabinet belonged to the Hales. At the back of the house are candle making and broom making demonstrations.

Other buildings that are original to the homestead property are the 1870 **Sheep Barn** which now contains a woodworking demonstration, an 1865 **Carriage Barn,** an 1852 **Farm Barn** where animals are kept, and the early-twentieth-century **Sugar House** in which the museum's Maple Sugaring Days are held.

The household garden's variety of plants is typical of farm gardens of the 1830s. An herb garden contains medicinal and cooking herbs. The **apple orchard** is located near the house, between the **north pasture** and the **garden barn.** The varieties of apples are those grown by the Hales during the mid-1830s.

On the east side of Oak Hill Road lies the **Western Reserve Village.** It is plotted in New England fashion on a village green.

The 1825 Federal-style **Law Office** from Jefferson belonged to Benjamin Wade, a U.S. senator from Ohio. Notice the partners' safe with two door locks so that both partners had to be present to open the safe.

A white Greek Revival church built in 1850 was moved from Streetsboro where it served a Baptist congregation. Called the **Mary Ann Sears Swetland Memorial Meetinghouse,** its pews and wainscoting are original. It has a large bathtub-style baptistery for total immersion.

The 1832 **Land Office** belonged to Ephraim Brown who sold Western Reserve land. The furnishings are original with the exception of a safe which belonged to the Mormon leader, Joseph Smith.

The 1816 **Log Schoolhouse** has unusual built-in log desks on a platform along the walls.

The 1832 transitional-style **Goldsmith House** is the most elaborate house in the village. Built over a cistern, the kitchen had running water brought up by a small pump. The dining room wallpaper, which is ten years older than the house, came from a similar house in North Bloomfield called Brownwood. Hearth cooking is demonstrated in the cellar kitchen. Next to the house is a fine walled garden. The flowers, herbs, shrubs, and vegetables are all varieties available in the 1830s.

Other houses include the 1830 **Saltbox House** which has an herb garden, the 1845 Greek Revival **Jagger House** noted for its paneling and stenciling, and the 1852 Greek Revival **Stow House** in which spinning and weaving are demonstrated. A potter works in the **Pottery Shed.**

The **Glassworks Exhibit,** housed in a log barn built in 1811 in Wellsville, contains the excavated remnants of an early Kent glassworks, as well as examples of early glassware.

Special events include Maple Sugaring in February or March, an Herb Fair the last weekend in May, a Music Festival in mid-July, a Harvest Festival in October, and a nineteenth-century Christmas.

Side Trips

Hale Farm is located in the **Cuyahoga Valley National Recreation Area,** a 33,000-acre urban recreation park along twenty-two miles of the Cuyahoga River between Cleveland and Akron. Its Ohio and Erie Canal Towpath provides a popular hiking trail. The park has two visitor centers: Happy Days Visitor Center is on SR 303 between SR 8 and Peninsula, (216) 650-4636, and Canal Visitor Center on Canal Road at Hillside Road in Valley View, (216) 524-1497 or (800) 445-9667.

The **Cuyahoga Valley Line Railroad** operates historic diesel locomotives pulling vintage coaches from the 1930s and 1940s through the Cuyahoga Valley National Recreation Area. The 40-mile round trip is on railroad tracks now owned by the National Parks. One of its stops is at Hale Farm, P.O. Box 158, Peninsula 44264-0158, (800) 468-4070. Admission charged.

ZOAR VILLAGE STATE MEMORIAL

Restoration of an 1830s communal society of German Separatists; NR, HABS

Address: P.O. Box 404, State Route 212, Zoar, OH 44697
Telephone: (216) 874-3011
Location: In east central Ohio between New Philadelphia and Canton; it is three miles southeast of I-77 exit 93 on Ohio 212
Open: Wednesday to Saturday, 9:30 A.M. to 5:00 P.M.; Sunday and holidays, 12:00 noon to 5:00 P.M., from Memorial Day weekend to Labor Day; Saturday, 9:30 A.M. to 5:00 P.M. and Sunday, 12:00 noon to 5:00 P.M., April to mid-May, September, and October
Admission: Adults, $4.00; seniors, $3.20; children 6 to 12, $1.00
Restaurants: Zoar Tavern; Inn on the River Restaurant
Shops: Zoar Store; antique, book, candle, and gift shops are in the town of Zoar
Facilities: Special events; demonstrations; orientation video; guided tours

WHERE TO STAY

Inns/Bed & Breakfasts: Garden Gate Bed & Breakfast, Zoar 44697, (216) 874-2693; Cider Mill B&B, Zoar 44697, (216) 874-3133; Cowger House #9 B&B, Zoar 44697, (216) 874-3542; Weaving Haus B&B, Zoar 44697, (216) 874-3318; Cobbler Shop B&B, Zoar 44697, (216) 874-2600
Motels/Hotels: Best Western Valley Inn, 131 Bluebell St. SW, New Philadelphia 44663, (216) 339-7731; Atwood Resort, 2650 Lodge Rd., Dellroy 44620, (216) 735-2211
Camping: Atwood Lake Park, Mineral City, (216) 343-6780; Tall Timber Lake, Rt. 1, Box 1158, New Philadelphia 44663, (216) 364-9930; Tuscarawas Co. Fair Grounds, Dover, (216) 343-3418; Bear Creek KOA, East Sparta 44626, (216) 484-4488

OVERVIEW

Zoar is a small, nineteenth-century Ohio town founded in 1817 by a pietistical religious group from Germany. Because of its relatively isolated location and peaceful setting in the Tuscarawas Valley, the town has re-

Zoar Village State Memorial, Zoar, Ohio
A rocking chair and candle stand provide a quiet place to rest in the 1835
Gardener's Residence attached to the Zoar Greenhouse. The 1830s communal
society of German Separatists was noted for its beautiful gardens.
At Zoar Village State Memorial, Zoar, OH.

Photo by Patricia A. Gutek

tained much of its simplicity and charm. Ten restored buildings maintained by the Ohio Historical Society constitute historic Zoar Village. Other Zoarite buildings are privately owned and used as residences, bed and breakfasts, and shops.

Under the leadership of Joseph Bimeler, 300 pietistical Separatists emigrated from Württemberg, Germany, so that they could openly practice their religion which deviated from the established Lutheran Church. Because of economic hardships, the community decided to become communal in 1819. Private property was eliminated, and work and assets were shared in exchange for food, lodging, and clothing. The Zoar Society disbanded in 1898.

The Ohio Historical Society acquired several Zoar buildings in the 1940s and 1960s. The buildings have been faithfully restored to their appearance in the 1830s, the period of Zoar's greatest prosperity. Zoar is an outstanding museum village because of its historical significance, its fine restoration, and its exquisite setting.

History

Zoar Village State Memorial is a museum complex of ten restored buildings maintained by the Ohio Historical Society within the town of Zoar. It is the location of a community that was established by a group of German Separatists headed by Joseph Bimeler. Persecuted in their homeland for their religious beliefs, 300 men, women, and children from Württemburg reached Philadelphia in August 1817. There they hoped to practice their religion in peace. The pietistical Separatists, who left the Lutheran church, did not believe in sacraments and refused to enter military service, pay taxes, or send their children to state schools.

In Philadelphia, Joseph Bimeler and his group were warmly received by the Quakers. With their financial assistance, the relatively impoverished Separatists purchased 5,500 acres along the Tuscarawas River in Ohio from Godfrey Haga for $16,500. When Bimeler and a few of his men visited the Tuscarawas Valley, they were delighted to find heavily wooded hills, fertile plains, and several good springs.

The first log cabin in the town the Separatists called Zoar was completed in December 1817. More houses were added during the winter and spring. The first two winters at Zoar were very hard, and the harvests were not adequate to feed the people. Because of the difficult financial situation, Johannes Breymaier, one of the group's early leaders, advocated a communal economy. There would be no private ownership of property, and all resources would be pooled. Although the idea met some resistance at first, eventually communalism was backed enthusiastically.

The Society of Separatists of Zoar was formed April 15, 1819. According to the Articles of 1819, property was owned communally. Members worked where needed in shops or fields in return for being provided the necessities of life: food, clothing, and housing. Officers of the society were elected. Joseph Bimeler held the office of cashier and agent-general from 1819 until his death in 1853.

The economic base of the Zoarites was agricultural. They raised wheat, oats, rye, barley, and vegetables. Beer and wine were produced from their own orchards and vineyards. Among their industrial pursuits were wagon, cooper, and tin shops; a saddlery; flour, woolen, saw, and planing mills; and two blast furnaces. A general store and hotel catered to outside customers.

By 1835, Zoar was practically self-sustaining. The society produced all its own food except tea, coffee, and rice and made its own cloth. The houses were built of Zoar sandstone, roofed with Zoar tile, and heated with Zoar stoves. The shops produced furniture, kitchen utensils, tools, and plows. Revenue from the sale of surplus products paid mortgages and taxes. The society made the last payment on its land in 1830 and reached the height of its prosperity in the 1850s. In 1852, Zoar property was estimated to be worth $1 million. The Ohio Canal crossed the property, opening new markets for Zoar products, and the community owned and operated four canalboats.

Celibacy was adopted at Zoar in 1822 primarily because of economic necessity. Two-thirds of the members of the society were women, which left a small work force of men; women were needed in the workplace, but childbearing interfered with work. By 1830, when the community had achieved a level of prosperity, celibacy was discontinued, and the ban on marriage was lifted.

In a similar effort to free women for the workplace, children aged three to fourteen were placed in nurseries in the care of the older women of the society. After 1840, placing children in nurseries became optional, and in 1860, the nurseries were abolished.

As the community prospered, crude log cabins were replaced with larger frame or brick houses with front and back porches. These houses had large, comfortable rooms but were simple in design. Joseph Bimeler's home, built originally as a home for the aged, was quite elaborate. The Zoarites built a second church in 1853 and a second school in 1868.

Zoarites were noted for their industry, cleanliness, and love of music and flowers. An entire block in the center of Zoar was occupied by a garden that was designed as a religious symbol. One of the most distinctive features at Zoar was its greenhouse, and the community became known for exotic and varied plants and bulbs.

The communal society that began in 1817 and ended in 1898 was most vigorous and prosperous in the 1830s and 1840s, when its membership increased from 300 to 500. Joseph Bimeler was the driving force behind the development of Zoar. He was a gifted orator, an untrained doctor who was able to effect many cures, a highly successful business agent for the community, and a pastor with an unselfish devotion to his people. Bimeler's death in 1853 was a severe blow to Zoar. Although other good men succeeded him, none had his combination of business sense and religious zeal.

As the first generation of Zoarites, the original immigrants, died off, their children did not have the same appreciation of religious freedom. The Civil War was difficult for the pacifist society, and in spite of their upbringing, fourteen Zoar boys ran off to enlist. Industries at Zoar failed to keep up with the technological changes of the nineteenth century. Their production methods became outdated, and they were unable to compete. Poor investments resulted in heavy financial losses. Discord resulted from hiring nonmember laborers, who not only introduced worldly ways but also received cash payments, which Zoarites never did.

The Zoar Hotel was a disruptive factor in the community. Although hotel business was vigorously pursued because it brought in income, good business meant numbers of people with different beliefs coming to Zoar. Employees of the hotel received cash tips, which they pocketed against society regulations. Many Zoar families started selling produce and craft items to the increasing number of tourists for cash. The best food was served in the hotel and was shared by employees, much to the displeasure of other Zoarites, who felt that they were not receiving equal treatment.

One frequent hotel visitor, Alexander Gunn, a retired businessman from Cleveland, liked Zoar so much that he purchased a log cabin there. He was not a member of the society nor even a German, a prerequisite for membership. Moreover, he used the cabin to entertain the society's leaders, alienating the envious membership from their leaders.

Business declines, outside influences on the membership, internal rivalries, and lessening religious commitment all contributed to the dissolution of the Zoar society. The membership decided to dissolve it on March 10, 1898. Property was distributed among the permanent membership, with families receiving a home, land, personal clothing and furniture, and some cash. Those involved in the society's industries received a share of those businesses.

TOUR

Begin your visit to Zoar at the **Zoar Store** which also serves as a reception center. The **Store** (1833) was the center for the community's commercial dealings with the outside world. It stocked items made in the community and other necessary goods. Society members could take what they needed from the store free. Today, the store has been restored to its original appearance. Visitors may purchase reproduction pottery, baskets, tinware, and other items.

After watching the video, your guided tour with a costumed interpreter will begin. Behind the Store is the **Community Dairy** which has only recently been restored. Zoarites came to the Dairy daily to get milk. Zoarites were noted for their cheese making skill.

The **Number One House**, built in 1835, was the home of Joseph Bimeler and the administrative center of the community. It was originally intended to be a home for the community's aged but was never really used for that purpose. A two-and-a-half-story red-brick Georgian colonial mansion, the house contained three separate living quarters for the Bimeler family and two of the trustees and their families.

Some of the furnishings are Zoarite pieces, which are simple and Germanic; some are more elegant Empire-style pieces. Bimeler conducted business from his office in the Number One House, and it contains a desk specially made for him at Zoar.

A deep cellar, where the temperature is an even fifty degrees Fahrenheit, was used by the community for storing fruits and vegetables.

A **Greenhouse** and a large **garden** are special features of the community. The formal garden, which occupies an entire block, contains beautiful annuals, perennials, shrubs, and herbs, reflecting the Separatists' love of flowers. The gardens of Zoar became well known and spawned a thriving business in the sale of plants and bulbs.

The garden's design is symbolic of New Jerusalem as described in the Revelation of Saint John the Divine in the Bible. A wide border path symbolizes the earthly road taken by the unredeemed, and twelve narrow walkways lead to a Norway spruce, the tree of everlasting life.

The greenhouse, with its attached **Gardener's Residence,** dates from 1835. The Zoarites raised oranges and lemons, regarded as exotic fruits for Ohio. The greenhouse was heated by a system of pipes under the floor that brought in warm air from an outside charcoal furnace. Seedlings for the garden were raised in the greenhouse, and people from Cleveland sent their best plants to Zoar for the winter.

The simple gardener's residence has been restored and is decorated with Zoar furniture. There is a parlor downstairs and a bedroom upstairs; the kitchen was outside.

The **Bakery,** built in 1835, provided daily bread for the residents of Zoar. Bread was baked in two brick ovens that could hold fifteen loaves each. The baker lived upstairs in the two-story stone and clapboard house.

Several craft shops, which required some reconstruction, are open and operative at Zoar. The **Tin Shop,** which was built in 1825, was torn down in the 1940s. Now rebuilt on its original foundation, the small two-room structure is of brick and timber. The building is a good example of the Zoar method of construction called *nogging:* soft bricks or sandstone were placed between framing timbers. The inside of the building was then covered with plaster, and the outside was covered with clapboards, brick, or stucco.

The tinsmith produced household products such as basins, cups, buckets, sconces, and milk pails. Similar items are produced in the restored shop; traditional tools and methods are used.

Buggies and farm wagons were built in the restored **wagon shop,** which dates from 1840. The nearby **blacksmith shop** produced any metal tools or parts required by the society. The charcoal-fired forge, with its huge bellows, is going again, demonstrating traditional methods.

The **Bimeler Museum** was the residence of Joseph's great-grandson, William. It is furnished as it would have looked in the 1890s, at the end of the communal experience.

The **Magazine/Dining Room/Kitchen** complex behind Number One House is currently undergoing restoration.

Many other Zoarite buildings that are privately owned and used as residences or businesses can be seen on a leisurely stroll around the town.

The **Zoar Hotel,** built in the 1830s as a popular resort hotel, was visited by distinguished Ohioans, including President William McKinley. The Hotel is now closed.

Special events at Zoar include the Quilt and Needlework Show, which alternates with a Toy Show and the Strawberry Social in June, the Candlelight Dinner Tour in July, the Harvest Festival, Winetasting, and Volkswalk in August, the Apfelfest in October, and Christmas in Zoar in December.

OLD WORLD WISCONSIN

Recreation of nineteenth-century ethnic farmsteads and 1870s village; State Historic Site

Address: S103 W37890 Hwy. 67, Eagle WI 53119
Telephone: (414) 594-2116
Location: In southeastern Wisconsin, 35 miles southwest of downtown Milwaukee, 75 miles northwest of Chicago; 1½ miles south of Eagle, off St. Hwy. 67
Open: Daily, 10:00 A.M. to 5:00 P.M., July to August and weekends in May, June, September, and October; 10:00 A.M. to 4:00 P.M., weekdays in May, June, September, and October
Admission: Adults, $7.00; seniors, $6.30; children 5 to 12, $3.00; tram rides: $1.50 per person
Restaurants: The Clausing Barn Restaurant
Shops: Museum Store in Ramsey Barn Reception Center
Facilities: Visitor Center with audio-visual presentation; tram rides; picnic areas; special events

WHERE TO STAY
Inns/Bed & Breakfasts: Eagle Centre House, W370 S9590 Hwy. 67, Eagle 53119, (414) 363-4700; The Green House, Rt. 2, Box 214, Hwy. 12, Whitewater 53190, (414) 495-8771, (800) 468-1959; Ye Olde Manor House, Rt. 5, Box 390, Elkhorn 53121, (414) 742-2450
Motels/Hotels: Hampton Inn Brookfield, 575 N. Barker Road, Waukesha 53186, (414) 796-1500, FAX: (414) 796-0977; Country Inn, 2810 Golf Rd., Pewaukee 53072, (414) 547-0201, FAX: (414) 547-0207; Holiday Inn, 2417 Bluemound Rd., Waukesha 53186, (414) 786-0460, FAX: (414) 786-1599
Camping: Kettle Moraine State Forest—Southern Unit, Hwy. 59, Eagle 53119, (414) 594-2135

OVERVIEW
The idea of gathering historic structures together into outdoor museums is a European one. The Scandinavian museum called Skansen is the prototype, and many European outdoor museums are simply referred to as "skansens." Old World Wisconsin is modeled after Sweden's Skansen.

Old World Wisconsin's unique concept has been to locate nineteenth-century Wisconsin farm buildings built by European immigrants and arrange them into farmsteads. Since each nationality mimicked the familiar architectural styles of their homeland, the agricultural structures they built reflected their ethnic origins as did their furnishings, clothing, crafts, and customs.

Calling itself "an outdoor museum of immigrant farm and village life," Old World Wisconsin's ten ethnic farmsteads and an 1870s crossroads village present a comparative study of ethnic pioneer farmers' adaptation of their European traditions in the Midwest. Rural structures have been carefully restored to their original appearance and furnished with appropriate artifacts found in the Wisconsin area. Farmsteads depict the lifestyles of German, Polish, Norwegian, Danish, and Finnish immigrants. Restoration has been based on extensive historical research on buildings and their owners. Each site is restored to a particular year, and costumed guides interpret a site as if it were still occupied by that time period's owner and his family. To add to the authenticity, farm and village residences are surrounded by gardens and field crops appropriate to the era and ethnic background of the family. The same standards have been applied in the selection of farm animals.

History

Old World Wisconsin, a State Historic Site administered by the State Historical Society of Wisconsin, is an outdoor ethnographic museum designed to preserve examples of European-style buildings built by the state's early settlers. A recreation, it illustrates the cultural and architectural contributions of ethnic immigrants to rural Wisconsin in the nineteenth and early twentieth centuries. Richard W. E. Perrin, an architect and expert on Wisconsin's historic buildings, led the movement to save the state's diverse rural architectural history. The concept of a museum of ethnic architecture was approved by the Board of Curators of the State Historical Society of Wisconsin in 1964. A site was selected in the southern unit of the Kettle Moraine State Forest. Old World Wisconsin opened in 1976 as Wisconsin's bicentennial project.

The museum's fifty historic buildings, moved from throughout the state, were built by pioneers, many of whom were from northern Europe. In addition to the ethnic farmsteads, there is a Yankee farmstead and an 1870s crossroads village.

Old World Wisconsin's 576 acres, located in the town of Eagle in the southwestern corner of Waukesha County, are within the boundaries of the southern part of the Kettle Moraine State Forest and the Ice Age National Scientific Area. This area was formed at the juncture of the Lake

Old World Wisconsin, Eagle, Wisconsin

The Koepsell House, an example of German half-timbered or *Fachwerk*
architecture, was moved from Jackson where it was built in 1858. It, along with
the 1855 Hilgendorf cattle and horse barn, is displayed in the German-Polish area
at Old World Wisconsin, Eagle, WI.

Photo by Patricia A. Gutek

Michigan and Green Bay glacial fields, two massive ice sheets, coming
from opposite directions, that deposited glacial materials to create the Kettle Moraine. When the ice melted, channels were cut in the gravel by
streams, and the melting buried ice produced depressions known as *kettles*.

TOUR

Old World Wisconsin is a 576-acre site which takes almost all day
to see. Farmsteads are spaced so that each one seems to be alone in the
midwestern wilderness, a deliberate attempt to recreate the isolation experienced on the frontier. Trams, which are highly recommended, leave from
the visitors' center and make frequent stops near each exhibit.

The **Visitor Center Complex** was designed to prepare tourists for the experience of returning to nineteenth-century rural Wisconsin. Information services are in **Leuskow House,** built in Herman in 1850 in the German *Fachwerk* or half-timbered style. The **Ramsey Barn,** built in 1841 in Fort Atkinson, is the museum's Reception Center. There an orientation program uses the diaries and photographs of immigrant settlers to tell of their journeys and experiences. The Museum Store sells reproduction items as well as books on Wisconsin history. The restaurant is in the **Clausing Barn,** built in 1897 in Mequon, Ozaukee County. It is one of a few remaining eight-sided barns built by German immigrants.

The **1870s Crossroads Village** served rural settlers as a social and commercial center. Many frontier businesses were also typically owned by European immigrants.

A Bohemian shoemaker, Anton Sisel, lived and worked in the **Sisel House and Shoe Shop.** The **Rediske Stable** belonged to another shoemaker, Carl Rediske from La Crosse. The **Four-Mile House,** a stagecoach inn from Rolling Prairie, had a unique barroom in that alcohol was not served because the owners believed in temperance. The 1881 **Wagon Shop** was built in Whitewater by Andrew Peterson, a Norwegian, while the **Blacksmith Shop** was erected in Waubeka in 1886 by Henry Grotelueschen, a German. The **Waterville General Store** was operated in the 1880s by Griffith Thomas, the son of Welsh immigrants. One home, the **Hafford House,** was occupied by an Irish widow named Mary Hafford, while the **Benson House** belonged to Wesley Benson from Fort Atkinson.

St. Peter's Church, built in 1839 to serve German Catholics in Milwaukee, has been restored to its 1889 Greek Revival and Gothic architectural styles. The altar, altar railing, and stations of the cross are wooden. The recessed aisle was meant to keep Wisconsin's cold winter air from creating a draft.

Harmony Town Hall, built in 1876 in Harmony, Rock County, exemplifies the frame clapboard town meetinghouse that settlers from New England brought to Wisconsin.

The **Yankee Area** has the only farmstead that did not belong to a European immigrant. The Sanford family moved west to Wisconsin from New York in 1845. The two-story, Greek Revival **Sanford House,** built in La Grange in 1858, reflects the prosperity of this farmer. On the first floor are well-decorated formal and informal parlors, an office, dining room, and a modern kitchen. Sanford was a businessman who hired men to run his farm.

There are three farms built by settlers from Germany in the **German Area,** and each reflects a different decade. The earliest era, 1860, is represented by the **Schulz Farm** which features a traditional Pomeranian half-timbered house with mud-straw insulation built in 1856 in Herman. It has a central black kitchen which is an interior smoke house used for baking, cooking, and smoking meat, the walls of which are blackened by smoke. Because these structures easily caught fire, smoke houses eventually were built separately, which makes this 130-year-old house quite a find. Both the stable and barn have thatched roofs.

At the **Schottler Farm,** the time period is the 1870s when a depression made economic survival difficult. Outbuildings at the Schottler Farm include the 1855 Held Barn, the 1875 Jung Barn and Jung Smokehouse, the 1865 Fassbender Granary, and the 1875 Kessel Summer kitchen.

Horse-powered dairy farming in the 1880s is portrayed at the **Koepsell Farm.**

The **Turck-Schottler House,** which is on the National Register, was built in 1847 in Germantown, Washington County, and is restored to its 1875 appearance. An example of German *Blockbau* style, the two-and-a-half-story house is constructed of logs with loam and rye straw chinking.

Koepsell House, built by master carpenter Friedrich Koepsell in 1858 in Washington County, has been restored to its 1880 appearance. The house is typical of Pomeranian *Fachwerk* style. This half-timber one-and-a-half-story house has a gabled roof, central brick chimney, and a central hall.

This farm has two barns, a machine shed, and an outhouse, all built between 1855 and 1880.

The **Kruza House** was built in 1884 in Hofa Park by a Polish immigrant. The small, rectangular structure is an example of stovewood architecture, in which stovewood-length logs are set in mortar. The house has two rooms, each of which has an outside door. One room is for people, while the other is for chickens.

Near the farmsteads are small gardens of onions, cabbage, berries, and flax and pens of livestock such as chickens, ducks, geese, and horses. Historical interpreters describe the various skills and crafts that were practiced by the German immigrant farmers.

The **Norwegian area** has two farms, the **Fossebrekke Farm** and the **Kvaale Farm,** as well as the **Raspberry School.**

Fossebrekke House was erected in 1841 in Newark, Rock County. It is constructed of oak logs.

Kvaale House, built in 1848 in Dunkirk, Dane County, and restored to its 1865 appearance, features a *svalgong,* or covered porch, which provided additional shelter from harsh weather.

The **Veggli House,** built in 1843 in Plymouth, Rock County, is restored to its 1865 appearance.

The **Sorbergshagen Barn** is a dogtrot barn, with one side built in 1872 and the other added in 1880. Horses were stabled in one half and cows in the other.

Raspberry School, built by three Norwegian families in Russell, Bayfield County, was named after Lake Superior's Raspberry Bay. It has been restored to its 1906 appearance. The school, in operation until 1914, was attended by the children of Norwegian and Swedish families. It is a good example of the one-room, rural school, which housed all eight grades and was taught by one teacher. The building contains educational materials of the period, such as books, papers, and maps.

Other structures in the Norwegian area are the **Dahlen Corncrib** (1875), the **Lisbakken Granary** (1860), the **Bosboen Barn** (1865), and the **Offeson Outhouse.** The **Danish Area,** adjacent to the Norwegian, contains the **Pedersen House,** built in 1872 in Luck, Polk County, and the **Jensen Barn,** 1886.

The queen of Denmark traveled to Wisconsin in 1976 to dedicate the **Pederson House** which has been restored to its 1890 appearance.

There are two farms in the Finnish area, the 1897 **Rankinen Farm** and the 1915 seven-structure **Ketola Farm.**

The **Ketola House,** built in 1894 in Bayfield County, has been restored to its 1915 appearance. It is an example of the log construction used by Finnish farmers.

Rankihen House, built in 1892, in Oulu, Bayfield County, looks just as it did in 1897.

The **Ronkainen Sauna** (1919) was built in Maple County. The sauna was an essential feature of Finnish farm life.

Other structures found in this area are the **Kortesmaa Dairy Barn** (1910), the **Makela Stable** (1911), the **Kortesmaa Granary** (1910), the **Lantta Barn** (1919), and the **Rankinen Outhouse** (1898).

Special events include Plowing and Planting in early May, Sheep Shearing in late May, Cookies and Kuchen in mid-June, Scandinavian Midsummer Celebration in late June, Independence Day Celebration on the Fourth of July, Children's Day in mid-July and mid-August, Pioneer Threshing in late August, a Civil War Weekend in early September, Woman's Work is Never Done in early October, Autumn on the Farms in late October, and Christmas Through the Years in December.

PENDARVIS

Restoration of 1840s Cornish lead miners' homes; State Historic Site; NR, HABS

Address: 114 Shake Rag Street, Mineral Point, WI 53565
Telephone: (608) 987-2122
Location: In south central Wisconsin, 54 miles southwest of Madison, 175 miles northwest of Chicago; off U.S. 151
Open: Daily, 9:00 A.M. to 5:00 P.M., May through October
Admission: Adults, $5.00; children 5 to 12, $2.00
Restaurants: In town: Ovens of Brittany; Red Rooster Cafe
Shops: Museum Store
Facilities: Visitors' Center; guided tours; special events

WHERE TO STAY

Inns/Bed & Breakfasts: Chesterfield Inn, 20 Commerce St., and Chesterfield Inn on Shake Rag, Mineral Point 53565, (608) 987-3682; The Duke House, 618 Maiden St., Mineral Point 53565, (608) 987-2821; Wm. A. Jones House, 215 Ridge St., P.O. Box 130, Mineral Point 53565, (608) 987-2337; The Wilson House, 110 Dodge St., Mineral Point 53565, (608) 987-3600

Motels/Hotels: Redwood, Box 43, RR 3, Mineral Point 53565, (608) 987-2317

Camping: Governor Dodge State Park, Rt. 1, Box 42, Dodgeville 53533, (608) 935-2315; Moe-Harding Camp Grounds, Hwy. 23, Mineral Point 53565, (608) 987-3456

OVERVIEW

Pendarvis is the name of a restored group of limestone cottages built in the 1840s by Cornish miners. Not a separate museum village behind a fence, the cottages are clustered together in a neighborhood of the small town of Mineral Point, population 2,500. The homes belonged to tin miners, migrants from Cornwall, England, who came to Wisconsin when lead was discovered in the 1820s. Pendarvis tells the story of both the mining business and the Cornish people who brought distinctive speech patterns, limestone architecture, and traditional food to rural Wisconsin.

In addition to being the site of a well-done historical restoration, Mineral Point is an interesting destination itself. Streets in the hilly country town are laid out irregularly, following miners' footpaths. Architecture is a mix of limestone cottages and Greek and Gothic revival mansions. Cornish food is still served in the restaurants. There are more than one-half dozen antique stores and at least two dozen art and craft galleries.

History

In 1827, Stephen Taylor, a nineteenth-century traveler, described Mineral Point as

> . . . a piece of land elevated about 200 feet, narrowing and descending to a point, situated in the midst of a valley, as it were—a ravine bounding the same both eastward and westward, through which tributaries of the Pekatonica River flow, uniting in a wider valley to the southward. It was upon this point that the "leads were struck," the fame of which spread, and so quickly become the center of attraction, the miners flocking to them from every quarter. . . .

By the mid-1830s, the town's population was more than 2,000. When Wisconsin became a territory in 1836, Mineral Point residents sought—optimistically though unsuccessfully—to have the territorial capital established there.

In cold weather, miners without homes lived near the mines in holes dug into the sides of hills. It was from these early miners, who "hibernated" in dugouts like badgers, that Wisconsin received its nickname, the Badger State.

The first permanent homes in the community were erected by Cousin Jacks and Cousin Jennies who arrived from Cornwall, England, during the 1830s and 1840s. The Cornishmen, among the best miners in the world, brought wtth them the techniques they had used in Cornwall's mines. They also brought an expert knowledge of stonecutting and masonry, which they used to build limestone houses like those they had left in England. Most of these stone and log houses, more than thirty of them, were built in a ravine along a street that became known as Shake Rag Under the Hill. (The miners' wives would shake rags to call their husbands to dinner when the men were working at nearby mines.)

Using Cornish construction methods, the miners quarried the limestone from under their houses. Only the stones on the street side of the house were dressed, or *faced,* and the face stones were cut carefully to fit together. On the sides of the house, the stone was cemented with mortar.

The rectangular houses with interior end chimneys had walls eigh-

Pendarvis, Mineral Point, Wisconsin
Polperro, built by Cornish miners in 1828 and now restored, is a three-story stone
and log house. At Pendarvis, Mineral Point, WI.

Photo by Patricia A. Gutek

teen inches thick, oak floors and trim, and square, handmade iron nails.
The gabled roofs were made of wooden shakes (shingles).

There were about 7,000 Cornish in the entire lead-mining region in
1850, settled in Hazel Green, Platteville, and Shullsburg, as well as Mineral Point. They were hard-rock miners, in contrast with the surface-min-
ing Americans. The Cornish introduced the safety fuse for blasting, a slow-
burning fuse that allowed miners to light it and still have ample time to
get out of the mine. The Cornish probably made up no more than a fifth
of the population in the lead country, but their colorful names, customs,
and speech were memorable. Giants and pixies were favorite folklore characters. Anyone who lost his way was said to be *pixilated* (bewitched). The
only method of avoiding a pixie spell was to wear clothing inside out. A
few Cornish expressions are: *to tough pipe* (to sit down to rest and smoke a
pipe); *put 'ome the door* (close the door); and *a dish o' tay* (cup of tea).

After 1847, lead production, and with it the importance of Mineral Point, declined. Some of the miners turned to farming; others joined the California gold rush or went to other mining areas. The houses along Shake Rag Alley fell into disrepair.

In 1935, Robert Neal and Edgar Hellum decided to save at least one of the log and limestone houses from destruction. They purchased a one-story cottage that they named Pendarvis, after a village in Cornwall, and began painstakingly restoring it to its 1830s appearance. They removed any additions or improvements and bought restoration materials from Cornish houses that were being demolished.

Neal and Hellum eventually restored several other houses and furnished them with antiques and mining artifacts. In 1971, the Wisconsin State Historical Society took over the site.

TOUR

Your first stop is the **Visitor Center.** From there, costumed guides will take you on a tour of six miners' cottages.

The lifestyle of the miners and their families was difficult and basic as evidenced by the simple furnishings and crowded living conditions of the cottages. Building interiors have small rooms and low ceilings despite the fact that miners' families were often large. Visitors can well imagine Cornish mining families' circumstances after being inside their small homes. Mid-nineteenth-century furniture and artifacts gathered from the area can be seen in the stone houses.

Pendarvis, a one-story structure, was the first Cornish house purchased and restored by Neal and Hellum in 1935.

Trelawny (1828), next to Pendarvis, is a two-story rectangular limestone house featuring an interior end chimney and a gabled roof. It has been refurnished as the 1940 residence of Robert Neal and Edgar Hellum, the site's founders.

Polperro is a three-story stone and log house built in 1828. Three families occupied Polperro, one on each floor. The low ceilings contribute to the cramped feeling inside the rather small space, where large families cooked, ate, and slept during long Wisconsin winters.

Tamblyn's Row is a three-unit row house. Athough the three structures were built at different times, they are contiguous. When Neal and Hellum began restoring Tamblyn's Row, they were surprised to discover a *kiddlywink* (a Cornish pub), completely hidden by dirt and undergrowth, on the lower level of the building. This charming room, with its stone walls, beamed ceiling, and end fireplace, is furnished with trestle tables and Windsor chairs. Here miners once played board games and enjoyed much-earned drinks and companionship. The attractive **Cornish gardens** have ferns, daisies, and columbines in bloom.

Mineral Point Hill, across the road from Pendarvis, is pockmarked with abandoned surface lead diggings and remnants of once-shafted lead mines. Here you'll find the **Merry Christmas Zinc Mine,** which opened in 1906, as well as the **badger holes.** Rusting mining equipment is strewn along the path. Mineral Point Hill offers a pleasing panorama of Pendarvis.

Tours conclude in the Museum Store which features craft items and books related to Wisconsin history.

Special events include lead smelting demonstrations in late May. There are many antique shops and art and craft galleries in town.

SOUTHWEST
AND WEST

FORT ROSS STATE HISTORIC PARK

Restoration and reconstruction of a Russian fur-trading post and fort, 1812–1841; NR, NHL

Address: 19005 Coast Highway 1, Jenner, CA 95450
Telephone: (707) 847-3286
Location: On California's northern coast, 75 miles north of San Francisco; 12 miles north of Jenner on Coast Hwy. 1
Open: Daily, 10:00 A.M. to 4:30 P.M.
Admission: $5.00 per car; seniors: $4.00 per car
Shops: Museum shop in Visitors' Center
Facilities: Visitors' Center with orientation film; picnic area; campground

WHERE TO STAY

Inns/Bed & Breakfasts: Timberhill Ranch, 35755 Hauser Bridge Rd., Cazadero 95421, (707) 847-3258, FAX: (707) 847-3342; Murphy's Jenner Inn, Jenner 95450, (707) 865-2377
Motels/Hotels: Fort Ross Lodge, 20705 Coast Highway 1, Jenner 95450, (707) 847-3333; Salt Point Lodge, 23255 Highway 1, Jenner 95450, (707) 847-3234; Timber Cove Inn, 21780 North Coast Highway, Jenner 95450, (707) 847-3231, FAX: (707) 847-3704
Camping: Fort Ross State Historic Park, 19005 Coast Highway 1, Jenner 95450, (707) 847-3286; Salt Point State Park, Jenner 95450, (707) 847-3221; Sonoma Coast State Beach, Jenner 95450, (707) 865-2391; Casini Ranch, 22855 Moscow Rd., Duncan Mills, (707) 865-2255

OVERVIEW

A Russian fort in California? Hard to believe, but true. The Russians had settlements on the northwest coast of North America before either the Americans or the Spanish. The Aleutian Islands and the mainland of Alaska were claimed for Russia in 1741 by explorers Vitus Bering and Alexei Chirikov. Russian interest in North America revolved around fur trading, and Russian hunters and traders pursued the seal and sea otters of the North American coast. Permanent Russian settlements for hunting expeditions and fur storage were founded on Kodiak Island in 1784, and the Russian American Company established a permanent headquarters on the island of Sitka in 1804. In 1812, Fort Ross was established eighty miles north of San Francisco as a hunting base and an agricultural base for supplying food to the Alaskan settlements.

Fort Ross's setting is as dramatic and unique as its history and architecture. Driving on California's Highway 1 north from Jenner to Fort Ross, you see breathtaking vistas of the Pacific coast, with waves dashing against jagged rocks, and dozens of sheltered bays, inlets, and tidal pools. Early morning mists merge with dashing waves. Herds of cattle and sheep graze on the deep hills and slopes, occasionally wandering onto the highway. Against this background standing on top of a cliff on this isolated wind-swept coast is the restored early-nineteenth-century Russian fort complete with wooden Siberian-style architecture.

HISTORY

North America was the site of European exploration and settlement both before and after the Revolutionary War. For centuries, Spain was the dominant European nation in the southeastern and southwestern parts of North America. The Seven Years' War in Europe ended in 1763 with an agreement to expel France from North America. Spain acquired France's Louisiana Territory, and England advanced to the Mississippi and north into Canada. The Pacific coast had been claimed and the southern portion, Baja California, had been settled by the Spanish. Spain feared that the English could drive through Canada to the Pacific Ocean and then move south along the California coast. Russia's claims on the Pacific coast, from Alaska south to Oregon, also worried Spain. Fear of further Russian expansion prompted the Spanish to finally colonize California in the late 1760s by establishing missions. By 1812, the Spanish had reached as far north as San Francisco Bay.

Russia's interest in North America began with two voyages of exploration led by Vitus Bering and Alexei Chirikov in 1728 and 1741. They explored the strait, now known as the Bering Strait, and discovered the Alaskan mainland and the Aleutian Islands, both of which they claimed for Russia. The expedition returned to St. Petersburg with a large quantity of furs and pelts. In the next half century, forty Russian fur-trading companies sent ships to the Aleutian Islands and Alaska.

In 1799, Tsar Paul I of Russia chartered the Russian-American Company, giving the company a monopoly on fur trading in Alaska, the Aleutians, the Kuriles, and other North Pacific Islands. The charter also authorized the trading company to use the coastal facilities of North

Fort Ross State Historic Park, Jenner, California
Visible through the stockade fence of the Russian Fur Trading Post and Fort are
the reconstructed Kuskov House, which served as the commandant's house, and
the Russian Orthodox Chapel. At Fort Ross State Historic Park, Jenner, CA.
Photo by Patricia A. Gutek

America from Alaska to fifty-five degrees north latitude, as well as the
right to explore and colonize unoccupied lands to the south.

The Russian-American Company established a permanent Russian
settlement at Sitka, Alaska, in 1804. Unable to grow enough food for its
own needs, Siberian supply ships, which often arrived late, brought food
to the Alaska base. Nikolai P. Rezanov, chief executive of the Russian-
American Fur Company, visited the Sitka colony in 1805 and found the
settlers dying from malnutrition and scurvy.

Moved with compassion, Rezanov sailed to San Francisco Bay in an
attempt to obtain food from the Spanish in exchange for furs. Although
Spanish ports in California were officially closed to trade with foreigners,
Rezanov's mission was successful. On his return to Sitka, he urged Alexan-
der Baranov, the company manager, to utilize an uncolonized stretch of
California north of San Francisco Bay as an agricultural and hunting base.

A cove and promontory up the coast from Bodega Bay was selected
as the best location for the colony because of good soil, timber, water

supply, and pasturage as well as relative inaccessibility from Spanish-occupied territory. Ivan Alexandrovich Kuskov, along with twenty-five Russians and eighty Native Alaskans, was charged with building the trading post on the Sonoma Coast in 1812.

Eighty miles north of San Francisco Bay, the fur-trading post was Russia's southernmost outpost in the New World. Located on a cliff-top plateau seventy feet above the ocean, Fort Ross occupied about one square mile. The quadrangular stockade wall was 276 by 312 feet. Both the stockade walls and the buildings were made of redwood. A seven-sided, two-story blockhouse and an eight-sided, two-story blockhouse defended the walls and were originally mounted with many cannons. Although built as a defensible fort, Ross was a commercial rather than a military outpost. It was never attacked. The Spanish protested the Russian intrusion into California but were unprepared to take action against the heavily armed fort.

Inside the walls were the manager's house, officers' quarters, barracks for Russian employees, a chapel, storehouses, and offices. The Native Alaskans and the Kashaya Indians, on whose ancestral lands the outpost was built, lived outside the wall in redwood huts. Also outside the stockade were a windmill, cattle yard, threshing floor, farm buildings, bakery, bath houses, a cemetery, vegetable gardens, and an orchard. On the cove below the stockade were a shipyard, tannery, blacksmith shop, and a storage shed.

Since the land the Russians chose for Fort Ross was the home of the Kashaya Indians, a tribe of hunters and gatherers, the Russians contracted with the Kashaya for the land accompanied by an exchange of gifts, mainly tools, clothing items, and trinkets. To prevent Spanish claims, the Russians decided to formalize their title with a deed of cession signed by the Russians and the American Indian chiefs in 1817. The treaty is the only one known to have been executed between American Indians and Europeans in California.

Good relations existed between the Russians and the American Indians, many of whom were employed as farm workers and paid in flour, meat, and clothing. The Russians, Native Alaskans, and Kashaya developed a cooperative three-way culture at Fort Ross that included intermarriage. The children who made up about a third of the residents by the mid-1830s were almost all born of these ethnically mixed unions. No more than four hundred people inhabited Fort Ross at any one time.

In addition to seal and otter hunting, the Russian settlement engaged in farming and raising livestock. Less than a decade after the Russians built their fort, the seals and sea otters in the area were almost exterminated. The quantity of skins hunted by the Alaskan Natives totaled about 40,000 in 1812 but was less than 400 by 1819. Despite the virtual end of fur trading, the fort remained a viable community which produced tools, farm implements, and household wares. They traded their products with the Spanish for food which they shipped to the Russian settlements in Alaska. Cattle was also raised.

Farming was not as successful as hoped since there was little level land in the area, too much coastal fog, and serious rodent problems. The fort managers realized that a move inland to better agricultural and grazing land would be the only way to increase the profitability of the economically marginal operation. Between 1833 and 1841, three inland ranches were maintained.

Political opposition to the Russian presence in California came from the American government when in 1821 Alexander I announced that Russian claims on the Pacific coast of North America extended south to the fifty-first parallel. In 1823, President Monroe declared to Congress that the United States opposed further European colonization in the Americas—the Monroe Doctrine.

Opposed by Spain and Mexico and with England supporting the American position, Alexander I bowed to the pressure. In an 1824 treaty with the United States, the southern limit of Russia's claims on the Pacific coast was set at the 54° 40′ line. The treaty also provided that trading and fishing in the North Pacific would be open to both the United States and Russia.

In 1839, officials of the Russian-American Company decided to abandon the fort as the sea otter population was depleted, and farming and stock raising did not create the kind of profits the company wanted. Also, the Russian government did not want to directly confront the Mexican government which encouraged its people to settle in the area. Americans were also moving to the area.

Alexander Rotchev was directed to sell the California holdings. A deal was struck with John Sutter from Fort New Helvetia in 1841. Sutter, a native of Switzerland and a naturalized Mexican citizen who ran a trading post near Sacramento, purchased Fort Ross and Bodega for $30,000 in installments, in both cash and produce. In January 1842 after thirty years on the northern California coast, the Russians returned to Alaska. By 1844, Sutter had removed everything he considered salvageable from Fort Ross and Bodega. He then leased the land to a former employee, William Benitz. Although Sutter's debt to the Russian-American Fur Company was supposed to be paid off in four years, Sutter still owed $19,000 seventeen years later. When the company tried to attach Sutter's property at New Helvetia for repayment, Sutter transferred title to the property to his son, John Sutter, Jr.

The Mexican government, which had never acknowledged Russia's claim to the California properties nor its right to sell them to Sutter, appropriated the property in 1845. It was then included in an 18,000-acre land grant given by the Mexican government to Manuel Torres. Benitz and his partner, Ernest Rufus, purchased Fort Ross and its adjoining 17,500 acres from Torres in 1847. The Benitz family lived at the fort for twenty years during which it became the headquarters of a large cattle ranch. In 1867, Benitz sold the property to James Dixon, and in 1873 the G. W. Call family purchased the fort and ranch.

Preservation of the Russian fort began in the early 1900s when local citizens purchased the fort and a few surrounding areas from the Call family and donated it to the state for a park. Twenty-seven days after Fort Ross officially became a historic site of the state of California, the massive earthquake of April 18, 1906, struck, causing structural damage to all the fort's buildings. The state began restoration of the fort in 1916 and subsequently acquired additional acreage now totaling 250 acres. Fort Ross State Historic Park is administered by the California Department of Parks and Recreation.

Tour

In the modern **Visitors' Center** is a small gift shop carrying books and Russian crafts; a slide show on Fort Ross is shown. Exhibits in the Visitors' Center are on the Kashaya Indians, the Native Alaskans, and the Russians at Fort Ross, along with the ranch period.

Only one original building still stands at Fort Ross. The **Rotchev House** is a one-story log building built in 1836 for Alexander Gavrilovich Rotchev, the last manager of Ross, and his wife, the former princess Elena Gagarina.

A few of the fort buildings and the stockade have been carefully reconstructed on their original foundations. The twelve-foot-high stockade fence is made of eight-inch-thick redwood timbers that enclose a quadrangle 276 by 312 feet. They are held together by a complex system of mortise joints locked by wooden pins.

The two **blockhouses,** one of which has seven sides while the other has eight, are built of heavy, hand-hewn timbers laid horizontally. Sentries are posted in these two-story blockhouses, which were equipped with muskets and cannon.

The **Russian Orthodox Chapel,** considered one of the most unique architectural structures on the Pacific coast, was built in 1828, collapsed in the 1906 earthquake, reconstructed in 1917, burned down in 1970, and reconstructed in 1974. The small redwood building has a cupola and a bell tower with a Russian Orthodox cross on top of it. Inside there is a small vestibule, and the main portion of the small church seems surprisingly large because the high ceiling extends into the cupola. There are icons of Jesus, Mary, and Orthodox patriarchs. Outside the chapel hangs a replica of the Russian chapel bell.

The **Officials Quarters** were the barracks for the Russian employees of the fur company. Several rooms contain cots, beds, and chairs. One room serves as a small carpenter's and tinsmith's shop complete with tools while another is the cooper's shop. There is a built-in bench alongside the large stone fireplace and a built-in floor-to-ceiling decorated chest in another room. The food storage room has barrels of food and utensils, including a samovar used by the Russians to make tea. In the kitchen is a large stove and baking oven, and there are icons in one corner of the dining room.

The large, two-story **Kuskov House** served as the commandant's house until 1836 when the new commandant's house was built. On the lower floor is a storeroom containing storage barrels, sacks of grain, farm tools, and rope along with an armory where weapons and gunpowder were stored. The living quarters upstairs include three bedrooms and a small office with a display of plant specimens, rocks, shells, and bones, and a storage room with cloth, blankets, and lanterns. The walls of this reconstructed building are of redwood logs, and both the floors and ceilings are wooden. The windows have large indoor wooden shutters.

In 1820 the Russians planted an orchard near the fort consisting of about one hundred peach, pear, cherry, and apple trees. Fifteen original trees still grow—two Gravenstein and three Bellflower apples, four Russian pears, and six seedling cherries.

EL RANCHO DE LAS GOLONDRINAS

Restoration of a early-eighteenth-century Spanish colonial ranch; recreated mountain village

Address: Rt. 14, Box 214, Sante Fe, NM 87505
Telephone: (505) 471-2261
Location: In north central New Mexico, 15 miles south of Santa Fe; I-25, exit 276
Open: Wednesday to Sunday, 10:00 A.M. to 4:00 P.M., June to August, for self-guided tours; prearranged guided tours are available daily in April, May, September, and October
Admission: Adults, $3.50; seniors and youths 13 to 18, $2.00; children 5 to 12, $1.00
Restaurants: Food service during festivals, and on weekends from June through August
Shops: Museum Shop
Facilities: Special events; festivals; living history weekends; picnic areas; changing exhibits in the exhibit hall

WHERE TO STAY

Inns/Bed & Breakfasts: La Posada de Santa Fe, 330 E. Palace Ave., Sante Fe 87501, (505) 986-0000, (800) 727-5276, FAX: (505) 982-6850; El Paradero, 220 W. Manhattan, Santa Fe 87501, (505) 988-1177
Motels/Hotels: La Fonda, 100 E. San Francisco St., Santa Fe 87501, (505) 982-5511, (800) 523-5002, FAX: (505) 988-4455; Eldorado Hotel, 309 W. San Francisco St., Santa Fe, 87501, (505) 988-4455, FAX: (505) 988-4455; The Inn at Loretto, 211 Old Santa Fe Trail, Santa Fe 87501, (505) 988-5531, FAX: (505) 984-7988; Hilton of Santa Fe, 100 Sandoval St., Sante Fe 87504, (505) 988-2811, (800) 336-3676
Camping: Hyde Memorial State Park, Hyde Park Rd., Santa Fe (505) 827-7465; KOA Sante Fe, RR 3, Box 95A, Santa Fe 87501, (505) 982-1419; Los Campos, 3574 Cerrillos, Santa Fe 87501, (800) 852-8160, (505) 473-1949; Santa Fe National Forest, Black Canyon Campground, Hwy. 475, Santa Fe, (505) 753-7331; Tesuque Pueblo RV Campground, Rt. 5, Box 360H, Santa Fe 87501, (505) 455-2661

El Rancho de las Golondrinas, Sante Fe, New Mexico
In the courtyard of the restored early-eighteenth-century walled adobe
Golondrinas Placita can be seen adobe ovens, or *hornos*, which were used for
baking bread. At El Rancho de las Golondrinas, Sante Fe, NM.
Photo by Patricia A. Gutek

OVERVIEW

El Rancho de las Golondrinas, the Ranch of the Swallows, was a
large Spanish colonial ranch which was also a *paraje* or stopping off place
where travelers, merchants, soldiers, and priests rested on their 1,500-mile
journey on the El Camino Real. The Royal Road or Real began in Mexico
City, went through the state of Chihuahua, and ended in the colonial
capital city, Santa Fe. The historic ranch was acquired from the king of
Spain in 1710.

The story of New Mexico as a Spanish colony, a part of the large
Spanish empire in North America known as New Spain, is told through
the life of the Baca family who lived on the ranch. This is a one-of-a-kind
museum that focuses on Spanish colonial history in the Southwest rather
than the usual emphasis in the United States on its English colonies in

the east. El Rancho de las Golondrinas, a living history outdoor museum, is not a well-manicured museum like Williamsburg. On more than two hundred dusty acres are all the structures essential to a self-sustaining Spanish rural hacienda. They include a restored early-eighteenth-century, walled, adobe ranch complex arranged around a courtyard and defended by a tower, a restored early-nineteenth-century ranch house, a variety of agricultural and industrial buildings as well as cultivated fields and a vineyard. There is also a small, recreated, nineteenth-century mountain village. Reflecting the central place that religion played in the Spanish lifestyle in New Spain, there is an unusual Penitente chapel, a cemetery, and a private family chapel.

HISTORY

New Mexico's Spanish heritage began when Francisco Vasquez de Coronado explored the region in 1540 while searching in vain for the legendary but mythical cities of Cibola, believed to be filled with gold and great wealth. The conquistadors—the explorers, soldiers, and adventurers—who established Spain's claims in the New World brought with them the Spanish language and culture as well as the Roman Catholic religion. Don Juan de Onate established the first Spanish colony in New Mexico in 1598. In 1610, Don Pedro Peralta founded Santa Fe, the colony's capital.

The American Indians who were living in this area received varied treatment at the hands of the Spanish. Some American Indians were enslaved and regarded as the property of estate owners. Missionary priests, at first Jesuits and than Franciscans, came to New Spain to bring Catholicism to the natives. While the Franciscan priests protected the American Indians, especially the Pueblo Indians, from exploitation, their concerted efforts to suppress the kachinas religious practices and to destroy the kivas where the Pueblo Indians practiced their ancient rituals made the priests unpopular. In 1680 the Pueblo Indians revolted against the Spanish, temporarily forcing their withdrawal from New Mexico. Spanish rule was reestablished when Don Diego de Vargas and his troops reconquered the territory in 1692.

When Mexico revolted against the Spanish in 1821, it won its independence. New Mexico then came under Mexico's jurisdiction for more than two decades. The Spanish had kept foreigners, Americans, out of New Spain to protect their economic monopoly. Under Mexican rule, American traders and settlers traveled the Santa Fe Trail, a 780-mile route that began in Missouri, to Santa Fe. Spanish and American cultures met in the old colonial capital, whose population was 3,000 in 1830, while developing a brisk trade in a wide range of goods.

War broke out between the United States and Mexico in 1846 over disputed territory in Texas and the Southwest. During the war, the U.S. Army of the West, commanded by General Stephen Watts Kearny, captured Santa Fe and proclaimed New Mexico's annexation to the United States. At the end of the war, the Treaty of Guadalupe Hidalgo ceded New Mexico and California to the United States for $15 million. New Mexico was organized as a United States territory in 1850 and became a state in 1912.

El Rancho de las Golondrinas was one of the estates, or *haciendas*, sold to prominent settlers by the king of Spain. In 1710, Miguel Vega y Coca bought the ranch from the Spanish crown. The property passed to the Baca family when some of Vega's seven daughters married that family's sons. The Baca ranch became famous for the shelter and hospitality that it provided to travelers who made it their last encampment before proceeding to Santa Fe, which was a day's horseback ride away. The ranch remained in the Baca family until 1932 when it was acquired by the Curtin family.

Y. A. Paloheimo Sr., a Finnish immigrant to the United States, married Leonora Curtin in 1946. Paloheimo was impressed with the cultural and historical significance of the ranch, and was familiar with museum villages in the Nordic countries. Paloheimo began restoration of the existing ranch buildings and the rebuilding of other structures on their original foundations. Additional buildings were moved to the site to recreate various aspects of Spanish colonial culture in New Mexico. Paloheimo's efforts at historic preservation and restoration led to today's 205-acre open air museum operated by the non-profit Rancho de las Golondrinas Charitable Trust.

TOUR

There are three areas to see at this sprawling ranch museum. The first is the Golondrinas Placita, built 1710 to 1720, and the Baca House, built 100 years later. The haciendas combine living quarters, food preparation and storage areas, craft production, and defensive fort. The second area consists of agricultural, industrial, and religious structures located around the land, some of which is farmed. The third area is the recreated mountain village composed of historic structures moved to the property.

The early-eighteenth-century **Golondrinas Placita** consists of a walled complex of solidly built adobe structures. The design of the living quarters which also include a look-out tower turned the home into a secure fort where residents could protect themselves from American Indian attacks. There are two doorways to the complex: the smaller door is for persons and the larger one is for animals and wagons. They open to a plaza, or *placita,* with trees, a well, and *hornos,* adobe ovens adopted from the Moors of North Africa, used for baking bread. The placita was used daily for socializing and household chores. Around the plaza is a variety of rooms in rectangular adobe structures. The chapel, dining room, and kitchen are original eighteenth-century structures while reconstructed buildings on their original foundations comprise the remainder of the rancho.

The **capilla,** or chapel, was an important place of worship for the Baca family who were devout Catholics, as were most of the Spanish settlers in New Mexico. Since the number of priests in colonial New Mexico was few, families on ranches conducted their own religious services while waiting for a visit from a priest. The altar features an antique reliquary, handmade wooden crosses, carved wooden statues of saints called *santos,* and candlesticks. The chapel's wooden candle-lit chandeliers are called *aranas* because of their spider-like shape. The floor is made of wooden planks, and the ceiling of log beams.

La sala de fundadores, one of the original ranch buildings, is the dining room that was used by the family and guests. **La cocina,** the kitchen, has a corner fireplace for cooking food. Clay pots were used to store food, and herbs were hung from the beamed ceiling to dry. A shelf over the fireplace, called a shepherd's bed, provided a warm place for weak baby lambs who were sometimes brought indoors at night. Corn and beans were the main dietary staples. Corn was hand ground into corn meal using a *mano* in a stone *metate.*

The **cuarto de recibo** was a receiving room used to greet and entertain guests while the **alcoba de huespedes** was the guest room. Hospitality was a high priority in the Spanish lifestyle and guests were welcomed and looked forward to as they brought news of the outside world.

The **torreon defensivo,** or defense tower, was built upon order of the king of Spain. From the fortified lookout tower, a sentinel would survey the landscape watching for bands of hostile American Indians, often Apaches, who raided both the haciendas of the Spanish settlers and the homes of the Pueblo Indians. When the sentinel would sound the alarm by blowing a ram's horn, those working outside would return to the safety of the thick hacienda walls. Men trained in arms would enter the tower, which was stocked with guns, swords, crossbows, and lances.

The hacienda complex had a carding room where wool was combed and prepared for weaving, a weaving room outfitted with looms, and a **dispensa,** a communal food storage room.

Adjacent to the eighteenth-century rancho is the newer **Casa de Manuel de Baca,** built in 1812. A two-room adobe dwelling, it resembles the later Mexican-style house more than earlier fortress-like buildings of the colonial ranch. Its two-foot-thick walls were designed for insulation and to keep out animals rather than raiding Apaches. Outbuildings of the Manuel de Baca ranch house include a village store, tinsmith shop, food cellar, corrals, chicken house, a barn, goat sheds, and a storage shed.

As you walk around the ranch, you will find threshing grounds, old and new molasses mills, a winery, a mill, and workshops where farm equipment was made or repaired including the **carreteria,** wagon shop, and the **Herreria Apodaca,** blacksmith shop, which has an adobe forge. Crops grown include varieties of all-important corn, several varieties of beans, squash, chilies, melons, watermelons, pumpkins, wheat, punche, which is a native tobacco, sorghum, and sunflowers.

Buildings in **Sierra Village** have been moved from other locations to create a nineteenth-century New Mexico mountain village. The **Casa Mora,** Mora family home, belonged to a prosperous family. The large house has an extensive porch covered by a portal. Adjacent to it is the *casa de la abuelita,* or grandmother's house. Its location near the main house meant that the family could care for the grandparents but still allow them the privacy of their own house. This house is simply furnished with a *camalta,* or high bed for the grandmother, and a *camita,* small bed for a grandchild. There is an iron stove for cooking which by the mid-1800s had replaced the fireplace.

The *casita primitiva* was a very simple dwelling where a young married couple began housekeeping. The exterior is of logs with an adobe veneer. The interior walls are plaster and the floor is hard-packed swept dirt. The 1820s *la choza del pastor,* shepherd's cabin, is a simple log cabin with plaster interiors and a dirt floor. Burro boxes used by shepherds to carry supplies, shears, and tools are in the cabin. Other village structures include a chicken house, hide storage barn, food storage cellar, and barn. Nearby is an herb garden.

One of the most interesting buildings at Las Golondrinas is the **Morada de la Conquistadora.** A *morada* is a chapel used by the *Penitentes,* a religious fraternity that developed when priests were scarce in New Mexico and Catholic lay people conducted their own religious services. The Penitentes developed their own religious rituals which emphasized mortification and penance. For example, during Holy Week, some of the Penitentes practiced self-flagellation, a practice not sanctioned by the Roman Catholic Church. The famous Archbishop Lamy, the subject of Willa Cather's novel, *Death Comes for the Archbishop*, opposed these rituals.

In the chapel, there is a large figure of Christ with movable arms, a handcarved wooden statue of St. Anthony that dates from 1720, a statue of St. Francis of Assisi that dates from 1690, and a crucifix which has a figure of Christ with a ministering angel. There is a **cemetery** and a small **family chapel** nearby.

Special events at Los Golondrinas include spring, summer, and harvest festivals which feature Spanish music, dancing, working craftspeople, and traditional food sales. In addition, there is a Civil War Weekend and a Fourth of July Celebration. Living History Weekends conducted throughout the summer vary from year to year but may include Adobe Making and Construction, Colonial and Territorial Lifestyles, Traditional Arts and Crafts, Riding, Working and Wild Horses, Santos and Santeros, Agriculture, and Southwestern Textiles.

SIDE TRIPS

Santa Fe is America's oldest capital city. It is a great tourist town with loads of atmosphere and plenty to do. Take your time as you are sure to enjoy exploring Santa Fe.

A BRIEF HISTORY OF THE SHAKERS

Ann Lee, a blacksmith's daughter born in Manchester, England, in 1736, founded the Shakers. The Shakers, a communal religious sect, established nineteen societies in America during the eighteenth and nineteenth centuries. The total membership reached 17,000.

In 1758, Ann Lee joined a group of Manchester Quakers, led by Jane and James Wardley, called *Shaking Quakers*, or *Shakers*, because of their physical movements during religious services. By 1770, Ann had become the accepted leader of the Shakers and was known as Mother Ann Lee. It was she who introduced celibacy to the Shakers. The need for celibacy was revealed to Mother Ann through a vision, though she herself was married and had given birth four times. None of her children survived infancy.

Mother Ann and her followers were persecuted and imprisoned for their religious beliefs, which emphasized work and worship. Again, acting on knowledge gained in a vision, Ann and eight followers sailed to America in 1774. The United Society of Believers in Christ's Second Appearing, as the Shakers called themselves, established their first communal society at Niskayuna (later called Watervliet), New York, in 1776.

Converts began to be attracted to Shakerism in 1780, and Mother Ann was one of the missionaries who traveled through New England seeking converts. Missionary work continued even after Mother Ann's death in 1784. It is estimated that at the sect's peak in the mid-nineteenth century, there were 6,000 members living in the nineteen communities.

Shaker communities usually began with missionaries holding worship services for local people in the home of a sympathizer or believer. Later, when there were enough believers to form a family, a communal site was agreed upon. Members donated or sold their possessions and gave their money to buy land. Shaker beliefs forbade private ownership of property; all property was held communally.

The meetinghouse was almost always the first structure built in the community, and many were designed by Shaker architect Moses Johnson (1752–1842). Typically, religious services were held on the first floor, with men entering through a left door and women through the right. They then sat on benches facing each other; the space between them was referred to as the *altar*. A section of benches was often reserved for the *world's people*, who were allowed to observe Shaker services.

Religious services, without following a formal ritual, included frenetic dancing and shaking, exhortations, and singing. Blue and white were thought to be heavenly colors, and worshipers dressed in blue and white for the services.

The second floor of a meetinghouse usually contained sleeping quarters for the community leaders, called *elders*.

Shaker communities were divided into families of approximately 100 people, who lived, worked, and took meals together. Each family's dwelling house was the center of domestic life, and all activity was strictly segregated by sex. Many dwelling houses, therefore, have double doors and stairways and wide halls to ensure minimum physical contact between the sexes.

Sleeping rooms were barely furnished; the wooden pegs that line the walls were used for hanging clothes. Because of the size of Shaker families, they often had separate laundry buildings. Brother David Parker of the Canterbury, New Hampshire, community is credited with inventing the first washing machine in 1858. It used water for cleaning and for mechanical power. The washing machine was exhibited by the Shakers at the Philadelphia Centennial Exposition in 1876 and was purchased for use in many large hotels.

Shakers believed in separation from the world, which was every place outside of their villages, because they felt that the world was sinful. They tried to make their communities self-sufficient so that they would have to purchase only a few things from the world. But since productivity often exceeded the community's needs and the quality of their goods was so high, Shaker products were regularly sold to the world.

Shakers strove for perfection through prayer and work to prepare for Christ's Second Coming. Their motto was "Hands to work and hearts to God." Manual labor was required, and adornment of either people or things was forbidden. This led not only to simple dress and functional buildings but also to furniture and artifacts carefully made of the finest materials. Shaker-made became synonymous with the highest quality.

By striving for efficiency and practicality, the Shakers devised many labor-saving inventions in addition to the washing machine: the flat broom, the circular saw, the clothespin, and the threshing machine among them. During the early 1800s, the Shakers monopolized the garden seed and medicinal herb industries because of the high quality of their products.

Shaker villages had schoolhouses even though Shakers did not produce children. Children were brought to the communities when whole families including children joined the sect or when Shakers took in homeless children. Boys and girls had separate buildings in which to live. They were supervised by adults and participated in all aspects of the Shaker way of life. They attended school four months out of the year; girls in summer, boys in winter. In addition to learning crafts and trades, children were taught the "3 Rs."

Within a Shaker society, all people were to be treated equally, including women, which put this sect ahead of the general population. However, the governance of Shaker societies was autocratic. Each family was governed by four people: two elders and two eldresses appointed by the church's central ministry at Mount Lebanon, New York. They were responsible for both the spiritual and the temporal affairs of their family, and their rule was absolute. They, in turn, were subject to the central ministry, composed of two elders and two eldresses, with the head elder or eldress being the official head of the church. Deacons, who were in charge of workshops and food production, and trustees, who conducted business activities with the world, were appointed by the elders.

From the 1830s to the 1850s, the Shakers experienced a period of spiritual renewal known as *Mother's Work,* in which gifts of songs, dance, and drawings were received from Mother Ann and other religious figures by Shaker mediums. Because the Shakers fundamentally banned all ornamentation, decorated Shaker artifacts almost certainly date from this period. *Spirit drawings* are watercolors in the folk art tradition and include pictures of the well-known Shaker tree of life, heavenly populations, and wreaths of flowers. Lyrics and tunes to songs were received and transcribed. The songs were usually about peace, work, and love.

Shaker membership reached its peak around the Civil War and gradually declined thereafter. By 1900, communities began closing; and by 1925, most had folded. By 1950, there were only two remaining communities, Canterbury, New Hampshire, and Sabbathday Lake, Maine, with small numbers of elderly Shakers. Today, only the Sabbathday Lake community is still active.

INDEX